5⁰⁰

BY SILENCE
BETRAYED

Also by John Crewdson

The Tarnished Door: The New
Immigrants and the Transformation
of America

BY SILENCE BETRAYED

Sexual Abuse of Children in America

John Crewdson

PERENNIAL LIBRARY

Harper & Row, Publishers, New York
Cambridge, Philadelphia, San Francisco
London, Mexico City, São Paulo, Singapore, Sydney

First PERENNIAL LIBRARY edition published 1989.

LIBRARY OF CONGRESS CATALOG CARD NUMBER: 88-45645

ISBN: 0-06-097203-3

89 90 91 92 93 FG 10 9 8 7 6 5 4 3 2 1

For Anders

CONTENTS

PREFACE

IN JANUARY 1984, ABC-TV broadcast a made-for-television movie called *Something About Amelia*. It was unlike anything seen on television before, the story of a white, middle-class, teenage girl who has a sexual relationship with her father. Deftly acted and dramatically understated, *Amelia* contained a message that child-protection workers had been trying to convey for years — that the sexual abuse of children in America is not uncommon, and not bound by class or culture. Nearly half of those who watched television that night were watching *Amelia*, and when it was over, child-abuse telephone hotlines across the country began to ring. The callers numbered not in the hundreds or the thousands, but in the tens of thousands. They included children who said they were being sexually abused, children who thought their friends were being abused, teachers who thought their students were being abused, mothers who thought their daughters and sons were being abused, grown women and not a few men who said they had been abused as children — even a handful of child abusers who wanted help.

Over the next few days, the hotline operated by the state of Illinois received thousands of those calls. I was then day metropolitan editor of the *Chicago Tribune*, and it was the story we printed about the reaction to *Amelia* that caused me to really think for the first time about child abuse and child abusers. I had known there were child molesters, of course; as a child I had been warned not to take candy from strangers — but no strangers ever offered me candy, and like most Americans, I had always assumed they were a rare species.

A couple of months later, in the hope of learning more, I flew to Washington, D.C., for the Third National Conference on the Sexual Victimization of Children. The opening address was delivered by Paula Hawkins of Florida, a formidable advocate for the rights of children during her six years in the United States Senate.[1] Putting aside much of her prepared text, Hawkins announced that she had been sexually abused by an elderly neighbor at the age of six. No one, not even the senator herself, was prepared for the national impact her speech would have. "I never realized it would be such a sensation," she said later. "I had been so involved in the subject that I thought it was commonly talked about. Victims must speak out."

That spring, when I left Chicago to take up a new assignment as the *Tribune*'s Los Angeles correspondent, I arrived on the West Coast a few weeks after the first indictments had been handed down in the Virginia McMartin's Pre-School case. Not just one or two children, the McMartin prosecutors were saying, but dozens of them, possibly hundreds, had been sadistically and ritually abused for a decade by a cabal of teachers at the school. The children represented an insignificant fraction of the six million toddlers who are cared for each day by someone outside their homes, but many parents who read and heard about the case were beginning to wonder about the nurseries, day-care centers, and preschools where they deposited their own children each morning. Before long, most of the state agencies that regulated day-care centers learned what the child-abuse hotline people had known for months: Americans were becoming worried about their children.

I spent most of the next year writing about the sexual abuse of children for the *Tribune*, and it was a wrenching experience. Before the year was over, I had become convinced that sexual abuse is one of the most pressing problems faced by this society, all the more urgent because there are so few apparent solutions. Even more disquieting, however, were the responses I received from those who politely inquired what I was writing about. A surprising number, including some people I thought I knew well, would cautiously acknowledge that "something like that happened to me when I was a kid," and go on to tell about having been molested by a father or an uncle or a teacher. Most of the others, including some whom I knew to be sensitive and humane individuals, had somehow become convinced that children who claim to be sexually abused are lying. Because it hadn't happened to them, it seemed, they simply couldn't imagine its happening to anyone.

To those who were abused as children, I hope this book will offer at least the faint reassurance that they are far from alone. To those who disbelieve the children, I hope it will offer some reasons to reconsider their disbelief. This book is not intended as a scholarly study, though for those who are interested in knowing more I have cited much of the currently available research. It is, rather, an overview of what is known about the sexual abuse of children in America. If I offer no ultimate solutions, it is because I know of none.

The large gaps in my knowledge of psychiatry and the law will be immediately apparent to members of those professions, but few journalists ever become experts in the subjects they write about. The reporter's task is to gather information from those who do have expertise, to sift it and synthesize it and then present it in a clear and balanced way. If I have managed to do that here, it is only because I received so much help and encouragement from so many people.

Above all, I must express my gratitude to Jim Squires, Dick Ciccone, and Doug Kneeland of the *Chicago Tribune*, who were among the first editors in the country to recognize the importance of writing at length about sexually abused children, and who provided me with the time and resources to pursue the subject as fully as I did. I am also grateful to Lynn Emmerman and Eileen Ogintz, my *Tribune* colleagues, who did most of the reporting on the Jordan, Minnesota, case.

Every effort has been made to ensure that the many trials and other legal proceedings mentioned in this book were reported accurately. All dispositions were up to date as of the summer of 1987, when the manuscript went to press, although some verdicts may have subsequently been reversed on appeal.

In the course of my research I spent many hours talking to men and women who were sexually abused as children or who have abused children sexually. All spoke to me in the hope that telling their stories might make a difference to the lives of uncounted others who share their grief and pain. They also spoke in confidence, and I have honored their requests that their real names not be used and that other identifying details about them, their families, and their lives be changed without affecting the substance of their stories.

Those to whom I can express my appreciation by name for having given so freely of their expertise include Jon Conte, Ken Freeman, Roland Summitt, Nahman Greenberg, and Bud Lewis, all of whom were kind enough to read the manuscript or portions of it, and to recommend important changes and clarifications. Their suggestions improved it enormously, as did the thoughtful editing of Bill Phillips, Doug Kneeland, and Prudence Crewdson. Thanks also to Henry Giaretto, Judith Becker, David Corwin, Ken Lanning, Bill Dworin, Paul Abramson, Anne Cohn, Bruce Selcraig, Steve Wolf, Lucy Berliner, Norm Coleman, Toby Tyler, Seth Goldstein, Mike Fondi, Terry O'Brien, Rob Freeman-Longo, Roger Smith, Michael Ryan, David Jones, Donald Bross, Donna Rosenberg, David Finkelhor, Diana Russell, Gail Wyatt, and others too numerous to mention.

All errors, of course, remain my own.

BY SILENCE
BETRAYED

ONE

Questions

I T WAS SOMETIME on the afternoon of September 26, 1983, that Judy Kath and Christine Brown, their ten-year-old daughters in tow, marched into the Jordan, Minnesota, police department. The two girls, their mothers said, wanted to talk to someone about James John Rud, a twenty-seven-year-old trash collector who lived by himself in a shabby mobile home at the Valley Green Trailer Park. Jordan's five-man department had no one on its staff who could qualify as an expert in child sexual abuse, certainly not patrolman Larry Norring. But when the girls announced that Rud had been abusing them sexually, Norring did not take their allegations lightly. Later that evening, while Rud was riding his motorcycle on one of the narrow county roads outside of town, Norring pulled him over and placed him under arrest. Had the matter ended there, with a suspect behind bars, it might have been worth a single headline in the Minneapolis papers. But the matter did not end there, and before it was finally over, it would occasion many headlines.

Norring's superiors took the girls' allegations as seriously as he had, and in the days and weeks that followed, the police interviewed a number of other children. Some of them were playmates of the two girls, others the sons and daughters of Rud's neighbors at the trailer park or of women he had befriended at meetings of Alcoholics Anonymous. To the surprise of no one more than the police, many of the children told essentially the same story. As residents of small American towns will attest, very little happens in such places that does not quickly become common knowledge, and no sooner had the investigation begun than dozens of worried parents, particularly those whose children had known Jim Rud or any of his victims, were asking their own sons and daughters whether anything had happened to them. Those who said it had were taken to talk with the police, who by now were struggling to cope with what would have been a major child-abuse case in a city many times the size of Jordan.

When the children were asked whether they knew of any others who had been abused, nearly every child supplied at least one new name. When they were asked who had abused them, many named several adults, often including their own parents. As it unfolded, the tale being told by the children of Jordan was a most improbable one — nobody in Minnesota law enforcement could remember anything remotely like it — and it was being told in a most improbable setting, a Minneapolis suburb distinguished only by the consummate ordinariness of small-town America. With its spired churches, main-street cafés, and simple, sturdy houses, it was possible from a distance to mistake the village of Jordan for a painting on a calendar, or perhaps for Garrison Keillor's mythical hamlet, Lake Wobegon. Seen from up close, Jordan was less picturesque, a little threadbare in places and beginning to sag, but most of those who lived there were the kind of phlegmatic, reliable folk that Keillor has in mind when he says no true Minnesotan accepts an offer of anything until it has been made at least three times.

At the beginning the investigation focused on the Valley Green trailer park, the first stop for those arriving in town and the last for those on their way to somewhere else, but before long it had expanded to include some of the middle-class families who lived in the large, pleasant houses that were, both literally and figuratively, on the other side of the tracks. By then it wasn't only the children who were talking. One morning a woman walked into the police department to report that Rud had been photographing her five-year-old twin daughters in the nude, and that he had probably abused them sexually as well. When she and her children visited Rud's trailer, the woman said, he often took one girl or the other into a back bedroom for a few minutes at a time. As she was leaving, the woman named three other children Rud had molested, not at his trailer but at the house of Judy Kath, one of the two original complainants in the case, who also happened to be Jim Rud's former fiancée.

Less than a month after Judy Kath and Chris Brown had taken their daughters to see Officer Norring, both women were under arrest themselves, Brown charged with abusing Judy Kath's daughter and one of her own, Kath with promoting a minor, her own daughter, to "engage in obscene works." Brown's current boyfriend, her ex-husband, her sister, and her brother-in-law would eventually be charged with the sexual abuse of several other children. So would a deputy sheriff, a truck driver, a printing-equipment operator, an auto-body painter, a waitress at the local truck stop, an employee of the county assessor's office, an eight-year veteran of the Jordan police department, and both of Jim Rud's parents. A few of the defendants in the case were strangers, a few others related by birth or marriage. Most had become acquainted in the ways that people get to know one another in any small town, as neighbors, parishioners, customers, and friends of friends. On the surface the defendants didn't seem much different from anybody else, but the tales their children were telling were growing more horrifying by the day.

One boy, seeking to pinpoint one of the many occasions on which, he said, he had been abused by his parents, remembered that "we had pizza that night, because Mom and Dad went shopping." A girl recalled being abused by a neighbor lady who had just finished fixing her hair into a ponytail. Another boy said he had been abused by his parents in his own living room while watching "Wonder Woman" on TV. A girl said her grandmother had abused her with a pair of scissors before giving her macaroni and cheese for lunch. But not all of the abuse had been so matter-of-fact. There had also been "parties" that sometimes included ten or fifteen adults and as many children, parties where everyone played hide-and-seek or baseball or some other game, the sort of get-togethers one might expect to find on a summer evening in a small Midwestern town — except that, the children said, the outcome of the games had been their parents' way of determining which adults would have sex with which children.

When they talked about the sex, the children described nearly every permutation imaginable — mothers and fathers with sons and daughters, aunts and uncles with nieces and nephews, grandparents with grandchildren, children with one another and even with their pets. At one party, they said, the abusive games were followed by a hot dog supper. At another, everyone had strawberry ice cream afterward. Though they were copied down in the stilted dialect that is the universal trademark of police reports, the children's stories managed to retain some of their innocent language. One boy said his parents had put their mouths on his "freddie." Another talked of being forced to put his penis in his mother's "chinese." A young girl spoke of having been penetrated in both her "front butt" and her "back butt." Some of the children said they were given drugs and liquor, mostly beer and wine but sometimes peppermint schnapps, to encourage their compliance. Others said they had been threatened with being hurt or "sent to jail" or even killed if they did not submit. Some of the children talked freely to the police. Others talked only to the half-dozen child therapists who had been brought in from Minneapolis to help them deal with the aftereffects of the abuse. A few, mostly very young children, were reluctant to talk at all, and a few older ones could not seem to stop talking. As winter gave way to spring, the pages of police reports numbered in the thousands, and still the questioning went on: Who else hurt you? Do you know any other children who were hurt? Is there anything else you haven't told us?

From the day it surfaced, the Jordan case enjoyed the full attention of Kathleen Morris, then thirty-nine, the local prosecuting attorney who had become known for an aggressiveness that bordered on flamboyance and a penchant for working seven-day weeks. Morris, whose waist-length hair and lack of makeup contrasted sharply with her tailored business suits, had already won a reputation beyond the borders of Scott County, the state's second smallest. As a young assistant prosecutor, Morris had made her first headlines when, while prosecuting a narcotics case, she told a reporter that she favored legalizing marijuana. The offhand remark caused a furor, but within a year Morris had been elected chief prosecutor. When she won six convictions in the first child sexual abuse case in Scott County history, she emerged a self-styled champion of children's rights, crisscrossing the state to make speeches about child abuse and to criticize her fellow prosecutors for steering clear of such difficult cases. It wasn't uncommon to hear people say that someday Kathleen Morris was going to be Minnesota's first female attorney general, or maybe its first female governor, but not everybody felt that way. "People either love me or hate me," Morris was fond of saying. "I guess I'd rather they love me, but I'm not going to worry about it if they don't."

By the spring of 1984 the "Jordan sex case" was beginning to attract some national attention, and most of the news reports reflected one of two points of view. According to the prosecutors and the police, what had happened in Jordan was beyond imagination — two dozen men and women, most of them married, most of them parents, many of them solid citizens, had forged a twisted conspiracy of sex and torture with their own children as its victims. According to the defendants and their lawyers, what had actually happened was just as incomprehensible — two dozen men and women, friends, neighbors, and churchgoers, were faced with the loss of their savings, their homes, their jobs, and their reputations because their children had lied. For a black fantasy such as the children described to have taken place, the defendants' lawyers said, was plainly impossible. The only thing more inconceivable, the authorities replied, was that the children had made it all up. Privately, not all the lawyers were quick to insist that all the other defendants were equally innocent, or that the whole case was nothing but a children's conspiracy of lies. Some children, most of them agreed, had clearly been abused, but by whom was another question.

The defense hoped to show that many of the children's recollections of times and places didn't coincide with the events they described, and the statements taken by the police and therapists did contain a number of inconsistencies. One five-year-old girl, when asked where she was abused, first said it had happened, "upstairs, by the TV." Reminded that the TV was downstairs, the girl corrected herself. When a four-year-old who told investigators she had been abused by one of the defendants two days before was informed that the man had been in jail for weeks, she agreed it must have happened earlier. To the defense lawyers, most of whom were more accustomed to cross-examining adult witnesses about the details of traffic accidents and barroom brawls, such contradictions were the stuff of which acquittals were made. Seeking a convincing explanation for the children's allegations, the lawyers settled on the idea that the children had been brainwashed by the therapists. But the half-dozen psychologists working on the case, who by now were seeing most of the purported victims at least once a week, were less concerned about the discrepancies. "Five-year-olds change their stories," one said. "When you discover the cookie on the floor and he's the only one in the room, you'll get five different stories on something as innocent as that. Now imagine your son being severely sexually abused over a long period of time, and you can imagine why they are telling different stories at different times."

The therapists pointed out that although nearly all the children were being kept in separate foster homes and hadn't seen each other for months, many had told essentially similar stories, and they were also impressed with the physiological details the children supplied. "They tell you what sex is like," said one therapist. "They say, 'He put lotion on his penis before he put it in my butt.' When a three-year-old tells you that, there's nothing for me to conclude other than the kid is relating something that really happened to them." Most of the questions asked during the interviews had been designed not to put words into the children's mouths, but were open-ended: "Did someone have you do something?" or "Who touched you?" The therapists also noted that the children had been discriminating in their allegations, that no child had accused every defendant and that most had accused only a few. "If they were just trying to make up things and say everybody's a terrible monster," one therapist said, "it doesn't make sense to me that they would really differentiate who did what."

Such distinctions were important, for as the Jordan investigation continued through the summer of 1984 the question of the children's veracity was becoming paramount. The police had been able to come up with next to nothing in the way of physical evidence to corroborate the children's stories, and what little they had found was inconclusive. When two children said their anuses had been penetrated with miniature bowling pins and candles at one defendant's house, the house was searched. A miniature bowling pin and some candles were recovered, and a laboratory analysis found that both were coated with an unidentified "organic material" that could have been feces. The tests gave no indication, however, of who had used the items or for what. But for the failure to search Jim Rud's trailer the night he was arrested, there might have been much more. Many of the children had told of being photographed naked by Rud and some of the other defendants, and a few mentioned having seen Rud's scrapbooks of nude photos of children. Had such pictures been found, the case against Rud and any of the other defendants portrayed in the pictures would have been airtight. But when Larry Norring searched Rud's trailer nine days after his arrest, there weren't any photos or scrapbooks to be found.

According to the official report he typed up later, when Norring arrived at the trailer he saw "a stack of approximately 12 VCR cassette tapes, a large box containing pornographic magazines in the living area and two green garbage bags of pornographic material in the bedroom area." There were also "numerous items of children's clothing," including some underwear. But then Jim Rud's parents, both of whom would be charged in the case less than two weeks later, showed up and stopped the search. So "abusive and threatening" was the couple, Norring reported, that he "vacated the premises to avoid an altercation." As he was leaving, he saw the Ruds carrying "unknown items of personal property in boxes and bags" from the trailer. When Norring returned at nine o'clock the next morning the tapes, the pornography, and most of the children's clothing were no longer there. Much later, a senior Minnesota law enforcement official brought in to review Kathleen Morris's handling of the prosecution admitted that search warrants weren't issued as they should have been. "Usually you get a search warrant with an arrest warrant," the official said, "particularly when you're looking for pictures." Inexplicably, the homes of most of the other defendants in the case were never searched at all.

The only potential corroborating evidence available to the prosecutors was medical, and some of that was compelling. When a professor of pediatrics from the University of Minnesota examined one of the older girls in the case he found she had suffered such severe physical damage that she could not control her bladder or bowels. At least ten of the other children examined by three different doctors showed evidence of some kind of sexual abuse, and four others showed signs of possible abuse. But the medical findings were by no means clear-cut. Many of the examinations had been performed by a family practitioner, and they had been rather rudimentary. According to the reports the doctor submitted, his technique consisted mainly of using his fingers to see whether the children's sphincters, vaginas, and hymens had been enlarged, a common method where sexual abuse is suspected, but one that many physicians dismiss as inaccurate in the extreme. For one thing, the human finger is something less than a precision measuring device. For another, hymens can be stretched and sphincters and vaginas enlarged for reasons that have nothing to do with sexual abuse. To confuse matters further, some of the medical findings contradicted statements by the children. One young girl who claimed that two of the male defendants had penetrated her rectally "lots of times" had a rectum that appeared to be normal. An older girl who said two defendants had had vaginal intercourse with her had a hymen that was "substantially intact."

As the Fourth of July came and went, the village of Jordan had divided itself into three camps. The first was made up of the defendants and their relatives, neighbors, and friends, all of whom protested that the case was at best a publicity grab by Kathleen Morris, and at worst a vendetta and a witch-hunt. In the second camp were the investigators, the prosecutors, and their relatives, neighbors, and friends, all of them convinced that what Morris was uncovering leaf by twig was the most heinous case of child sexual abuse in the history of Minnesota or any other state. Some Jordanites joined one camp or the other right away; in the best Minnesota tradition, most chose to wait and see. But the tension around town was not only palpable, it was visible and audible — coffee-shop arguments, street-corner debates, even face-to-face confrontations between the accusers and the accused. One eleven-year-old victim complained to police that one of the female defendants had been "giving me the finger around town"; another defendant, she said, had confronted her in the grocery store and warned her to "stop your damn lying."

A small-town criminal justice system can overload in short order, and the management of the Jordan case was rapidly becoming more than seven police and sheriff's investigators, several prosecutors, a half-dozen therapists, and an equal number of social workers could handle. The case records were beginning to reflect the overload. Many of the police reports and some of the criminal complaints were being so hastily assembled that children's names were misspelled and their birthdates and even their sexes listed incorrectly. Only a handful of the interviews had been recorded on tape, which meant that most of the interview reports were paraphrased rather than verbatim, something that would eventually make it impossible to know precisely which questions had been asked of which children, and also precisely which answers they had given.

Not only were the investigators overwhelmed, they were mostly untrained in the intricacies of interviewing small children about sexual abuse. Only one, Pat Shannon of the Minnesota Bureau of Criminal Apprehension, could qualify as an expert, but Shannon hadn't entered the case until it was already nine months old. One of the others had attended a week-long seminar on the subject of child sexual abuse, and two had taken a four-hour course in "family relations." The rest had no training at all. Larry Norring had been taken off patrol duty to work on the case, and another investigator had a background as a crime-scene technician. Though they were not really part of the law enforcement team, the therapists were acting as surrogate investigators themselves. Any revelations made by the children during therapy were passed on to the police, and the police in turn fed the children questions through the therapists. The law enforcement types, one therapist said later, had been "well-motivated people," but she shuddered at the interview techniques of "guys who were writing speeding tickets one day and questioning kids the next."

Whatever their other failings, they were methodical to a fault. Whenever a new allegation arose, the investigator who heard it first would not only ask each of the other children about it, he would pass it on to his fellow investigators, who would raise it in all of their own interviews. The result was that the children in the case were being called upon to repeat their stories over and over, many of them as often as fifteen or twenty times, not counting the interviews they gave to prosecutors, therapists, and social workers. The children, living in foster homes and missing their brothers, sisters, pets, the familiar objects of their childhood, and even their parents, were on their way to becoming professional witnesses, and they were growing weary of the constant questioning. The prosecutors defended the incessant re-interviewing by pointing to the scope and complexity of the case. In an ordinary sexual abuse case, they said, where there was a single victim and a single victimizer, one or two interviews might be enough. But in a case like this one, with so many victims and so many suspects and so many separate instances and allegations, how else were they to sort it out?

As July faded into August the prosecutors were forced to face the uncomfortable fact that, while the investigation was far from complete, they were due in court in less than a month. The first trial, that of a couple named Bob and Lois Bentz, who were accused of abusing their three sons and three unrelated children, was scheduled to begin on August 27. Though lawyers for several of the defendants had asked for extra time to prepare for trial, the Bentzes' lawyers were not among them. "I wanted to be first," Earl Gray, the couple's lead counsel, told Eileen Ogintz of the *Chicago Tribune*. "I was scared of having somebody else be first." Had he asked for a continuance everything might have turned out differently, but Gray sensed that Kathleen Morris was not ready to go to trial, and his instinct proved to be right. Morris, whose case rested on the testimony of the children and some ambiguous medical evidence, had been hoping against hope that at least one of the defendants would "roll over" by pleading guilty and agreeing to testify against the others. A guilty plea would solve much of Morris's problem, not just by reducing her caseload and encouraging other defendants to enter similar pleas, but by giving her the thing she needed most of all — an adult witness who could take the stand and say, "I was there when it happened."

The prosecutors had already discussed plea bargains with several defendants, in some cases on the same day that they were arrested. At first the discussions were of the kind that take place as a matter of course in any conspiracy case — an offer to allow a defendant to plead guilty to reduced charges in return for testifying against the other suspects. But as the Bentz trial neared, it became clear that nobody was eager to accept Morris's offer, and the pressure to make a deal with someone — anyone — became intense. The prosecutors had insisted at the beginning that anyone who pleaded guilty and agreed to testify would have to serve at least some token time in jail. But as time grew short, some of the defendants were being told that the prosecutors would recommend probation in return for a plea of guilty, and a few were even promised that they would not have to testify at all. "They looked hard for somebody to roll over," one of the defense lawyers said. "I'm usually offered one deal. I've never been offered so many deals. They weren't prepared to take these cases to trial. They weren't ready to go."

In the end, the only defendant to accept Morris's offer was Jim Rud, the first person charged in the case and the one who had the most to lose. With a previous conviction for child sexual abuse in Virginia, where he had been stationed when he was in the Army, and another in nearby Dakota County, Minnesota, Rud was in danger of becoming a three-time loser. If he were convicted a third time in Minnesota, then the only state that had strict sentencing guidelines for child sexual abusers, Rud would be seventy-five by the time he emerged from the state penitentiary. Under the terms of the plea bargain, however, he would have to serve only six years. The Minnesota legal community, watching the Jordan case with fascination, was stunned — not that Rud had taken the deal, but that it had been offered in the first place. "For Kathleen Morris to offer Rud the deal she did," another prosecutor said later, "she had to be very desperate."

In return for leniency Jim Rud promised to tell all, and on August 14 he started talking. He kept at it for most of the next four days, until he had delivered a 113-page, single-spaced statement implicating eighteen of the twenty-three other defendants in the case, including his own parents. Yes, Rud said, he had been there when it happened. He had attended the sex parties and some of the other gatherings, had taken part in the abusive games described by the children, had seen adults and children having sex with one another. Everything the children said was true.

When the Bentz trial opened two weeks later, the first witness to take the stand was the prosecution's star, Jim Rud, the man who was supposed to wrap the whole case into one neat package. The Bentzes, looking tense, were seated with Earl Gray and his co-counsel at the defense table a few feet away. But when Morris asked Rud to point out Bob Bentz for the record, he couldn't. Morris tried gamely to continue, but as Rud babbled on, his testimony wandered far afield. Too far, the Bentzes' lawyers thought, and they quickly objected. When the judge ruled that the prosecution had improperly allowed Rud to testify about crimes with which the Bentzes had not been charged, Rud disappeared from the courtroom, but his testimony was only disaster number one. Disaster number two was the second witness, an eleven-year-old boy who had told the police that Bob Bentz had forced him to have anal intercourse. The boy repeated his accusation from the witness stand, then proceeded to chip away at his own credibility on cross-examination. Was he a believable witness? asked Earl Gray. Not really, the boy replied. Did he exaggerate things a lot? Well, yes, he did. Did he hate Bob Bentz for having abused him? No, he liked Bob Bentz. Was it true, as he had told the police, that Lois Bentz had made him put his finger in her anus? No, it wasn't true. Was that a big lie or a little lie? A big lie, the boy replied.

The boy was followed by an eleven-year-old girl who said she had been forced to perform fellatio both on Bob Bentz and on the Bentzes' dog. Asked during cross-examination whether she had ever lied about anything, the girl replied, "Of course. Kids aren't perfect. Everyone doesn't always tell the truth." Then another girl, a ten-year-old, admitted under cross-examination that the six young witnesses in the case had discussed their testimony over dinner the night before at the Howard Johnson motel where Kathleen Morris had put them up during the trial. For Morris, who had previously assured the judge that the witnesses were being kept apart to prevent the comingling of their stories, it was disaster number three.

Those who attended the trial were as puzzled by Kathleen Morris's strategy as by the performance of some of her witnesses. Her own interrogation of the children was limited mainly to questions that could be answered yes or no, and which left very little room for the sort of elaboration that juries find most convincing. Earl Gray and his defense team were more vigorous, sometimes even engaging in shouting matches with some of the children, but Morris remained seated during much of Gray's cross-examination, rising only occasionally to object that the children were being badgered. Then, when Gray called a Minneapolis psychologist to testify in the Bentzes behalf, Morris did not object to his credentials as an expert, a standard prosecution move. Nor did she cross-examine the psychologist on his pronouncement that the children had been subjected by the therapists and the police to the same brainwashing techniques perfected by the Chinese Communists. When Bob and Lois Bentz took the stand to deny the allegations against them, Morris didn't cross-examine them either.

Not that the disasters were unmitigated. Several of the children, including the Bentzes' six-year-old son, testified in what many observers thought was a convincing fashion that they had been abused by Bob Bentz, Lois Bentz, or both. A particularly dramatic moment occurred when the six-year-old, having told of being forced by his father to submit to anal intercourse, turned toward the judge with tears in his eyes and asked for an assurance that "he won't do that no more." The twelve jurors deliberated for twenty-two hours before acquitting the Bentzes on all counts. The trial had been an ordeal for everyone, not just for the defendants and the jurors but also for the witnesses, some of whom cried and vomited after leaving the stand. But the trial and its outcome were equally devastating for the children waiting to testify in the cases yet to come. For months they had been reassured by Kathleen Morris and her staff that all that mattered was that they tell the truth. If they did, they would be believed, their parents would "get help," they could go home again, and everything would work out.

Now things weren't working out, either for the children or for the prosecutors. While the Bentzes were appearing on "Nightline" and the "Phil Donahue Show" to express their relief at having been acquitted and their outrage at having been put on trial in the first place, Morris and her assistants were preparing to go back into court. The second trial in the case was scheduled to begin in less than a week, this one of a Scott County deputy sheriff and his wife, charged with sexually abusing their two daughters and two other children. This time, however, there would be no star witness, and Kathleen Morris had another problem as well. The prosecutors were under a court order to provide their investigative files to the defendants' lawyers, but there were 126 pages of police reports they had not yet turned over. The defense lawyers knew about the reports, but they had no idea what the files contained. When Don Nichols, the second couple's lawyer, asked the court to order that he be given the documents, he was acting on a hunch. "If somebody doesn't want to give me something," he told Eileen Ogintz, "I always like to know what it is." As soon as Nichols got his hands on the files, the reason for the prosecutors' reluctance became clear.

Early in July, a few of the children had begun suggesting to police that the assaults by their parents had extended beyond sexual abuse into some nether region they could not, or would not, name. Finally one of the boys came out with it. At one of the parties, he said, a child had been murdered. As was by then their habit, the investigators summoned most of the other children in the case to ask what they knew about a murder. The idea seemed so improbable as to be beyond serious consideration, but six of the children agreed that a murder had taken place. The victim, they said, had been a young black boy with curly hair who had shown up at one of the parties unaccompanied by an adult. Before he was killed, the boy had been tortured with a knife by the grown-ups. It was there, however, that the children's accounts began to diverge. One child said the boy had worn a red and blue shirt and pink, yellow, and red pants. Another said he wore a jacket with zippers on the front, "like Michael Jackson." A third child described the victim as dressed in a light-blue shirt and cutoff jeans. A fourth said he had worn a black shirt and black pants. Nor could the children agree on whether the boy had been shot, stabbed, or drowned, or whether his body had been buried in the woods or thrown in the Minnesota River. A couple of the children even said there had been more than one murder.

While the Bentz trial was getting under way, the investigators had been out looking for bodies, but the murder investigation was running into one brick wall after another. It didn't take the investigators long to conclude that some of the children's accounts were fanciful on their face — the assertion, for instance, from the same eleven-year-old who admitted having lied at the Bentz trial, that the murdered child had been the drummer in a band hired to perform at one of the parties. But some of the other accounts seemed to ring true, and the police continued to puzzle over how so many children who had seen one another only briefly or not at all over the past several months could have provided essentially the same physical description of the murdered child. When one young witness described for a therapist how the boy had gone into convulsions, the therapist thought it was "a piece of medical detail that I felt uncomfortable with a child knowing."

It was during a child custody hearing in family court that one of the seven children who had talked about the murders, a nine-year-old girl, finally admitted that she had lied — not about having been abused, she told the judge, but about having watched a child die. There hadn't been any strange boy, and there hadn't been any murder. The girl's recantation — which she would later recant again, after it was too late to matter — left Kathleen Morris with no other choice. Just as the second couple was about to go to trial, Morris called a press conference to announce that all of the charges against the twenty-one remaining defendants in the sexual abuse case — the original two dozen minus Jim Rud and Bob and Lois Bentz — were being dropped.

Morris left the reason for the dismissals vague, saying only that to pursue the remaining sexual abuse cases would jeopardize another, unspecified investigation of "great magnitude." But to those who knew what was going on behind the scenes, the reason was crystal-clear. The seven children who had made the murder allegations were the key witnesses, and in some cases the only witnesses, against ten of the twenty-one remaining defendants. As a group their credibility was shot, and without their testimony, half of Morris's remaining cases went up in smoke, since how could any jury possibly believe that children who had lied about a murder were telling the truth about having been sexually abused? "Those children," one of the defense lawyers said later, "would have been destroyed on the witness stand." The six other children who had told about the murder were sticking to their stories, but now the FBI had entered the investigation on the grounds that the murdered child might have been brought to Minnesota from another state.

Most of the FBI agents assigned to the Jordan case had been extensively trained in sexual abuse investigations, and they brought with them a professionalism and an air of efficiency and authority that the children were not used to. Most important, the federal agents had no investment in the outcome of the case. "We'd say, How do you know this happened? When? Where? What were the other people doing?" one of the agents said. "Let's say a kid saw someone dump a body at a certain location on the river. We'd take the kid out there, and he'd positively identify the location. We'd ask him when it happened, and he'd give us a certain date. We'd check the conditions on the river that day and find out the river was flooded, that it was impossible to dump a body there." Faced with such intensive scrutiny, it wasn't long before the other children began to recant. One boy had insisted that the body of the murdered child had been carried across a particular bridge. When the FBI discovered that the bridge had been washed away by a flood the year before, the boy broke down and cried. He had lied about the murder, he said, because he thought that the lie would keep him from being returned to his parents. A second boy, the one who said the murdered child had been the drummer in a rock and roll band, admitted that he had gotten the idea of ritualistic torture from a television program he had seen. He had lied about the murder because he wanted to please the investigators, whom he had come to think of as his friends and who seemed always to want something more from him. The four other children who had been counted by the police as among the seven who claimed a murder had occurred told the FBI they had never said any such thing. What they had meant, they said, was that some of the children who were abused had also been hurt.

In Jordan and around the country, the reaction to the dropping of the charges was one of utter astonishment. For months, out-of-state reporters had been visiting the town, talking to those on both sides of the case and to the townspeople caught in the middle, and then filing stories — always with the standard disclaimer that no one had yet been found guilty — that portrayed the case as among the most sordid crimes in recent memory. Now, in a flash, the whole thing had simply evaporated. Within the criminal justice community, particularly among those who had been involved in some aspect of the investigation, the anger at Kathleen Morris was intense. Certainly mistakes had been made, the investigators agreed, but they were mostly mistakes of procedure and preparation, not mistakes of fact. The investigators also pointed out that most of the children who had fouled things up by talking about murderers had been considered loose cannons from the beginning. There were still a number of younger children who had said nothing about any murder and who were prepared to testify against half of the erstwhile defendants. Perhaps the case could not be resurrected in its entirety, but a large part of it seemed salvageable. The only question was, Who would do the salvaging? Two days after the charges were dropped, Hubert H. Humphrey III, the Minnesota attorney general and son of the late senator, announced that his office, in conjunction with the Bureau of Criminal Apprehension and the FBI, was taking over the Jordan case.

Then, another explosion. Jim Rud, promised leniency in return for the truth, was now telling investigators that the statement he had given them three months before, the one that corroborated many of the children's accounts, was a tapestry of lies. Rud wasn't professing his own innocence; he still admitted having abused sixteen of the children in the case. What he was saying now was that he knew nothing about any abuse by the Bentzes or any of the other adults. "I worked on my own," he told Lynn Emmerman of the *Chicago Tribune* from his cell at the Scott County jail. When he began talking to the police, Rud said, he didn't plan to lie. But his lawyer had routinely been sending him copies of the police reports provided by the prosecution, reports that summarized the investigators' interviews with the children, and he had used them as a basis for his fabrications. "Put yourself in my shoes for a minute," Rud said. "Think of forty years behind bars. You'd probably do anything to get out of that." Even to falsely accuse his own parents? "I love my parents dearly," he said. "They know I lied. I have lots of guilt."

Rud's recantation was a blow, but he had only implicated just over half of the twenty-four defendants in his statement, and he was not the only one who had said he was present at the gatherings and parties. Most of the children had said so too, and they had said it months before he did. But the biggest mystery surrounding Rud's recantation was what he hoped to gain. His provisional sentence of six years had been predicated on his telling the truth, and now the plea bargain agreement was out the window. By claiming he had lied, Rud was looking at maximum hard time, forty years in the Minnesota Correctional Facility at St. Cloud. The state and federal agents didn't have any answers, and when a polygraph examination failed to determine whether Rud was really lying, they just put him and his unfathomable motives aside. "He's got so many stories," one said, "who knows what he's saying anymore?"

The agents had better things to do, poring over the thousands of pages of interview reports assembled by police and therapists during the first investigation and painfully cross-indexing each accusation by every child by date, time, place, and corroborating witness, then interviewing the children yet again to sort out the inconsistencies. "We're starting over," one of the federal agents said. "We have our own methods for conducting an investigation. I'm not saying that their way was wrong or our way is right, but I can tell you that our way is successful."

The cross-checking produced some interesting insights. "Some of the kids are liars," another agent said. "Some are telling the truth. We just don't know which is which." The more the agents learned, the more they were convinced that at least some of the adults were guilty. "It isn't just James Rud who's involved in this," a senior investigator said, but a third agent warned that it would be foolish to equate all the former defendants. Three or four, he said, appeared to be genuine psychopaths. The rest, including most of the women, were followers. "Maybe they didn't do anything, but they knew what was happening," the agent said. "They went along with what their husbands wanted. They were very passive, dependent people who had had hard lives. They were victims like their children." Despite their conclusions, the agents were not optimistic about their chances of bringing new charges. "We'd have to find something new," one agent said. "I'm very realistic about what we have to deal with. These kids have suffered some credibility problems."

Two months later, the Jordan case was closed forever. In a twenty-nine-page report titled "Scott County Investigations," the attorney general's office explained that there was "insufficient evidence to justify the filing of any new sex abuse charges." All of the obstacles that couldn't be overcome, the report went on, stemmed from the mishandling of the original investigation, and the list of errors was long. Some of the defendants had been arrested before they, or even their children, had been interviewed. Standard electronic and physical surveillance techniques were not used. Search warrants were rarely obtained. "The tragedy of Scott County," the report said, "goes beyond the inability to successfully prosecute individuals who may have committed child sexual abuse. Equally tragic is the possibility that some were unjustly accused and forced to endure long separations from their families." Attorney General Humphrey suggested that Kathleen Morris might want to resign.

She didn't, but her methods, like those of the police and the therapists, were being questioned in other quarters. When they were asked for their opinions of what had gone wrong, most of those familiar with the full scope of the case included the name of Kathleen Morris somewhere in their answers. "It's hard for me to explain why Kathleen did a lot of the things she did," said one. "Kathleen's tough to figure," said another. "It just got away from Kathleen," said a third. Among the questions was why Morris had charged two dozen people before she had obtained a single verdict, rather than trying to win a conviction in her best case and using it as a foundation to charge and prosecute the others. "You go for your best stuff first," one Minneapolis lawyer said. "You don't charge the world and try to beat the world. Nobody's that good."

Morris replied hotly that she had acted to protect the children from further abuse. Only by charging their parents as soon as an allegation had been made, she said, could she ask a judge to remove the children from their homes. It sounded like a reasonable explanation, exept that in Minnesota, as in most states, children can be taken from abusive or neglectful parents who have not been charged with any crime. Another question being asked was how the twenty-four defendants had been chosen from among the forty-five adult suspects listed in police records, particularly since some of those not charged had been accused earlier, and of more serious abuses, than some of those who were charged. Morris stood her ground. "I'm supposed to be the villain," she replied. "Let me be the villain. They have to have somebody to blame. There's a lot of wrong happening in the world. Wrong is what's happening to kids. It's not fair for the kids, so why should it be fair for me? I've got a whole bunch of kids I've got to worry about. They don't want to believe what's going on? Let them blame me."

As the questions continued to resound, Minnesota governor Rudy Perpich appointed a commission of inquiry to pass judgment on Morris's handling of the case. When Morris decided she needed a lawyer to represent her before the commission, she chose Steve Doyle, her ex-husband. Doyle had also been one of the defense attorneys in the case, but by then nobody in Scott County was very much surprised by anything Kathleen Morris did. Among the first to testify at the Morris hearing was Officer Larry Norring, who had worked full time on the case since arresting Jim Rud more than two years before. If Norring hadn't been a child abuse expert when the case began, he was one by now. Norring thought most of the cases had been solid ones, "excellent cases" that should have been taken to court.

Several of the investigators who had worked on the murder angle followed Norring, and despite the FBI's conclusions, they still weren't certain that no murders had taken place. "Something terrible happened to those children," said a Jordan police detective named Norm Pint. "You could see the fear and distress in their faces when they talked about it. But whenever we got into locations of where the bodies were buried, it was like the clouds rolled in. It was never clear what happened to the bodies." Earl Fleck, a policeman from neighboring Shakopee, even suggested an explanation. "I wonder," he said, "if the children weren't speaking to us metaphorically, in a sense reporting to us their own deaths. I think the children were crying out to us in reporting the death of their own inner soul, their own spiritual life, and they were screaming to us in a sense and saying, 'I'm dying here, this is killing us.' "

After hearing two weeks of testimony and examining five thousand pages of documents, the commission faulted Morris for keeping the murder investigation a secret from the defense and for misleading the judge about where the witnesses at the Bentz trial had been housed. But it reserved its strongest criticism for her decision to drop the remaining charges in the case. "Those defendants who were guilty went free," the report said, "and those who were innocent were left without the opportunity to clear their names. Those children who were victims became victims once again, abandoned by the system and by the system's representative, Kathleen Morris." Merely dropping the charges did not constitute malfeasance, however, and there was not sufficient cause to recommend that Morris be removed from office. Governor Perpich, who had agreed to abide by the commission's findings, made it official: Kathleen Morris would remain as prosecutor until the voters of Scott County had a chance to speak. In November 1986, the voters made their feelings clear. By nearly a two-to-one margin, Morris was defeated for reelection by a challenger fresh out of law school.

To most of those who didn't live there, the Jordan sex case was a string of newspaper headlines or a series of disconnected images fluttering across a television screen — handcuffed parents being led away in ones and twos followed by thirty-second interviews with somber investigators, angry defense lawyers, grim-faced defendants, and a self-righteous-sounding prosecutor. Incomprehensible to begin with, the case was also unrivaled in its complexity, and many of the details and nuances had long since gotten lost. As Kathleen Morris's prosecution fell apart piece by piece, Jordan became "that little town up in Minnesota where all the children lied." When the case finally disintegrated in full public view, it was perhaps inevitable that "Jordan" would become a paradigm of sorts, a one-word metaphor for the combination of anger, repulsion, and incredulity that the subject of child sexual abuse evoked in most of those who thought about it.

Many people were thinking about it, for by the end of 1984, it was becoming difficult to pick up a newspaper or turn on a television set without reading or hearing of someone else who had been convicted of sexually abusing a child, including a surprising number of prominent and respected men and women: school principals and military officers, police officers and doctors, nursery school owners and university professors, professional athletes and television stars, socialites and rock musicians, even clergymen. More than the names and numbers, though, it was the suddenness of it all that didn't make sense. Not many Americans were under the impression that their society didn't have its share of troubles, but now they were being asked to believe that they faced yet another enormous and urgent problem, one that had been there all along, hidden from their view.

It was asking a lot, and not only because the uncounted thousands of children claiming to have been sexually abused were telling Americans something unpleasant about themselves. Children also seemed to have acquired the power to point a finger and send an adult to jail, and some of those who were not frightened for their children were becoming frightened of their children. Parents were thinking twice before letting a child awakened by a nightmare crawl into their bed, for fear of what the child might say at school the next day about having "slept with Mommy and Daddy." Preschool teachers who had once rewarded good behavior with a hug and a kiss were telling children instead to "give yourself a pat on the back." Fathers playing tag with their children at the neighborhood pool pretended not to hear when children they didn't know asked to join the game. Neighbor ladies who had earned extra money baby-sitting began to look for other sources of income.

Had children gone mad? Possibly, some thought, recalling the Salem witch trials. What seemed more likely, though, was that ambitious prosecutors, overzealous police officers, and the news media were putting ideas into children's heads. The news media, perhaps the most sensitive to criticism of all public institutions, soon began trying to make up for its perceived excess. "A lot of the graphic horror stories in the press are themselves little more than child porn," wrote Michael Kinsley, *The New Republic*'s respected editor. "And when they're not being salacious, the media are being mawkish, which sells almost as well." On "60 Minutes," Mike Wallace reported the story of Erin Tobin, a University of Texas coed accused of sexually abusing the three-year-old twins for whom she occasionally baby-sat; her arrest had been highly publicized before a grand jury decided there was insufficient evidence to bring her to trial.

"Are we in the media responsible for all the attention," Wallace asked, "all of the lurid details of this kind of thing coming out now?" An equally concerned voice belonged to Phil Donahue, whose producers assembled a panel of people, among them Bob and Lois Bentz, who claimed to have been unjustly accused of sexually abusing children. "What is child abuse?" Donahue demanded. "And should children be able to accuse you? And is that information enough to convict you? And who's watching the prosecutors? We are scared to death of child abusers in this country, and it appears that on more than one occasion we have perhaps gone too far and railroaded innocent people." Leo Buscaglia, the University of Southern California psychologist who wrote best-selling books urging people to love one another, was also moved to wonder whether "the cure isn't worse than the disease." As deplorable as child abuse was, he wrote, "it would be more' harmful to eliminate all physical contact between adults and children. Children need to be cuddled and hugged for health reasons and for the security that is conveyed by a gentle hand, a reassuring touch."

The growing public concern was perhaps best expressed by a member of the Jewish Big Brothers Association of Los Angeles, who wrote to a local newspaper that "in the current climate of accusation, the concept of innocent until proven guilty is forgotten. When that happens, we've committed a crime even worse than child sexual molestation. If this hysteria continues unabated, a generation from now someone is going to ask the question: What is worse, molestation or starvation of affection, the disease or the cure?" Sensing the wind's shifting direction, twenty-six accused child molesters in the Bakersfield, California, jail went on a hunger strike, demanding that prosecutors allow them to take lie-detector tests to establish their innocence. The strike followed a protest outside the jail by a new organization called VOCAL, short for Victims of Child Abuse Laws, whose 120 chapters around the country were composed of men and women claiming to have been unjustly accused of abusing children. Leslie Wimberly, the head of VOCAL's California chapter, spoke for many when she said, "The consensus that a child does not lie is wrong and behind the times."

It wasn't that anybody, aside from the child molesters, was in favor of adults having sex with children, or even that anybody thought that child sexual abuse didn't exist. Rather, the concern seemed to focus on the question of how many children were being sexually abused, of just how large the problem really was. To judge from the current increase in child abuse reports, it seemed quite large. A decade ago, only about twelve thousand American children were reported each year as having been sexually abused. By 1985 the number had passed 150,000, and no state or region seemed to be exempt. Reports in Georgia were up by 102 percent, in Iowa by 40 percent, in North Carolina by 43 percent, in Rhode Island by 51 percent. Even largely rural Maine was reporting a single-year increase of 300 percent.

Startling as they were, such numbers were almost certainly too low. Not all states kept child abuse statistics, and those that did tallied them in different ways. Some states counted the number of families where abuse had been reported, not the number of victims in each family. Some states only counted the number of children who were abused, not the number of times they were abused or the number of adults who abused them. Some states didn't even distinguish between physical and sexual abuse, or between abuse and neglect, and most didn't count abuse by neighbors or day-care workers or other non-relatives.

Those who wished to dismiss the problem of child sexual abuse as *de minimus* suggested that many of the reports were simply untrue, a notion that can be traced to an article by Douglas J. Besharov that appeared in the summer of 1985 in the *Harvard Journal of Law and Public Policy*.[1] Besharov's assertion that 65 percent of the child abuse reports made in this country proved to be "unfounded" received a surprising degree of publicity, in part because he spoke with considerable authority — Besharov was a former director of the National

Center on Child Abuse and Neglect, the chief federal agency charged with promoting the protection of children. Among those who seized upon his research were Paul and Shirley Eberle, the authors of *The Politics of Child Abuse*,[2] who toured the country to argue that child protection advocates were conducting a "child abuse witch hunt" and "profiteering on the ruin of innocent people."

Like the Eberles, most of those who cited the Besharov paper as evidence that children were lying about sexual abuse hadn't read it very carefully. For one thing, Besharov's statistics included all types of child abuse reports, not just sexual abuse but physical abuse and neglect. For another, most child abuse reports come not from children but from adults. Some of the overreporting, Besharov said, doubtless resulted from mistaken expressions of concern by well-intentioned adults. He also acknowledged that "few of these 'unfounded' reports are made maliciously; rather, most involve confusion over what types of situations should be reported. Approximately half involve situations of poor child care which, though of legitimate concern, are not sufficiently serious to be considered 'child maltreatment.' "

Also largely overlooked in the debate Besharov's article generated was the fact that *unfounded* did not mean untrue, but only that the allegations in question could not be proved one way or the other. Besharov noted that while they have gotten better in recent years, state-run child-protection bureaucracies have not increased their capacity to investigate suspected child abuse by anything resembling the exponential increase in the number of reports. Because of highly publicized child abuse hotlines and relatively new laws requiring a wide range of professionals to report any instance of suspected child abuse, many more reports are being funneled to such agencies than they can effectively investigate. California's child protection system has long been pointed to as a model for other states, and it is better than most, but the California Department of Social Services admits that it investigates fewer than half of the fifty thousand child abuse reports it receives each year.

Most states now have laws requiring that child abuse reports be investigated, and some determination made, within what is proving to be an impossibly short period of time. In many states an investigation must be begun within twenty-four hours of the receipt of a report, but in practice such deadlines are often ignored. In order to keep the case alive, harried child protection workers routinely certify that they have met the deadline for beginning an inquiry, even when they cannot find the victim's home. If they cannot determine within a week or ten days whether an accusation of abuse is true, the report in question is either labeled "unfounded" or purged from the state's central registry altogether.[3] During an average month in 1985, nearly five thousand Los Angeles children who were suspected of being physically or sexually abused were never visited by a child protection worker at all.

The social workers, police officers, and prosecutors assigned to handle such cases also point out that the reports of child sexual abuse are the most difficult to prove. Many children who have been starved or beaten will carry with them some visible evidence of mistreatment, but in cases of sexual abuse there may well be no evidence at all. If a child is too young or too frightened to talk, or if there is no physical or medical evidence to support his allegations, the only choice is to mark the case "unfounded."

Because so many children who are sexually abused never tell anybody about it in the first place, all the numbers being tossed about were misleading anyway. But with all the doubt and confusion that had sprung up around the issue, such nuances were largely lost. If 1984 had been the year of the sexually abused child, then 1985 was fast becoming the year of the child abuse backlash, an understandable reaction to an issue that had assumed in some minds the proportions of a hysteria. There were, after all, something like sixty-three million children in America, and while a problem that afflicted a few thousand children every year was to be dealt with expeditiously, it didn't necessarily demand any more urgency than suicide or drug abuse or a dozen equally compelling problems. To many of those who had initially been alarmed by what they heard and read, child sexual abuse was beginning to look like a rather modest social problem. But that was before anybody knew that thirty-eight million American men and women had been sexually abused as children.

TWO

Numbers

THE STORY THAT appeared on the front page of the *Los Angeles Times* for Sunday, August 25, 1985, was thoroughly unequivocal: "At least 22% of Americans," it began, "have been victims of child sexual abuse, although one-third of them told no one at the time and lived with their secret well into adulthood." As the article went on to show, the *Times* had done something no one had ever attempted. Using the techniques of an ordinary public opinion poll, it had conducted a random survey in which thousands of Americans were asked not whom they planned to vote for or what they thought about arms control, but whether they had been sexually abused as children. In trying to get a handle on the true extent of child sexual abuse in America, the *Times* had taken a retrospective approach. If, as the child advocates maintained, many of the children who were being sexually abused were not talking, and if, as the doubters made clear, many of those who were talking were not being believed, then why not ask adults about their sexual experiences as children?

It wasn't exactly a new idea. One of the first to try such a backward-looking survey had been Alfred Kinsey, the zoology professor from Indiana University who became this country's pioneer researcher in the field of human sexuality. When it was finally published, in 1948, Kinsey's *Sexual Behavior in the Human Female* was a national best-seller for weeks.[1] Although viewed by those who hadn't read it as something of a risqué document, the Kinsey survey was 842 pages of the most dispassionate and clinical language imaginable, reinforced with charts, graphs, and tables.[2] By illuminating what Americans really did inside their bedrooms, as opposed to what they pretended to do, Kinsey had made a giant stride toward the demystification of sex in America. Among his most important findings was that, during the first half of this century, sex between adults and children in America was fairly commonplace. Nearly a quarter of the four thousand women who answered Kinsey's questions said they had either had sex with adult men while they were children or had been approached by men seeking sex.

Even more remarkable was the degree to which that part of Kinsey's report was almost completely ignored, not just by the public but by his fellow researchers. In 1955, when S. K. Weinberg published what was then considered a landmark study of incest, he estimated that its victims totaled only one English-speaking child in every million.[3] One of the first contemporary researchers to follow in Kinsey's footsteps was David Finkelhor, a sociologist from the University of New Hampshire who handed out written questionnaires asking eight hundred students at six New England colleges whether they had been abused as children.[4] Finkelhor's numbers were a little lower than Kinsey's — 19 percent of the women students and 9 percent of the men said they had had some sort of sex with an adult while they were children — and the problem with Finkelhor's findings, as had been the case with Kinsey's, was that the people he questioned had not been randomly selected. The women who talked with Kinsey's interviewers had volunteered to be questioned about their sex lives, which by itself meant that they weren't representative of the general population. Finkelhor's subjects were not only volunteers, they were also college students, which set them doubly apart from the average American man or woman.

The first truly random sexual abuse survey wasn't begun until 1979, when Diana Russell, a British-born sociologist with a Harvard Ph.D., set out to interview more than nine hundred randomly chosen San Francisco women about their childhood sexual experiences. It was then the largest and most complex survey of its type ever undertaken, and Russell spent the next five years assembling and analyzing the results. What she found was that 38 percent of those questioned — nearly four women in every ten — had been sexually abused by an adult relative, acquaintance, or stranger before reaching the age of eighteen.

Sexual abuse is a term more of art than of science. It can cover a multitude of sins, from exhibitionism and fondling to sexual intercourse, by a multitude of abusers, from parents and teachers to baby-sitters and strangers. It can happen once or it can go on for years. It can be violent or not violent. Russell's survey raised the question, not as facile as it sounds, of what, precisely, constitutes sexual abuse.

The instinctive answer is that any sexual contact between an adult and a child is abusive, and yet the same degree of seriousness cannot be attached to intercourse as to fondling. Because of the disturbing impact they can have on young children, experiences such as exhibitionism, in which the victim's body is never actually touched, must also be included.

Russell divided the experiences reported by the women in her survey into three categories: very serious abuse, which she defined as vaginal, oral, and anal intercourse, cunnilingus, and analingus; serious abuse (genital fondling, simulated intercourse, penetration of the anus or vagina with a finger); and least serious abuse (fondling buttocks, thighs, legs, or other body parts, clothed breasts or genitals, and kissing). Nearly two-thirds of the incidents recalled by women who said they had had sex with parents or other relatives, and four-fifths of those recalled by women who said they had been abused by non-relatives, qualified as either very serious or serious. When exhibitionism and other "noncontact" experiences were added in, the number of women in the survey who reported some sort of sexual abuse as children rose to 54 percent.

Any discussion of child sexual abuse must also include the question of what a child is, and the answer is not as obvious as it appears. A century ago, sex between children and adults was illegal in most states only if the child was younger than eleven. Today the generally accepted age at which a child becomes an adult is eighteen, which also happens to be the age of consent in most places, although not in all. In South Dakota and Virginia the age of consent is fifteen, and in Colorado, Hawaii, and Georgia it's fourteen. Not only are some statutes inconsistent in their definition of a child, they reflect an inability to decide what child abuse is. When a forty-year-old Tennessee dairy farmer had sex with the thirteen-year-old girl who lived on the next farm, prosecutors prepared to charge the man with statutory rape. But Tennessee law prohibits having sex with a thirteen-year-old girl only if she's not your wife; the farmer married the girl and remained a free man.

A sexual relationship between a grown man and a thirteen-year-old girl, while illegal in most states, cannot be looked at in quite the same way as one between a grown man and a six-year-old, and most state laws make allowances for age differences among the victims of sexual abuse. In California, any sexual activity with a boy or girl between the ages of fourteen and seventeen is statutory rape. If the child is under fourteen, the offense is child molestation, and for children under ten the penalties are even more severe. But Russell's survey helped to refine the question by making a distinction between victims who were younger than thirteen and those who were older. What she found was that 28 percent of the women who said they had been seriously abused had been abused before reaching the age of fourteen, 12 percent by someone in their families.

Like Kinsey and Finkelhor before her, Russell had an advantage over most people who ask the public questions — she didn't have to worry very much about being lied to. People might tell a poll taker they're going to vote Democratic when they're really going to vote Republican, but it's hard to think of a reason for anyone to say she was sexually abused as a child when she really wasn't. Much more likely was the possibility that some of the women in Russell's survey had lied when they said they hadn't been sexually abused as children, which meant there was a good chance Russell's figures were too low.

When Russell published her findings at the end of 1983, it was in a relatively obscure journal, and almost nobody noticed outside the small community of child advocates who read such publications, the same people who for years had been trying to tell the public that the sexual abuse of children was a far larger problem than anyone knew.[5] But Russell's figures were so far beyond those reported by Kinsey and Finkelhor that even some of the experts didn't trust them completely. Random sample or not, some of Russell's colleagues suggested that any survey conducted in San Francisco was bound to be unrepresentative of the rest of the country. Even if 38 percent of San Francisco women had been sexually abused as children, one ought not to assume the same was true for the women of Oshkosh or Cedar Rapids. When Russell pointed out that many of the women she interviewed had moved to San Francisco from somewhere else, her critics replied that perhaps women who moved to San Francisco were not the same as women who didn't.

As the debate over the validity of Russell's findings continued, Bud Lewis was watching from the sidelines. Lewis was the director of the *Los Angeles Times* poll, and his careful and scholarly approach to questions of public opinion had made the poll one of the most respected anywhere. Like most big-city newspapers, the *Times* had been devoting a lot of space to the subject of child sexual abuse, and some of the editors who worked there were beginning to ask the same question as their readers: Could this really be happening to so many American children? What was badly needed, Lewis thought, was a random national survey, one that included men as well as women.

Lewis looked over the current literature, but when he asked some of the scholars for suggestions about how to proceed, the responses were not encouraging. "They thought that I would screw it up," he said. Bud Lewis, who probably knew more about telephone polling than all the sociologists in the country put together, went ahead. Over a period of eight days in July 1985 telephones began ringing across the country, in Cape Cod cottages and Midwestern farmhouses, in Manhattan apartment buildings and Southern California condominiums. By the time Lewis's poll takers were done, they had questioned 2,627 men and women, from every state in the nation. [6]

Because of the cleverness with which the survey had been designed, nearly all the people who answered their phones were willing to talk. "I had a couple of innocuous questions at the beginning," Lewis said, "and then I told them what the survey was going to be about and asked whether it was going to give them any difficulty to talk about it." Only three people in every hundred said it would; the rest plowed bravely through the next ninety-seven questions. What Lewis most wanted to find was the number of sexual abuse victims among them, but his approach was indirect. "I moved into general attitudes about child sexual abuse that anybody would answer," he said, "and then I got into questions like how prevalent they thought it was. And then I asked them, 'If you were a victim, would you tell about it?' And of course, most people said they would. And then I just said, 'Well, were you?' And they sort of hooked themselves, because they said they'd tell."

Twenty-two percent of those questioned, 27 percent of the women and 16 percent of the men, said they had been sexually abused as children. [7] If those percentages were applied to the current population, it meant that nearly thirty-eight million adults had been sexually abused as children, several hundred thousand more than voted for Walter Mondale in 1984. [8] Lewis's poll takers didn't question any children, but if the experiences of American children were the same as those of their parents and grandparents, more than eight million girls and five million boys then alive will be sexually abused before they reach their eighteenth birthdays.

Many of the abuses uncovered by the *Times* survey were of the most serious kind, and they cast doubt on a number of myths about the sexual abuse of children — that intercourse between adults and children is relatively rare, that most sexual abuse is accompanied by the use of physical force, that boys are almost never the victims of abuse, and that most abusers are people the child doesn't know. The survey also provided a clue to just how well hidden sexual abuse has been over the years, since a third of the victims said they had never told anyone about their experiences, not even their husbands or wives. Even when they had told someone, in most cases nothing had been done; only 3 percent of the cases were ever reported to the police.

Apart from providing by far the clearest picture yet of the magnitude of child sexual abuse in America, the *Times* survey helped answer an equally important question: Who are the victims of child sexual abuse? In some ways the victims didn't seem much different from the nonvictims. They were slightly better educated, more of them were employed, and those that were working held somewhat better jobs. Most of the victims lived in the suburbs, were slightly less religious and somewhat more liberal politically. It was just below the surface, however, that the important differences began to emerge. Though a number of the victims had grown up in families headed by women, they hadn't been as close to their mothers as the nonvictims had. The victims had come from smaller families and had been more isolated as children. They described their families as significantly less happy than those of the nonvictims, and their adult lives also seemed more disjointed. More of them were separated or divorced, and more had also remarried. Least surprising of all, their adult sexual relationships had been much less satisfactory.

For decades the sexual abuse of children has been popularly perceived as a "lower-class phenomenon," which is a polite way of saying that it is mostly a problem among the poor, especially blacks and other minorities. Researchers have tried to change this perception by pointing out that child sexual abuse must really be a mainstream crime, since there are more white, middle-class sexual abuse victims flowing through the courts and child protective agencies than any other kind. The retrospective studies do suggest that white, middle-class children are most often abused, but there are also more white, middle-class children living in this country than any other kind. To emphasize abuse among the middle class is to risk overlooking abuse among minorities; the *Times* survey found that the incidence of sexual abuse among blacks and whites is almost exactly the same, about 21 percent for men and women combined.

Why do so few black victims show up within the criminal justice system? One answer is provided by Gail Wyatt, a professor of medical psychology at UCLA who spent two years interviewing a random sample of 248 adult women in Los Angeles County, half of them black and the other half white. In all, 59 percent of the women Wyatt questioned reported at least one unwanted sexual experience with an adult while they were children — the highest number of victims uncovered by any survey thus far.[9] But Wyatt also asked the women whom they had told about being abused. "For those people who told nobody," she said, "I also asked, 'Why didn't you tell?' It's fascinating to see what those people said. 'I didn't tell because I thought I'd be blamed, or because no one would believe me, or that something about my behavior would be the issue, like "Why did you walk down that street?" or "What were you doing in that house?" more than "Who is this person and where can we find him?" ' " Even when a black child did tell, Wyatt found, her family was not likely to involve the police. "They tended to try to take care of the situation themselves," she said, "to go out and try to find the perpetrator. White families get involved in the system much more readily."

As Bud Lewis began breaking down the responses to the *Times* survey by age and geography, he discovered a couple of curious things. One was that there appeared to be some merit to the criticism of regional bias lodged against Diana Russell's findings. In most parts of the country, Lewis found, the number of victims closely matched the distribution of the population. But 21 percent of the victims lived in the five-state Pacific Region — California, Alaska, Hawaii, Oregon, and Washington — an area that has only 14 percent of the nation's population. Did a proportionally greater number of victims in the western United States mean that more children had been abused in the West than in the North, South, or East? It was certainly a possibility, but there was no way of knowing where the Pacific Region victims had actually grown up, because Lewis hadn't asked them.

Potentially more significant was Lewis's discovery that many of those who acknowledged having been abused were younger than those who said they hadn't been. Not that there weren't any old victims — one in three was over forty-five and one in ten over sixty-five, which meant there was nothing very new about sexual abuse in America. But the largest group of victims was between eighteen and twenty-nine. This might simply mean that older Americans were more reluctant to talk about their experiences. But it might also mean that more children have been sexually abused in the years since World War II.

Has the sexual abuse of children increased in recent years? Reports of sexually abused children are clearly on the rise, but some of that increase is doubtless a result of what statisticians call a "reporting phenomenon"; more reports don't necessarily mean more victims in an absolute sense, only that more victims are coming forward. But

Lewis's numbers suggest that not all of the increase is attributable to an increased willingness to report, and there is some other support for such a conclusion. Diana Russell found that, except during the two world wars, when millions of American men were absent from the country, the incidence of incest increased from about 9 percent of girls "at risk" in 1916 to 28 percent in 1956.

Because of the loopholes in the retrospective studies, it's difficult to say with any certainty whether more children are being sexually abused now than before, but a number of demographic trends suggest that more children are at least running the risk of being abused. More than four American workers in ten are now women; more than half of the women with children under six, and half of those with children under three, work full time. For the first time in history, it seems, more American children have mothers who work than have ones who stay home. Many of those women are married, but many others are not. The number of single-parent families, nearly all of them headed by women, increased by more than 40 percent during the 1970s. The number of divorces in America is also rising steadily, and a fifth of all babies born in this country are born to unmarried women. By 1990, at least a third of all families with children will be headed by only one parent. More working, single, and divorced mothers means a greater demand for day-care centers, nurseries, and baby-sitters to look after preschoolers, and a greater demand for youth groups, sports teams, and other activities to fill the after-school hours of older children. Because some child abusers take jobs in day-care centers and other surroundings that provide them with access to children, more surrogate child-tenders may create more avenues for contact between abusers and potential victims.

There is another aspect to such demographics. As the divorce rate rises, so does the number of women who marry for a second time, and even a third. Fifteen years ago only a quarter of the marriages performed in this country were second marriages; today the figure is 34 percent. More second marriages mean more stepfathers, and step-daughters seem particularly vulnerable to sexual abuse. Diana Russell found that women who had a stepfather as a principal male figure in their childhoods were six times more likely to have been abused than those with a biological father. [10] As some researchers have begun to suspect, it may be the case that a growing number of stepfathers are really "smart pedophiles," men who marry divorced or single women with families as a way of getting close to children.

The recent recognition that many abused children grow up to

become child abusers raises the possibility that child sexual abuse may be increasing of its own accord. When groups of men who admit abusing children are asked whether they themselves were sexually abused as children, the great majority say that they were. Not every sexually abused child grows up to become a child abuser — if that were the case, one American in every four or five would be having sex with children. But as the number of current victims increases, so does the population of future abusers, and because many abusers have more than one victim, the sexual abuse of children threatens to become an upward spiral.

Is the sexual abuse of children a uniquely American problem? It doesn't seem to be. In late 1983 the government of Canada set out to do what the government of this country has not yet done, by commissioning the Canadian Gallup organization to conduct face-to-face interviews with more than two thousand men and women on their sexual experiences as children. The survey, which filled thirteen hundred pages, found that more than one out of every two Canadian women, and more than one in three Canadian men, had been subjected to some kind of sexual abuse as a child.[11] It also found that Canadians of all ages reported about the same incidence of abuse, a strong indication that sexual abuse has been occurring there with about the same frequency for most of this century. Said the parliamentary committee that oversaw the project, "Sexual offenses are committed so frequently, and against so many persons, that there is an evident and urgent need to afford victims greater protection than that now being provided."

Except for the United States and Canada, only a handful of countries have carried out any serious research into the incidence of sexual abuse. Reports of child abuse in Great Britain have risen by some 70 percent over the past six years, but that country has been curiously late in recognizing child molestation as a substantial problem. Public attitudes in Britain began to change last year, when two researchers interviewed 2,019 English men and women over the age of fifteen. Twelve percent of the women and 10 percent of the men acknowledged having had sex with an adult while they were children.[12] Though lower than the figures produced by similar surveys in the United States, those numbers suggest that at least five million Britons now alive were sexually abused as children. "Two issues dominated British people's lives this year and last, world famine and child abuse," says Keith Bradbrook, an official of Britain's National Society for the Prevention of Cruelty to Children. Bradbrook estimates that some fifty thousand British children fall victim to sexual abuse each year, not a small number in a nation of fifty million people.

Much less is known about child sexual abuse in the rest of the world. Though having sex with children is technically a crime in most European countries, child abuse there is not ordinarily considered a matter for law enforcement. All but the most egregious cases are treated as a public health problem best left to social service and child protection agencies to resolve. As a result statistics are sparse, and those that are available may reflect just a fraction of the real incidence. Fifteen thousand cases were reported in West Germany in 1985, and the Italian Association for the Prevention of Cruelty to Children says it knows of about the same number of reports in that country. Underreporting may be particularly high in Italy, however, where closely knit families resist intervention by neighbors or outsiders. In Holland, where the Ministry of Health has established special bureaus staffed by pediatricians and social workers to treat the victims of sexual abuse, an average of three thousand cases a year are recorded from among a total population of four million children.

Almost everywhere else in the world, the sexual abuse of children is low on the list of official priorities. Dick Willey, who heads the Los Angeles County Sheriff's Department task force on sexually abused children, recalls attending a conference in Europe where he was lectured by a woman from a drought-stricken African nation. "I can understand your concern over children that are being beaten and children that are being sexually abused," the woman said. "But I have ten thousand children a year dying of starvation." At another conference in Cairo, Willey said, "we got into a debate with some of the government people over there. They didn't even want to address the question of child sexual abuse. They didn't want to talk about it. We would start to get into the issue and it would be shifted over to something else. In many of these countries, children are a secondary or tertiary concern. They don't put the priority on children that we do here. There are a lot of caring people in every country who are doing what they can do, but they're placing their major emphasis on caring for children that have nowhere to live and nothing to eat, trying to keep them alive. It's the hierarchy of needs. Survival comes first."

In some very poor countries, sex with children, while not officially condoned, is unofficially tolerated. Under the regime of Ferdinand Marcos, the economy of Manila's Ermita district depended largely on the profits from child prostitution. The same is true in sections of Bangkok, and the "baby brothels" of Bombay are well known throughout the Indian subcontinent.

No modern society openly endorses sex between children and adults, but such has not always been the case. Egypt's nobility was once permitted to have sex with young family members, and sex was once allowed within the Hawaiian royal family as a means of ensuring that heirs to the throne would be of pure blood. There are a few accounts of more contemporary societies, most of them small and isolated tribes, where some form of sex with children is openly sanctioned. One is the Lepchas of Sikkim, high in the Himalayas, who are said to believe that early sex is necessary to promote the normal physiological development of a young girl.[13] Lepcha girls are betrothed at the age of eight to boys who are slightly older. If a girl does not soon begin her sex life with her intended spouse, an adult member of the village will volunteer to undertake the task. Anthropologists report that something similar occurs among the Chewa of Africa and the Ifuago of the Philippines. Sex between men and boys is also said to be encouraged in the Siwa Valley of North Africa and by some Australian aborigines.[14]

For the rest of the world, sex with children is nominally taboo — nominally, because the extent to which it apparently occurs raises the question of whether such a taboo really exists. The strongest taboo involves sex with one's own children; in that desire human beings appear to be quite alone, since no species of animal has yet been discovered in which adults display a genetic propensity to breed with their own young.[15] But whether the taboo is against having sex with children or, as some anthropologists maintain, merely against talking about having sex with children, its origins are obscure. It may be that, as Roland Summitt has suggested, sex with one's own offspring is such a convenient and appealing idea that the taboo arose as a practical defense. against a natural experience with unfortunate biological consequences. It's possible for two close blood relatives to produce a perfectly healthy child, but such a child also has a much greater than average chance of inheriting some serious genetic flaw.

Another reason for the incest taboo might be economic. Claude Levi-Strauss, the French anthropologist, has suggested that the prohibition arose as a way of guaranteeing the exchange of women among families. If daughters bear their fathers' children instead of marrying and beginning families of their own, there will be no new families and the society will cease to flourish. A third reason could be cultural. At the end of the movie *Chinatown*, the character played by actress Faye

Dunaway startles the audience by revealing that her sister is also her daughter, a phenomenon known to anthropologists as "role strain." In family-based societies especially, it is important that relationships be crystal-clear. Parents must be parents, children must be children, and siblings must be siblings. Incest scrambles these relationships, and the resulting confusion weakens not only the family structure but the fabric of the society as well.

The question of how often the incest taboo has been violated in different societies over the centuries is as murky as the taboo's origins. "We know a lot about what the rules are in other societies," one anthropologist says, "just like we thought we did in this society up until ten years ago. What we don't know is how often the rules are broken in other societies. That's where the big gap is. A lot of research really focuses on the regularities of cultural behavior rather than the deviance. We collect incest taboos, but it's very difficult to get at the question of how many people really broke them."

In many earlier societies, clear distinctions were drawn between sex with one's own children and sex with other peoples' children. While incest in fifteenth-century Venice was punished by long prison terms and even beheading, sex between adult men and unrelated girls was commonplace, so common that the average age at which girls married was fifteen.[16] The prohibition against sex with unrelated children does not appear to predate the idea of childhood itself, and the idea of childhood — which is to say, the recognition that children are not like adults — is a fairly recent one. Not until sometime in the seventeenth century were children recognized as requiring special protection from the rigors of the adult world. Philippe Aries, the cultural historian, points out that children portrayed in medieval and Renaissance paintings have the faces of grown men and women.[17]

Because children weren't accorded special status, there wasn't much concern about whether sex between adults and children was good or bad. Aries quotes from the memoirs of Heroard, physician to the French court in the early seventeenth century, in which he describes the rather raucous sex play engaged in by little Louis XIII and other members of the royal household, including Louis's mother. Little Louis, Heroard wrote, "made everybody kiss his cock. The Marquise [de Verneuil] often put her hand under his coat. He got his nanny to lay him on her bed where she played with him, putting her hand under his coat. The Queen, touching his cock, said: 'Son, I am holding your spout,' " When, at fourteen, Louis wed the Infanta of Spain, his mother watched while the couple consummated their marriage. "Nowadays," Aries writes, "the physical contacts described by Heroard would strike us as bordering on sexual perversion and nobody would dare to indulge in them publicly. This was not the case at the beginning of the seventeenth century."

Fueled by a moral and religious reformation, the growing predominance of manners, the Industrial Revolution, and the first child labor laws, such behavior began to give way to the notion that children ought to be shielded from the baser elements of life. But despite the gradual recognition that having sex with adults was probably not in children's best interests, a gap remained between word and deed. It was the children of the nineteenth century for whom the first fairy tales were written, but the Victorians have become notorious for preaching one thing and doing quite another where sex was concerned. In 1835, the Society for the Prevention of Juvenile Prostitution reckoned that four hundred Londoners depended for their livelihoods on the earnings of child prostitutes. London hospitals, it was said, had recorded twenty-seven hundred cases of venereal disease among children during the preceding eight years. One of the major accomplishments of England's Victorian-era child welfare brigades was to raise the legal age for prostitution from nine to thirteen.

Things were not much different on the Continent. Between 1858 and 1869, three-quarters of the French citizens charged with rape were accused of raping children, mainly girls, half of them younger than eleven. Alexandre Lacassagne, who held the chair of legal medicine at the University of Lyons, concluded in 1886 that as many as a third of the cases before the French criminal courts at any one time involved the sexual abuse of children.[18]

When the sexual abuse of children was rediscovered in Vienna a generation later, it was quite by accident. Sigmund Freud was just beginning to lay the foundations of what would become modern psychoanalysis, a field then regarded by most who had heard of it at all as a plaything of the idle rich at best and a brand of scientific witchcraft at worst. During the 1890s Freud treated a small group of women who complained of what he called "hysterical illness" — hypochondria, anxiety, hallucinations, and obsessive-compulsive behavior including unfounded fears and uncontrollable impulses, the sort of afflictions that today would be labeled neuroses. There is no detailed record of precisely what Freud's patients told him, but all acknowledged having been sexually abused as children, most by their fathers, a few by their brothers or some other close male relative.

Freud's research might have marked the first retrospective study, except that his patients did not make up a very good cross-section of nineteenth-century Viennese society. Then even more than now, psychoanalysis required a good deal of time and money, and those who availed themselves of Freud's services tended to be well-off and well educated. It was the backgrounds of his patients, in fact, that caused Freud so much astonishment at their recollections. There had been no suggestion in the medical literature of the time that sex with children was anywhere near as widespread as his patients were suggesting, especially among the privileged classes. But it wasn't just a few of Freud's patients who were recalling such abuse, it was every one of them.

So perplexed was Freud that he considered and reconsidered his findings. Were his patients lying? It didn't seem likely, since each of them had apparently repressed all memory of the abuse, dredging it up only after many hours of analysis had overcome what appeared to be their enormous resistance. Conscientious to a fault, Freud began to wonder whether he had inadvertently influenced his patients' recollections by unconsciously suggesting that he wanted them to remember such events. But that didn't seem likely either, in view of the shame and revulsion his patients had displayed while telling their stories.

Try as he might, Freud could see no alternative except to accept that what the women were telling him was the truth, and in 1896 he published his conclusion in a paper entitled *The Aetiology of Hysteria*. Elegantly written and faultlessly argued, it was and still is an extraordinary document. When Freud read the paper to a gathering of the Viennese Society for Psychiatry and Neurology, it marked his first major address to his fellow psychoanalysts, and what he proposed was nothing less than a revolutionary theory of mental illness: the idea that sexual experiences during childhood were the principal cause of neurotic behavior in adults. Freud called his idea the "seduction theory," and the implications were staggering. Since there was no apparent shortage of neurotic adults, the sexual abuse of children must be rampant.

The reaction to his address was immediate, though it was not what Freud had had in mind. The last thing the fledgling psychoanalytical community needed in its struggle for respectability was for one of its members — and a Jewish member at that, in a city that had just elected an anti-Semitic mayor — to announce his conclusion that the Vienna of Wittgenstein, Mahler, and Schoenberg was a city of child molesters. Five days after his speech, Freud wrote to Wilhelm Fliess, a Berlin surgeon who was then his closest friend, that his paper had "met with an icy reception from the asses" — and this, Freud said, "after one has demonstrated to them a solution to a more-than-thousand-year-old problem, a source of the Nile! They can go to hell." Freud's colleagues apparently felt the same way about him. Around Vienna, he wrote, the word "has been given out to abandon me."

Less than two years passed before Freud began to doubt his own conclusions. In September 1897, when he wrote to Fliess about "the great secret of something that in the past few months has gradually dawned on me," the secret proved to be his growing conviction that most of the incidents of childhood abuse recounted by his patients had never actually occurred.[19] His error, Freud said, had been both in believing their stories of childhood seductions and in assuming he had thereby discovered the common root of their neuroses. Freud wasn't suggesting that no children were ever sexually abused. The explanation he gave to Fliess was his delayed recognition that it was highly unlikely that so *many* women had been abused, that "surely such widespread perversions against children are not very probable."[20]

Now that it was clear to Freud that many of the stories were only fantasies the patients had made up, he would have to look elsewhere for the causes of his patients' disorders, and for an explanation of why they had contrived such lies. The new theory that emerged would become the cornerstone of Freudian psychoanalysis. Freud called it the "oedipal theory," named after Oedipus, Sophocles' mythical King of Thebes, who unwittingly murders his father, Laius, and marries Laius's wife without realizing that she is really Jocasta, his mother. In the course of his own self-analysis, Freud had become aware of a vague sexual attraction toward his mother and an undefined anger toward his father. Now he wondered whether the patients who had "recalled" sexual experiences with their parents or other close relatives might not be expressing "wishful fantasies" that had begun taking shape while they were still tiny children.

As a natural consequence of such feelings, Freud thought, the child unconsciously fantasized about making love to its mother or father.[21] But the conundrum that inevitably arose in the tiny uncon- scious mind was how this could be accomplished without first doing away with the other parent. For the young boy, Freud thought, the fear was that his father might discover his murderous intentions and punish him with castration. So horrifying was the prospect that the boy quickly repressed all thought of mother-love, walling the idea off in the deepest part of his mind.[22] Though it is a reaction to the most primitive of fears, the repression of the oedipal impulse as conceived by

Freud also represents the child's first act of conscience. The outcome, Freud thought, was the formation of the "superego," that part of the psyche where the child's sense of self-esteem resides. Having done the right thing by not having done the wrong thing, the child is now entitled to feel proud of himself.

But what of the young girl unconsciously in love with her father who harbors murderous thoughts about her mother? For her castration is not a concern; Freud surmised that it was her disappointment at not having a penis that caused her to turn her affections toward her father in the first place. The girl's fear is that her mother, discovering in her daughter a rival for her husband's affections, will murder her. She is naturally frightened by this prospect, and the repression of her own oedipal impulse follows. But her fear of murderous revenge from her mother is seen as somehow less intense than that of the boy who fears castration, and for the young girl the repression is less complete and effective. Because there are a few chinks in her mental wall, she retains some sexual feelings for her father during childhood and even for the rest of her life, feelings that may play an important role in explaining the dynamics of father-daughter incest.[23]

At last, Freud thought, he had the riddle solved. The oedipal experience was not only the central event of childhood and the major determinant of the adult personality, it was also the "nuclear complex of every neurosis." Neurosis in adults wasn't caused by childhood sexual experiences after all, but by the unconscious desire for such experiences and the subsequent repression of that desire. Only when those repressed wishes had been summoned up from his patients' unconscious minds during psychoanalysis had they begun to "recollect" such scenes. Most of all, it wasn't that large numbers of children were actually having sex with their parents, merely that they unconsciously wished to do so.[24]

Since the seduction theory and the oedipal theory seemed mutually exclusive, it looked like the end of the seduction theory. It almost was, but not quite. In the early 1930s a brilliant Hungarian analyst named Sandor Ferenczi, one of Freud's closest colleagues and widely respected in his own right, began to wonder whether Freud hadn't been right the first time around. Like Freud, Ferenczi was seeing a number of patients who claimed to have been abused as children. Had he faithfully followed Freud's map of the psyche, he would have treated such claims as fantasy. But Ferenczi was also seeing something Freud hadn't seen. Several of his patients were admitting during analysis that they had had sex with children themselves after they became adults — admitting that they were child molesters.

Fantasies about having been sexually abused were one thing, Ferenczi thought, but fantasies about doing the abusing? As he thought it over, Ferenczi wondered whether the oedipus complex might be "the result of real acts on the part of adults, namely violent passions directed toward the child, who then develops a fixation, not from desire [as Freud maintained], but from fear."[25] It was in the final paper of his career that Ferenczi broke with his friend and mentor. "Even children of respected, high-minded, puritanical families," he declared, "fall victim to real rape much more frequently than one had dared to suspect . . . the obvious objection, that we are dealing with sexual fantasies of the child himself, that is, with hysterical lies, unfortunately is weakened by the multitude of confessions of this kind, on the part of patients in analysis, to assaults on children."[26]

When Ferenczi read his paper to the Twelfth Internationl Psycho-Analytic Congress in Wiesbaden in September 1932, it received a reception very much like the one accorded Freud in Vienna more than three decades before. This time, however, Freud himself was among the dissenters. Irretrievably committed by now to the oedipal theory and the body of psychoanalysis he had built up around it, and no doubt feeling betrayed by an old and trusted colleague as well, Freud tried to stop Ferenczi from reading his paper. Ferenczi's age and stature prevented such an affront, but when Ferenczi died a few months later, his ideas went with him.

Jeffrey Masson, a psychoanalyst and former secretary of the Freud Archives, attributes Freud's abandonment of the seduction theory to his desire to restore his credibility among his colleagues, a decision Masson calls "a personal failure of courage" and a "momentous about-face that would affect the lives of countless patients in psychotherapy from 1900 to the present." There is some evidence that he is not overstating the case. For much of this century, women who have sought psychotherapy to relieve the lingering agony of the sexual abuse they suffered as children have been told by Freudian-trained analysts that they were merely fantasizing about such experiences. When Judith Becker, who directs the sexual behavior clinic at the New York State Psychiatric Institute, studied four hundred women who were victims of childhood sexual abuse, she confessed to having been "amazed at some of the stories" they told about their therapists. "Either the therapist did not focus on the issue," Becker says, "or the women were made to feel responsible."

The irony, of course, is that in view of what the retrospective studies show about the probable extent of child sexual abuse, it is entirely possible that more of Freud's patients were telling the truth about their childhood experiences than he was ultimately prepared to believe. Especially in light of Ferenczi's discoveries, the principal question that arises is whether Freud was right the first time around, whether the seduction theory was essentially correct. If it was, then what are the implications for the validity of the oedipal theory with which it was replaced? Freud's daughter, Anna, has maintained that had her father clung to the seduction theory, "there would have been no psychoanalysis afterwards."[27] But what remains unclear is why, as Ferenczi appears to suggest, there cannot be a duality of theorems.

While Freud's original thinking has been questioned and modified over the years, hardly anyone in the mainstream of psychoanalysis argues with the importance of some kind of oedipal experience in children. Suppose that children who are not sexually abused do follow some variant of the oedipal path and that, for them, the desire for sex with the parent of the opposite gender is ultimately repressed. For those children who are abused, the repression of the oedipal desire and the consequent formation of the superego are simply interrupted by the intrusion of a real sexual experience that brings the unconscious forbidden fantasy to life. If this is so, it may explain why so many victims of child sexual abuse, and particularly victims of incest, enter adulthood so utterly lacking in self-esteem, and why so many sexually abused children grow up to become child abusers themselves.

THREE

Victims

N OT ALL SEXUALLY abused children grow up to become child abusers. Though Alison, Caroline, Hugh, and Karen were all abused as children, none of them has ever abused a child. But their lives as adults have been defined nonetheless by the anguish of their experiences as children, and the stories they tell compose a fairly comprehensive map of the psychological terrain of sexual abuse.

It was in the summer of her eleventh year that Alison was invited to visit the New England farm of her best school friend. Encouraged by the caretaker, a man in his early fifties who lived in a house up the road, she spent much of the time trying to train a chestnut foal that had been born a few weeks before. "The caretaker and his wife always seemed to enjoy having children around," Alison says. "I remember they had puzzles and games at their house, and I remember feeling very welcome there. The afternoon it happened must have been fairly hot, because I was wearing a sleeveless top and matching shorts and sneakers. It was dark inside the barn. We must have been standing on the lower level, because I remember looking up and seeing sunlight filtering through the dirty windows. There was lots of hay tied in bundles all around me, and I remember how nice it smelled.

"I remember standing in the barn, and I remember the caretaker grabbing me around the waist from behind, saying he was going to tickle me. I had grown up in a very reserved family, and I did not like to be touched by strangers. I did not want to be tickled, but I also remember thinking that children should behave. I was an eldest child and had always been told to set a good example. I was taught never to question what adults did or said. So when the 'tickling' started I didn't do anything. But soon the man was pulling my shirt up and pulling the elastic waistband on my shorts away from my body. I remember feeling afraid, but not really knowing why. Then he put his hand down my shorts and began rubbing between my legs. I remember being horribly embarrassed and upset and pulling away from him, saying something about not wanting to be tickled any more. I remember trying to find the door and trying to get away from the barn and being absolutely terrified that he would follow me. I have no memory of the rest of the day. Before I left to go home, I wanted to tell my friend's mother about what happened, but I was afraid that I would be blamed or that I would be punished for doing something so awful. My parents expected me to be perfect. So I didn't tell anyone.

"In the ninth grade, my best friend and I began spending Friday nights at her house or my house. We would stay up until three or four in the morning, talking about everything, eating Popsicles, watching reruns of 'Sea Hunt' and monster movies, listening to records and the radio, occasionally sneaking a beer or a Bloody Mary. We made dreadful Bloody Marys, but we didn't know the difference. We had adolescent crushes on everyone from boys at school to rock stars. Our high school was hosting an exchange student from Austria, blond, charming, and a good soccer player, very popular. On the night that winter vacation began, my friend's parents went away, and we decided to stay at her house, in the basement, which had twin beds, a TV, a stereo, and easy access to the kitchen.

"My friend's brother and the exchange student had gone to a party somewhere and came back about midnight, very drunk. The four of us ran around the house, having pillow fights and chasing each other. Down in the basement, where we went to 'talk,' the exchange student put his arm around me, and we began kissing. I remember feeling terrified and at the same time very aroused. Then he started to unzip my jeans. I felt instant panic — guilty and afraid, as though I were doing something disgusting and horrible. I felt awful. For months afterward I felt very ashamed, as though I'd done something that would ruin my life forever. I tried to convince myself that I hadn't been responsible — and that I hadn't liked it. But I hated myself for enjoying it even for a minute.

"I didn't think consciously of that day in the barn, but I'm sure that's what terrified me so much. I'm sure that my subconscious feelings about that day were what threw me into such a panic and made me later convince myself that I had almost been raped. That's how I felt, as if I had been violated in some way. It was just about that time that I began to gain a lot of weight. I began to eat compulsively.

I've never been sure why, but it would be eight years before I took the weight off. I think now my conflicting notions about sex probably contributed enormously. If I were unattractive I wouldn't have to worry about sex. And I didn't. I studied hard, became editor of the school paper, assistant director of the school show, author of the senior class play.

"I wanted to please everyone, my parents, my teachers, my friends. I gave myself as little time to think as possible — and no time to worry about boys. By the time I graduated I weighed a hundred and sixty pounds. I had to ask an older friend to take me to my senior prom because no one else had asked me. All during my adolescence and my twenties I never completely trusted men. I didn't like to be near people I didn't know, and I never talked to strangers. I remember one morning, fifteen years after that day in the barn, when some man grabbed my rear end as I was crossing Times Square, turning around and hitting him. I felt sad and angry all day long, and that night I had a nightmare about a barn. I was depressed for weeks afterward.

"At twenty-one, only a few months after I graduated from college, I started working at a high-pressure job at a very high-pressure organization. The depressions that had plagued me occasionally during high school and college started again. I 'cured' them by eating obsessively, or moving to a new apartment, or getting myself way too involved with work or in relationships with the wrong men. There were bright spots — a fairly long and stable time with a very kind older man when I was twenty-three — but when these ended the depressions got much worse. When I was twenty-four, in the space of two weeks my older man friend ended our relationship, my roommate moved out, and I switched jobs.

"I channeled all my efforts into losing weight, though I'd already lost about fifty pounds and really didn't need to lose any more. I became more than a little obsessed with food, dropping twenty pounds in six weeks, becoming so angry with myself that I'd cry if I ate more than a hard-boiled egg for dinner, exercising constantly. Fortunately my doctor caught on to what I was doing and helped, and my job turned out to be fun, and that helped. Things began to improve. I had about one and a half relatively unturbulent years, although they were marked by the fact that I dated no one during this time and spent an enormous amount of time shopping and living at my parents' house.

"Another slide into depression began about Christmas of the year I was twenty-five. I met a man on vacation, had a wild affair, came back to New York, and started sleeping with everyone. It was about this time that I became increasingly unhappy, a sadness that shaded everything I did and everywhere I went. I just couldn't seem to snap out of it. I think I understood that I should be seeing someone about this, but I felt too depressed to even bother. I don't remember any specific thoughts about killing myself, something I'd considered at least twice before, but I do remember thinking for days on end that if things didn't get better I would do it, that I couldn't bear feeling this terrible for years and years to come.

"Suffering through a long period of depression is hard to describe — it was like feeling trapped and helpless, unable to control my emotions, to be excited or happy about anything, sometimes unable even to get out of bed. Most of the time I could get dressed and go to work and do my job. But I cried all the time, frequently in the bathroom at work over nothing, more often at night, at home alone. The days I'd have to stay in bed were when I was so tired of crying and caring that I'd just go numb all over. I remember feeling that anyone could do anything to me and it wouldn't make any difference. This went on for nearly a year. I solved it once again by moving, this time two thousand miles away, to a new job in a new city where I didn't know anyone. At first the sheer craziness of all the things I had to do, from meeting people and learning my job to finding a home and a car, kept me so busy that I felt OK.

"About six months into my new job, the depression started again. I worked harder. I tried to do other things. It would abate for a while and then get worse again. Occasionally, because my job was so intense, it would go away completely for a while, only to creep back again. About twelve months into my new job I began to hate it, and to regret moving. That's when I started to apply to medical school — instead of dealing with the problem, I tried to escape once again. Six weeks after I began school, the crying jags and emotional upsets began again, nearly destroying my concentration and the friendships I was beginning to make.

"I chose to pursue a ridiculous relationship and became deeply depressed when it didn't work out. I studied myself into total exhaustion. I worried about everything. I couldn't sleep for days at a time. I tried to overcome the growing emptiness by making myself indispensable to my friends — cooking their meals, washing their clothes, typing their papers, a method of holding on to people I fell into frequently when I was depressed. Most of the men I've treated this way react similarly. They get used to it and then get angry if I stop. Then I don't feel appreciated, as though I will never be good enough, that if I were good enough I would be loved. I hate myself, and I hate other people for not loving me."

*   *   *

Caroline remembers clearly the night her brother Franklin, then twelve, first woke her from a sound sleep, remembers telling him to "stop playing around," pleading that she had to get up early to fix her younger brothers' school lunches. But Franklin did not stop, not then and not for years to come. Instead of telling her parents about what was happening, Caroline made excuses for her brother. "Before it happened, I loved him a lot," she says. "I figured he's mentally ill, he doesn't know what he's doing. I didn't want to send him to prison." When her two younger brothers, the ones she still calls "my angels," walked into her bedroom while Franklin was there, Caroline screamed at them to get out. She can still see the bewildered look on their faces. "In the morning we talked about it," she says. "I told them I didn't know what to do. But they were pretty young. I don't know if they really understood what I was saying."

Until then Caroline had been doing well in school, getting mostly A's and B's. But in the fourth grade she simply gave up, and her grades took a plunge. She sees it now as a cry for help, but it was so muffled that no one heard. Once, in a conversation with her father, she hinted at what was happening. "I said, 'Dad, if somebody did something to me, what would you do?' " When her father answered, "Kill him," she thought it best to let the matter drop. Only when Franklin began turning his attention to one of her younger brothers did Caroline, then fourteen, decide to act. "That just blew it," she says. "I raised them. When they first started to talk, they were calling me Mommy. I won't let anybody hurt my little brothers. They're my babies."

By then her parents were divorced, her mother remarried to a man Caroline neither liked nor trusted. When she finally decided to tell someone about Franklin, it was her junior high school counselor. The woman, she said, "almost had a heart attack. She called the police and everything. I was so scared." There was a hearing, and Franklin was committed to a psychiatric treatment center. It was after he went away that Caroline began "having bad dreams, losing all my emotions, hardening up so I wouldn't be hurt anymore." About the same time, she acquired her first real boyfriend. "I started trusting him, opening up, we talked. Then he wanted to take me into his bedroom, and I said, 'That's the end of that.' I never saw him again." After a few months Franklin was released. But despite a court order that he was not to come within a mile of his sister, Caroline's mother allowed him to return home.

Franklin began where he had left off. Since reporting the abuse hadn't solved her problem the first time, Caroline tried something different. She ran away, losing herself in the swarms of children who make the boulevards and back alleys of Hollywood their home, living with whoever would have her for a week or two and then hitting the streets again until someone else took pity on her. She moved in with some members of a motorcycle gang for whom she became a "house mouse," looking after their children and cleaning their shabby pad. It wasn't much of a life, but at least Caroline was safe until the gang members tired of her and tossed her out.

Her only real friend was Darla, a twelve-year-old runaway from Cincinnati who had made her way to Los Angeles by cadging rides from truckers. When they met on the corner of Hollywood Boulevard and Las Palmas Avenue, a favorite hangout for child prostitutes, "Darla was out there hustling. That was her only means of support. She didn't know what else to do. She showed me the burn marks on her stomach where her mom took lighted cigarettes and put them out, and told me stories about being raped by her stepfather." Her maternal instincts aroused, Caroline gathered the girl up and took her to the North Hollywood home where she had found a job keeping house for a young couple who had picked her up hitchhiking, "nice people who were helping me get back on my feet." But when the couple insisted that Darla leave because she wouldn't give up her Quaaludes, Caroline left with her.

Back on the street with no place to live and no money for food, Darla suggested that they turn a trick. When Caroline made a face, the younger girl assured her that it really wasn't that bad. Like most child prostitutes, the two girls didn't have a pimp or a madam behind them. When they went into business they did it on their own, the fifteen-year-old redhead and her twelve-year-old sidekick standing on High-land Avenue with their thumbs out, pretending they were hitchhiking and waiting for someone to stop. When someone finally did, he was old enough to be Caroline's grandfather. The man offered her a hundred dollars and Caroline agreed, but only if Darla could come along. He drove to a secluded spot in the Hollywood Hills, where Caroline performed oral sex while Darla acted as the lookout. "I just blocked it all out," Caroline said later. "It was a way to get money so Darla and I wouldn't be on the street. I thought he was an asshole. He shouldn't be coming out for young girls."

Besides the hundred dollars, the man gave the girls a motel room for the night, filling out the registration form and telling the desk clerk they were his granddaughters from out of town. The room would be their home for much of that summer, the rent paid each morning from the receipts of the night before. "I always figured prostitutes were sluts and tramps," Caroline said. "But after a while I sort of loosened up a little bit, and I started understanding the prostitute's viewpoint. They don't figure it's wrong, you know. You make love to your husband and he gives you money and buys you clothes. It's the same thing, in a way. I figured Franklin didn't give me anything, so at least I was getting something from it."

The girls developed a routine, taking one or two customers a night, three at the most. Though they always worked together, only one provided sex. "We'd let the man pick which one he wanted," Caroline said. "Whoever he didn't pick had the knife, in case he was a maniac." Most of the men were older, and they seemed to Caroline like regular people. "Me and Darla figured they were lonely, or that their wives were dead or something. We made up stories." They also established rules. They offered only oral sex, and only in the customer's car, at "this place way up in the hills where you can just park, where nobody thinks anything of it." Their price remained at one hundred dollars, substantially more than the regular Hollywood rate for street sex, because "the younger you are, the more you get. The tricks are looking for nine- and ten-year-olds now, and there's a lot of them out there too. I met this one little kid who had run away from home. He was eleven. I remember thinking, It's bad enough that I'm out here, let alone a little child."

Only once did they encounter any trouble, when a customer began to slap Darla after she refused to have intercourse with him. Caroline's knife was out in a flash. "I told him that if I ever saw him again I'd kill him. He said, 'Take my money, don't kill me.' We took his money, almost a thousand dollars. I held the knife to him while Darla took off his pants, and we got out of the car and took off. Then we set his pants on fire."

Caroline met another man who offered her a job making pornographic movies. "He wanted to see if I could play the little-girl virgin type," she said. "He said, 'Oh God, you'd be great for porno.' He said for every picture I'd get five hundred dollars." The money was tempting, but Caroline turned him down. "I figured I'd already lowered myself so far down that I wasn't going to lower myself any more."

It was during an abortive journey to Cincinnati to rescue Darla's younger sister, who was enduring the same sort of abuse at the hands of her mother and stepfather, that the two girls finally became separated. "A trucker dropped us off at a truck stop someplace in Arizona. We were going to dine and dash — eat and run — because we didn't have much money. The waitress called the police because she figured we were runaways. They came in and picked us up." Unaccountably, the Arizona officers let Caroline go. On her own again, she returned to Los Angeles, not to Hollywood this time but to the San Fernando Valley, on the other side of the hills. Hollywood was where the "real prostitutes" hung out, and in her own mind Caroline still wasn't one of them.

It was in the Valley, on the corner of Ventura Boulevard one warm September evening, that Caroline solicited a middle-aged undercover policeman who she mistakenly thought was "too old to be a cop. I propositioned him, and he flipped his badge and says, 'You're under arrest.' I almost had a heart attack. He handcuffed me and off I went. He said, 'I have a daughter around your age. If I ever caught her out here, I'd kill her.' And I'm going, 'Oh, my God.' " Because there was a longstanding runaway warrant for her arrest, Caroline was remanded to a juvenile facility in Los Angeles, where she spent eight months in intensive psychotherapy. When the state finally let her out, Caroline went back home. But even though Franklin is living elsewhere, Caroline is uncomfortable with all the memories. She talks of going to live with her grandparents in Colorado, of finishing high school, of studying to become a computer programmer. And when she insists that selling sex "wasn't for me," that she "did it because I had to," she sounds as though she mostly believes it.

*   *   *

"It was a relationship Mother and I had that was special," Hugh says. "When she took a bath, she would call out to me to bring her a towel, sometimes wash her back, sometimes get in the tub with her. I have vague recollections of her washing my penis, me washing her breasts. I'm talking about up through like the fourth, fifth, and sixth grade. There was a lot of enjoyment. A lot of it was enjoyable, and it kind of cemented the relationship, I suppose. I know that it was a form of attention. It was not necessarily unpleasurable. My dad's not real talkative. Mother always used to complain about the fact that he didn't have feelings or emotions, and I did. And with coaching and teaching, he worked late, until seven or eight o'clock every night.

"When we would go to the lake every summer, my dad would stay home and only come up on the weekends. He wasn't usually around. I was kind of her counselor. I listened to her. I felt that it was my job to help with the kids at a very early age, to kind of help take care of the family. I became aware fairly young that I had to kind of take care of my mother. That also increased the bond, I supposed, between her and me. There was some feeling of jealousy and competition between my dad and me all the time, when I was a kid. We would compete in sports. I suppose part of it was Mother. Attention, affection, that kind of thing. I would have to keep a low profile. There were times when he would play with her buns and squeeze her breasts right in front of me and wink at me. The things I was knowing I had to keep to myself.

"She was aware that I had sexual desires, and I think it gave her some kind of enjoyment that I had those desires. She would embarrass me sometimes with her sexuality, if her dress got up too high on her legs, if her dress was unbuttoned too far. She would have me actually help her get dressed and undressed sometimes. She had good tits and she had a good body. She did. She was well built, and she was attractive, and she was sexy. She used to talk all the time about men's bodies, because my dad coached. She was always talking about this guy's body and that guy's body, and doesn't Uncle So-and-So have a beautiful physique. I have a recollection of seeing her suck a guy's cock who was a boarder at our house. I have a vague recollection of her with a doctor at the lake. Those things don't bother me that much. If it happened, it happened."

It was not until Hugh's mother drew her younger sister into their relationship that the boy began to grow uncomfortable. "I think they had been out in the kitchen. I don't know if they had had any wine or not. They weren't supposed to be drinking anything, according to the church, but they did. I had taken a bath. I had a towel around me. And my mother talked me into going into the bedroom with her and her sister, closing the door, putting a chair up underneath the door. Margaret, that's my aunt, took off her dress and her slip, sat down on the edge of the bed, and Mother said to help her off with her bra. And I did.

"We got into bed, and the idea was that Margaret got embarrassed and was uncomfortable around men. She wasn't married. And the idea was that we would show Margaret how to enjoy sex. So Mother and I showed her. Mother played with me, with my penis, and I got an erection. Then Margaret did the same thing. Then my mother told me to help her take her pants off. I remember my mother coaching me to do things with Margaret, Margaret resisting, my mother telling me to go ahead, that Margaret doesn't really mean it when she says don't do that or slow down or stop, that the reason Margaret is unhappy and not having any sex is because she's always saying no. The next thing I remember happening is that the three of us were under the sheets, playing around."

The next summer, at the lake, when Hugh was thirteen, his mother walked into his bedroom late one night. "I remember it was stormy. We had electrical storms back there. She came in and asked me to come sleep with her because she was frightened. It was the only time she'd ever been frightened, but I went into the bed with her. What I remember is that when I woke up she was sucking on my toes and rubbing my legs and whimpering. And I'm turned on. I am turned on. And then I got on top of her, and I can remember touching and kissing and intercourse, and her crying afterwards and sobbing, saying how sorry she was and that she couldn't control herself, and that she missed my dad." The last incident Hugh remembers happened in a rowboat on the lake the summer before he entered college. "Mother was in the boat, and she said, 'Let's sunbathe, take off our suits.' We lay down in the bottom of the boat. I sat up every now and then, because it was my job to be sure that nobody discovered us."

They did not make love that day, though Hugh remembers wanting to. "I didn't like being seduced and not being able to complete it. There's still a lot of anger about it. Let's either do it or don't do it." During college, the sexual part of their relationship came to an end. "All through college I lived at home. We had a shower down in the basement. I'd go down there and take a shower rather than stand in the bathtub. And invariably my mother would find a reason to come down into the shower and see me naked. I started to complain about her invading my privacy. Her comment would be, 'Don't be ridiculous, you haven't got anything I haven't seen before.' I had a feeling that what she wanted to do was see me with an erection."

Hugh thinks he must have had "an awareness that the things we were doing we weren't supposed to be doing." But he also remembers thinking that "I had some power with this relationship, because it's mutual blackmail. She can blackmail me and I can blackmail her. I could get by with things that my dad couldn't get by with. And I still can to this day." Thirty-five years and hundreds of hours of therapy later, the anger still filters through his voice as he talks about his feelings for his mother. "I didn't like playing second fiddle. If I'd have

had my choice, I would have usurped my dad. Period. I would have.
I didn't like it that my dad was sleeping with my mother."

It was not until his own children were grown that the repression
finally gave way. "I would be out watering the yard, and I would see
scenes. Me in the bathtub. Me with my mother and my aunt in that
bedroom. Me and my mother at the lake. Things started falling into
place. So I started going to therapy." When Hugh decided to confront
his mother about what had happened, "she denied everything. She
said, 'I guess if you've got to hate somebody, you might as well hate
me.' She said, 'You're not going to be invited to my funeral. I don't
want anybody there that doesn't love me. You cannot possibly love me
and be saying these horrible things about me.' She's seventy-seven
now, and I guess she sees everything falling apart as far as I'm
concerned, and she wants me to save her ass. And I'm not going to do
it anymore. I've done it. For many years, I carried a resentment and
an anger. I waited for her apology. I waited for her admission of reality.
Then my therapist said, 'How come you're so angry at your mother?'
I let it go. She doesn't owe me anything. There's no debt owed
anymore. I wish that it had never, ever got started in the first place, of
course. Maybe I'd still be married. Maybe I wouldn't have become an
alcoholic. I almost killed myself, you know. But she was my mother.
And I loved her. And I forgive her. And I forgive myself for being
sexual."

*   *   *

"I've never met a man like him," Karen says. "His name was
Clay. He was a very close family friend. I can't remember when I
didn't know him. His daughter Cathy, who was my age, was my best
girlfriend. I remember the way that it all came about. I think I was
seven when it started. The game was that we little girls would walk on
his back like the Japanese women in the bathhouses, however that's
done. It evolved very, very easily. It just wasn't difficult at all, either
physically or emotionally. And I always loved being with him.

"The first time, it started with the walking on his back and ended
up with us sitting in his lap. I can't really remember, but I think Cathy
encouraged it. And he was quite ready for it. It was like grown-up
intercourse. I didn't know very much about where babies come from
at that age, but I don't think I thought it was shocking. I thought it was
fascinating. It happened a lot after that. I don't imagine that it was
more than once a week, but it was at least that. He would call, or I'd
just go by his house. I don't remember being frightened. He was a

doctor, and he had treated me as a doctor, and I obviously had a lot of confidence in him. I found him very gentle. He sewed up my head when I fell off the swing and had to have a lot of stitches, that sort of thing. And he was a nice, handsome doctor. He looked like Douglas Fairbanks to me.

"Cathy had told me about being with him before, so I think I was pretty forewarned about what we were getting into. I think she was getting a real giggle out of it. She took me down to his room to show me, 'Look what Clay can do.' His wife was gone a lot. She had a boyfriend herself during those years. I didn't know exactly what their relationship was, but I knew that she went and stayed with him a lot. Clay never told me to keep it a secret. I think it was understood, just understood. It's the same kind of thing as little boys and little girls going out in the garage and playing doctor. I was pretty aware that you don't go home and tell your mother that either. He gave me a lot of nice presents. It wasn't part of the deal, but I was always rewarded by being his special little girl. I really loved him romantically, like a man and a woman. He was very exciting to be around. I got pleasure from it in a cuddly way, being held and petted. The payoff wasn't orgasms, it was something else. But I liked the sex part. I like a man's body, especially a nice, healthy man like him. Even when I was very little I liked that. There is something quite thrilling about the opposite sex, especially when you don't know what men look like or feel like or taste like.

"It went on with Clay until I was nine or ten. I truly don't remember feeling guilty about it, even when I was a teenager, getting out of high school and going into college and beginning to have normal relationships with boys. I never connected that with Clay.

"When I started seeing boys my own age, I didn't think of them the way I thought of Clay. I might as well have been a virgin. I had a steady boyfriend, petting in the backseat at the drive-in, all through high school. They were two different tracks, different experiences. I was everybody's favorite daughter-in-law type. And I wasn't promiscuous. I first had intercourse with somebody other than Clay between high school and college. It was somebody I worked with. It wasn't nearly as much fun. It was like the first time, but it wasn't any fun at all. It wasn't not nice, it was just nothing.

"I married a nice guy. The marriage was not passionate. I married him because he was a real good catch at the time. I don't think I ever regarded it as a marriage made in heaven, or even very romantic. It was a very convenient marriage for both of us. He was very boring. He wanted a house in the suburbs. I wanted to do a lot of different things. My husband always said that I was frigid. That's a joke, but he really thought so. I had a lot of career ideas, and I was becoming very subordinated to my husband's ambitions.

"I had enough affairs that I remembered what it was like, that I didn't get out of practice. Every so often there's a real good man that comes along. Men seem to like me. I'm pretty selective with them, and the ones I like, I like a lot. They've always been older, more powerful. They tend to have white hair. I'm going to run out of older men soon. They don't last too long past seventy."

FOUR
Abusers

E XCEPT FOR THE FACT that they like to have sex with children, child abusers look and act pretty much like everybody else. Many of them are men and women with jobs and families, liked by their coworkers and neighbors and respected in their communities, the sort of people whose friends will say, "It can't be true. I know that guy. He's a nice guy." Researchers who have spent lifetimes searching for the profile of a typical child molester have concluded that there simply isn't any such thing. Child abusers can be rich or poor, smart or stupid, boorish or charming, failed or successful, black or white. Even some of the judges, prosecutors, police officers, and social workers whose job it is to put child molesters behind bars, and to protect their victims, have been convicted of molesting children.

How many child abusers are there? Nobody knows, mainly because those who abuse children sexually are far less inclined than their victims to talk about their experiences. The conventional wisdom among child protection workers, one founded on instinct rather than fact, has been that perhaps one adult male in every hundred abuses children sexually. If true, that would place the number of child molesters in America at a little over one million. But there is some new and persuasive evidence that even that remarkable number may be far too low. In addition to being the first to ask a random, nationwide sample of Americans whether they had been sexually abused as children, Bud Lewis of the *Los Angeles Times* was also the first to inquire into whether they had sexually abused any children. In conducting his 1985 survey, however, Lewis's poll takers didn't directly ask the 1,260 adult men they spoke to whether they were child molesters. To do so, Lewis thought, would surely produce denials from abusers who were frightened of being found out. Instead, he gave the men an opportunity to disguise their answers through the use of a little-known polling technique, called the randomized response, that depends on the flip of a coin.

If someone flips a coin an infinite number of times, in exactly half the cases the coin will come up heads and in the other half it will come up tails. But flipping a coin even a few hundred times will produce results that are exceedingly close to a fifty-fifty split. Those who responded to the *Times* survey were told at one point that they were about to be asked a sensitive question, but that they would be able to answer in such a way that the poll taker would not know what their answer was. In fact, a set of two questions was posed to each respondent — the first an innocuous question, either about whether they were members of a labor union or whether they rented their homes, and the second a question about whether they had ever sexually abused a child. Then the respondents were asked to find a coin and flip it. If the coin came up heads, they should answer the innocuous question. If it came up tails, they should answer the second one.

Because the respondents didn't tell the poll takers how the coin toss turned out, the poll takers had no way of knowing which question was being answered. But it really didn't matter, because after 1,260 flips of the coin the chances were excellent that half the men had answered one of the two innocuous questions and the other half the question about child molesting. Depending on which of the two innocuous questions was asked as part of the coin-toss series, the other innocuous question had been inserted into the main body of that respondent's questionnaire. That told Lewis the average percentage of labor union members and home renters among his respondents, and it also made it possible for him to extrapolate the number of admitted child molesters in the survey.

The number he came up with was astonishing. About one man in ten, it seemed, acknowledged sexually abusing a child. Even when the standard margin of error was added, the conclusion was that between one man in five and one in fifteen was a child molester. A special margin of error had to be added to account for people who didn't understand the relatively complicated directions or who had simply lied. But even then, the absolute minimum figure — one abuser in every twenty-five American men — was four times higher than anyone had dared to speculate, and it brought a new order of magnitude to the question of how many child abusers there are.

Whatever the number of child abusers, many therapists continue to classify most of them into one of two very broad categories developed several years ago by Nicholas Groth, a psychologist who works primarily with inmates in the Connecticut state prison system. According to Groth, the first category, the "regressed" child abuser, is an adult male who has led a relatively ordinary life. Because he has teenage girlfriends while he's a teenager and adult women friends when he becomes an adult, the chances are good that he will marry and become a father. But at some point, usually during his thirties, his sexual interests suddenly expand to include children; because he's likely to be a heterosexual, it's also likely that the children to whom he's attracted are girls.

Most fathers who sexually abuse their own children fall into the regressed category by default, since to have fathered children in the first place they must have had some sexual attraction to an adult woman. What triggers the regression is usually a mystery to the abuser, who will frequently say something like, "I just don't understand why I did that. I've never been turned on by kids." When the incident is examined in retrospect, however, it usually becomes clear that the abuser was suffering from some unaccustomed stress at the moment he turned to his children for sex. In Jerry's case, it wasn't until his wife went back to school and left her husband to run the household that he started having sex with his daughter.

"Diane worked all day, and she went to school at night," Jerry recalled. "She was taking some very heavy classes, and she wouldn't settle for anything below an A. To do that, you have to keep your nose in the books. Because I was dealing with all the kids at home, it was me who took the responsibility for the kids doing well in school. I would tell her, 'I need your help, I want you to talk to the kids once in a while, I want you to see that they get some homework done. I want you to see that they take their baths.' She'd just say, 'Oh, don't worry about it.' And then something would happen, one of the kids would get in trouble or something, and she would still say, 'Don't worry about it.' I was very upset about that." Jerry found the changes in his life-style traumatic, and his sexual relationship with his wife was suffering as well. "We didn't have any kind of sex life," he says. "I don't call going to bed and her sitting there with a book and all of a sudden putting it down and wanting love something that's going to turn me on. I couldn't do that, so we just kind of shut off the sex. We were just one step away from getting divorced."

Until then, all of Jerry's physical and emotional relationships had been with women his own age. But as his marriage deteriorated, Jerry found himself turning for companionship to his daughter Judy, who was also feeling abandoned by her mother. "Judy and I were close," he says. "We went to the store, we went to the shopping center, we went everywhere, holding hands. We made jokes, we talked a lot. She wanted attention, and I wanted attention. After a while I started getting turned on by her. She used to take showers and then walk from the bathroom into her room just wearing a little towel. To me that was very erotic. It started off with a lot of petting and so forth. She was in the house, we were very close, and Diane wasn't there. The first time she was very curious, very willing. When it got to where she was masturbating, me, she was about ten, probably, or eleven. When we got into oral sex, it went on for at least two or three years. We got together maybe three or four times a week."

According to Nicholas Groth, the second category of abuser, the "fixated" abuser, is a different personality altogether. His sexual interest in children develops early, even while he is still little more than a child himself, and it becomes the central focus of his life. As he grows older, the fixated child abuser remains so enamored of children that he may never feel any attraction for someone his own age. Because most fixated abusers are unlikely to marry and to have children of their own, their only recourse is to abuse other people's children. When they do, they act not on impulse but with a lifetime's worth of premeditation.

Mike is a college graduate, self-employed, intelligent, and articulate. He is also an acknowledged pedophile whose victims so far number a dozen, all of them girls. His girlfriend of the moment is thirteen. Like most pedophiles, Mike becomes angry at the suggestion that his attraction to children is anything but a conscious choice. "I can relate to older women," he says. "I am not afraid of them. Having sex with women my own age is as simple as getting a beer out of the ice box. But I'm no more interested in having sex with one of them than with a buffalo." Mike was in his early twenties when he realized he was a pedophile, but the realization came gradually. "I dated girls my own age through high school," he says. "Then sometime during my college years I noticed that I had an attraction to girls much younger than I. It wasn't that noticeable for a college boy of twenty-one and a girl of fifteen to be seen together. But after I graduated from college, the girls stayed the same age and I got older. I became concerned enough about it to see a friend who was a psychiatrist. The only answer I got was that there is no answer, that it was not a treatable malady or a disease, simply a sexual preference that is much more prevalent in this country than you would think."

Mike is dead-set against child abuse; it's just that he doesn't see himself as a child abuser. "If we're ever going to do something about child abuse," he says, "we're going to have to define it. Sex is going to have to be separated from child abuse. Forcing a child to have sex is the most reprehensible crime I can think of. But having sex with a willing, healthy girl is simply not an abnormal act. People just don't want to face the fact that a young girl becomes a sexual animal when she reaches the age of puberty. No amount of stupidity will ever convince a healthy thirteen- or fourteen-year-old girl who has just had an orgasm that she was a victim of abuse. I am not a pedophile according to the laws of science and nature. I guess it depends on which law you go by."

The clinical descriptions of regressed and fixated abusers appear to fit Jerry and Mike rather well, and they also apply to many others like them. But to classify every incestuous father as a regressed abuser would be incorrect, because a sizable minority of men who have sex with their own children are really fixated pedophiles. The existence of this third category of "crossover" abusers, fathers whose primary sexual attraction is toward children in general, has not been recognized until quite recently, and for good reason. Because of the notion that most incestuous fathers are regressive personalities whose abusive tendencies are only triggered by some trauma in their lives, such men are seen by many prosecutors and judges as a less serious threat to children. As such they stand a good chance of avoiding jail, and if they have also abused children besides their own, it's to their advantage to keep quiet about it.

The first researchers to break through this barrier of silence were Gene Able and Judith Becker of the New York State Psychiatric Institute.[1] Able and Becker assembled a group of 142 men who appeared at first to be typical incestuous fathers. All had admitted having sex with their own children and denied abusing any unrelated children, or even being sexually attracted to children in general. Before beginning their study, Able and Becker secured a promise from the police that none of the men would be charged with additional crimes if they admitted abusing other children in the course of treatment. Then they hooked the men up to a plethysmograph, a machine that can use a small collar filled with mercury to measure the erection of the penis — a sort of erotic lie detector.

The men were shown pictures of children, not pornographic

pictures but suggestive ones that only a true pedophile would find erotic. Many of the men developed erections, and when they were interviewed again, more than half admitted for the first time that they had abused children other than their own. Even so, the admissions did not always come easily. Judy Becker recalled one man who, insisting that "the test must be wrong," left the clinic in a huff. An hour later he telephoned to say he had just remembered abusing two unrelated children. "A hard thing to forget, I would think," Becker said.

By discounting the idea that all incestuous fathers, or even most of them, are necessarily regressive, the Able-Becker research adds an important dimension to the understanding of child sexual abuse. But an even more important dimension is still lacking. Labeling men as fixated, regressed, or crossover abusers may be a good way of describing their behavior, but it isn't much help in explaining why some men want to have sex with children while others do not. Freud suggested that human beings, in a cultural vacuum, are capable of being sexually attracted to just about anyone or anything, including children. Since no one lives in a cultural vacuum, Freud's theory of the polymorphous perverse can never be tested. The nature of sexual attraction remains so murky, in fact, that nobody really knows where any sexual preferences come from, even those that are considered normal. The consensus among those who have studied child abusers is that a sexual attraction to children is learned behavior and not inherited, but most researchers admit that they haven't a clue about what the learning mechanism is or how it works.

Despite the superficial differences among child abusers, is there some common experience or personality trait that links such individuals with one another? One thing many abusers have in common is that they themselves were sexually abused as children. Forty percent of the men in the Able-Becker study said they had been childhood victims of abuse, and other researchers have reported numbers as high as 80 percent. Such findings cannot be a coincidence, but to say that many child molesters were sexually abused as children still does not explain why a person grows up to treat children as he was treated when he was a child. Nor does it explain the behavior of all child molesters, since it leaves room for those who were not sexually abused as children. The closest anyone has come to a universal description of adults who are sexually attracted to children is that nearly all of them are narcissists. But what is narcissism, and how does it contribute to the sexual abuse of children?

The mythical Narcissus was a beautiful Greek youth who loved no one until he saw his own reflection in a pool of water and fell hopelessly in love with himself. So transfixed was he by his own image that, unable to leave the pond to eat or sleep, he withered and died. It was Freud, seeking to describe the kind of intense self-love characteristic of tiny infants, who coined the term narcissism. But it was Sandor Ferenczi who first recognized the existence of a personality disorder in adults that seemed to stem from an oversupply of infantile narcissism.

During the 1950s and 1960s, the concept of narcissism was refined and expanded by students and followers of Ferenczi, notably the late Heinz Kohut of the University of Chicago. As with most things, Kohut suggested, narcissism is a matter of degree. Everyone is narcissistic to some extent, since to be entirely without self-admiration would be no longer to exist. Moreover, the range within which varying degrees of narcissism can be viewed as a positive asset is fairly wide. It is only when an individual's self-image becomes grossly unrealistic that the borderline between a healthy personality and unhealthy one is traversed.

The extreme narcissist portrayed by modern psychiatry has aspects of the mythical figure in his character. His sense of his own superiority, and his certainty that everyone is as interested in him as he is in himself, can be suffocating. Outwardly, he retains a childish and unrealistically inflated view of his appearance, his abilities, and his intelligence, all of which are in his own eyes unique. The narcissist is forever mentioning the important people he knows, whether he knows them or not. He finds it hard to keep a secret, because telling secrets is a way of showing how important he is. He lies about both his real and imagined achievements, alternately taking credit that could not possibly be due him and disparaging the accomplishments of others. He indulges in grandiose and totally unrealistic fantasies — becoming a millionaire, becoming a movie star, becoming President — and whenever one of his schemes for gaining wealth or power collapses, he's got an even grander one just up his sleeve.

On paper, the extreme narcissist comes off as something of a cartoon character, an insufferable buffoon not unlike Ted Baxter, the preening anchorman on "The Mary Tyler Moore Show." But there are many quieter and less easily recognizable, though no less debilitating, forms of narcissism. Kohut, who was the first to propose a systematic approach to the treatment of narcissistic disorders, describes the more typical narcissist as someone who will wander the streets of an unfamiliar city for hours rather than expose his lack of knowledge to strangers by asking directions. Or who, when asked whether he has read a certain book, is forced by his grandiose view of himself to say yes even when he has not — sometimes, as Kohut notes, with the indirectly beneficial result that he now has to rush and quickly read the book.[2] Even the seemingly modest and self-effacing person who persists in giving all credit to others for things he himself has accomplished is narcissistically attempting to win the gratitude and admiration of those others while refocusing the spotlight on himself.

Beneath the surface, the narcissist is so monumentally insecure, so profoundly unsure of himself, and so desperate for external reinforcement of his fragile self-image that he devotes his life to seeking the admiration of family, friends, colleagues, even casual acquaintances and strangers, anyone who will comply, and by whatever means necessary — hence the often-heard reaction among those who know someone accused of sexually abusing children, that "It can't be true. He's a nice guy." He may be a nice guy, but there's a method to his niceness. Whether he is being subtle or blatant, boastful or self-effacing, the narcissist is constantly maneuvering people and events to provide himself with the affection and attention he so badly needs. When they are not forthcoming, he often refuses to admit the obvious, and imposes his own interpretation on the behavior of others. The woman who chances to smile in his direction while passing on the street isn't just making a friendly gesture toward a stranger, she's making a pass.

In deference to the myth, narcissism is often misconstrued as simply an overweening vanity and sense of self-admiration. But the true narcissist is as familiar with self-hate as he is with self-love. No matter what he pretends to others or even to himself, deep inside he knows that his exalted self-image is a sham. Secretly he feels powerless, unworthy, and ashamed. When his grandiose view of himself is being nurtured by those around him, when he's being praised and rewarded and loved by his family and friends, the narcissist may feel magnanimous and "full," in concert with his false self-image, since the strength he draws from love and praise allows him to ignore his internal contradictions. But the slightest interruption in the flow of admiration intensifies the ever-present conflict between his grandiose view of himself and his realistic one. In an effort to relieve his private anguish, he may resort to acts of self-degradation and defilement, perhaps as an unconscious reminder to himself that he is not who he pretends to be.

Sexually abusing a child, particularly one's own child, is the most self-demeaning act of all, but there are also things about sex with children that help repair a wound to the narcissistic ego. Gratification

of any kind is the narcissist's drug, his way of giving himself the reward
he has been denied by those around him and which he is certain he
deserves. Eating and drinking are two sources of gratification, which
may be why some narcissistic individuals tend toward obesity and
alcoholism. But the physical pleasure from sex can be more intense
than that from either food or drink, and many narcissists are conse-
quently addicted to sex and to what it implies. The narcissist who is
struggling to maintain his facade of superiority can never be loved
enough. More than most people, he equates love with sex, to the point
where sex becomes what Kohut calls an "incessant, self-reassuring
performance." What the narcissist really seeks from intimate encounters is yet another piece of evidence that he is both desired and
desirable, worthy and acceptable. More than wanting to make love, he
wants to be loved — to be worshiped would be better still.

When the adults in his world are no longer willing to supply him
with the uncritical love his ego craves, the narcissistic child abuser
responds by turning for affection to children. With their naïveté and
their natural capacity for affection, children are far more capable of
idolatry than any of the adults the abuser knows. Anyone who secretly
feels insignificant will try to recoup by seeking power over others, and
children can be manipulated and dominated to a much greater degree
than most grown-ups. No matter how impotent or insignificant the
abuser feels in the world of adults, in the world of children he is a
supreme authority figure, one who is indisputably in charge.

The grossly narcissistic nature of most child molesters may
explain some of the distinctions between child abusers and rapists.
Most rapists also seek power and control, but they do not ask love or
even admiration of their victims. Their aim is to demean and
humiliate, or at least to horrify and shock. If the rapist leaves his victim
broken and bleeding, why not? For him the rape is the end of the
relationship, not the beginning. Most child abusers, on the other
hand, have sex with children they know, usually ones they know well,
and often over a long period of time. While rapists may resort to
physical violence, most child abusers do not, since it is difficult to
solicit love and admiration from a child who has been beaten into
submission. Far from wishing to see their victims suffer, most child
abusers have a narcissistic need to believe that a child enjoys sex with
them as much as they do with the child.

Beyond merely suggesting why some adults find children sexually
appealing, the narcissistic theory of sexual abuse helps explain some
other aspects of the child abuser's personality — his impulsiveness, for

example, and his remarkable ability to overcome the social and personal inhibitions that deter other people from having sex with children. Most narcissists practice self-denial in few aspects of their lives. All of their needs and wants, sexual and otherwise, are very strongly felt, and for them sex with children can easily become another compulsion. Whenever the narcissistic abuser feels rejected, which is often, his first impulse is to seek a quick fix from his most reliable source of ego gratification, his child victim of the moment.

Because he's less concerned about the possibility and the consequences of getting caught, and because he secretly believes that rules and laws are meant for others, the narcissist is much better equipped to overcome the taboos that prohibit others from having sex with children. Because he's so self-centered, such an individual can more easily surmount the internal inhibitions most people have about sex with children. Since his world revolves around the satisfaction of his own needs, he finds it nearly impossible to empathize with his victim. And because the piece of his psyche that allows him to put himself in his victim's place is missing, the narcissistic abuser doesn't even try. For him, the child is just an extension of his own ego.

The narcissist may be a failure as an empathic human being, but not all narcissists are failures in the world. Those who have the intellectual or emotional wherewithal to realize their grandiose fantasies may indeed become senators, or movie stars, or chief executives of giant corporations. "For all his inner suffering," writes Christopher Lasch, "the narcissist has many traits that make for success in bureaucratic institutions which put a premium on the manipulation of interpersonal relations, discourage the formation of deep personal attachments, and at the same time provide the narcissist with the approval he needs in order to validate his self-esteem."[3] But even the narcissist who holds a high political office or runs a giant company can never accept that those who support or work for him are truly loyal, and he lives in perpetual fear of being "found out" for the fraud he secretly believes he is. For such powerful and successful narcissistic personalities, the need for reassurance to fill the inner void is even greater.

Because not all child sexual abusers were sexually abused as children, to say that the majority of adults who abuse children sexually were sexually abused themselves does not fully explain the root cause of child sexual abuse. When physical and emotional abuse are added to the equation, however, a common theme begins to emerge. Whether they were sexually abused, or beaten, or merely made to feel worthless, nearly all adults who have been caught having sex with children were badly mistreated by somebody when they were children. The answer, as simple as it is complex, appears to be that abuse begets abuse. But in order to understand why mistreated children grow up to mistreat children, it is necessary to see how the adult narcissistic personality develops.

Most babies are at the center of a universe populated by a mother and father who fulfill all their physical and emotional needs. When they cry out, their cries are answered immediately with food, or a change of diaper, or a hug. Denied nothing, they soon become accustomed to getting whatever they want whenever they want it. Eventually, however, most parents begin to put some distance between themselves and their children. This is clearly not the choice of the child, who would much rather remain the focus of attention. But as the child grows older, he probably begins to feel less privileged than he did as an infant or a toddler. Unless his parents continue to baby him, when he cries now there is sometimes no answer; sometimes it is late in coming, and sometimes it is the wrong answer altogether.

Not only is the child actually being denied some things, he is beginning to make mistakes and get into trouble. At first his narcissistic ego is gravely wounded — how dare his commands go disobeyed, his desires unfulfilled, his motives questioned? As the distancing process continues, however, the child eventually discovers that his parents aren't as crucial to his physical and emotional survival as he thought, that he can fulfill some of his own physical requirements and some of his emotional ones as well. When he was smaller, everything he did seemed to elicit praise. But when his mother and father fail to praise him now, it isn't the end of his world, because he's tapped into his own internal sources of approval as a means of bolstering his self-esteem.

The distancing process ideally continues through adolescence, until the narcissistic umbilical cord that links the child to his parents has been stretched to near the breaking point. Like any learning experience, however, such distancing must take place gradually, through a series of small disappointments and recoveries. Even though the child is no longer absolutely worshiped or adored, it's vital that he continue to feel loved and respected. Should his parents withdraw their emotional support too abruptly, his external sources of admiration and esteem would be completely cut off before he had taught himself to provide internal substitutes — as though the training wheels were taken off his bike before he was ready to ride it on his own. This sort of narcissistic trauma can result when a parent dies or is physically absent for some·other reason, and it can also occur when a parent puts a great emotional distance between himself and his children. Not coincidentally, many adult narcissists describe their parents, particularly their fathers, as distant, demanding, even tyrannical. But the surest way of all to deny a child the time and space to discover his capacity for self-love and self-admiration is to abuse him physically, sexually, or emotionally.

Children who never make the transition from their infantile narcissism to a more realistic view of themselves enter adulthood still desperately dependent on the love and approval of those around them to reinforce their childish self-image.

John Wayne Gacy's father demanded perfection from his son and beat him with a razor strop whenever he failed to deliver it, which was often. "His father was after John all the time," Gacy's mother said at her son's trial. "He always called him stupid. My husband didn't show any love and affection for the children. He was cold-blooded." Gacy's sister agreed. "No one ever praised him," she said. "My dad never once said to my brother, 'Hey, John, you really did good for a change.'"

Despite his unpromising beginnings, John Gacy did well in life, mainly because his IQ placed him in the top 10 percent of the population. "He was a very smart, a brilliant person," his ex-wife said. "He had a memory like an elephant." Gacy became a prominent Chicago businessman and a successful building contractor, but his narcissism was never far beneath the surface. Though Gacy never went to college, he often pretended to have degrees in psychology and sociology. Even more improbably, sometimes he would pass himself off as a Cordon Bleu chef. Despite his Polish heritage, Gacy bragged about his connections with the Mob, confiding that his cousin was Tony (Big Tuna) Accardo, the Chicago Mafia boss. His friendships with big-name politicians were somewhat less imaginary. Among Gacy's proudest possessions was a photo of himself with First Lady Rosalynn Carter, taken during a Polish Constitution Day celebration in Chicago (the photo shows Gacy wearing a special security clearance pin issued by the Secret Service). "He said he was big with politicians and that if I ever got in trouble, just to let him know," said one of the many teenage boys Gacy hired to work part-time in his construction business. "He was a jolly type of guy, but he liked having things his own way. He liked the sense of power."

John Gacy also liked having sex with young boys, including some of his teenage employees, and strangling them afterward. But it was not until after his arrest that John Gacy's narcissism achieved full flower. Without much ado he confessed to at least thirty-three murders, and the psychiatrists who examined him reported that he was behaving "like a star, the center of attention." His surface self-image, the psychiatrists said, was characterized by a "pervasive sense of power and brilliance, a sense that he is entitled to more than the average person." His lack of control under stress was "alarming," and so were his subsurface feelings of inadequacy and his lack of empathy. When Gacy talked about the murders, one psychiatrist said, it was "as though he were describing taking a drink of water."

Gacy was fully capable of behaving in what looked like a normal fashion, but underneath he lacked a conscience; one psychiatrist said he had a "Swiss-cheese superego." Gacy was a skilled manipulator of people who had the wives of the guards at the Cook County jail bring him his dinner each night. But whenever his grandiose sense of himself was threatened, Gacy erupted in a hostile, violent rage. "When he starts to express impulse and emotion, he has a minimum of control over himself," one psychiatrist reported. "When he has lost control, he explodes." In March 1980, John Wayne Gacy was convicted of the thirty-three murders to which he confessed. He awaits execution on Illinois's death row.

For the child who is physically, emotionally, or sexually brutalized, the pathway from victim to victimizer is clear. But to suggest that narcissism lies at the root of child abuse is not to say that all narcissists are child abusers, or that all abused children grow up to abuse children. The child who is emotionally "smothered" by his parents is just as likely to grow into a narcissistic adult as the child who is beaten or seduced.[4] When such children succeed, they're the smartest, prettiest, best-behaved children in the world; when they fail, their failure is ascribed to somebody else — a teacher, a coach, or whoever caught them up short. A child who can do no wrong is equally denied the opportunity to discover a realistic sense of himself. He receives so much attention, affection, and praise that the narcissistic cord is not only never cut, it is never even stretched, as if the training wheels were left on the bike forever. Such a child is likely to become a highly narcissistic adult, though not necessarily an abusive one.

Still, emotional smothering can be viewed as another form of child abuse, and it is possible for the narcissism of a child who was never seduced or brutalized to express itself as a desire for control through having sex with children. "I have a young woman now in treatment," says a Chicago therapist. "She's the perfect adolescent.

She's sixteen years old, she's responsible, she makes good grades, she's neat and tidy, and she comes from a nice suburban home. Her family is intact, she's a cheerleader, she's got all kinds of goals in mind. And she molests kids. She wasn't abused herself, though I was hoping she had been because that would be much easier to deal with. There's no sexual abuse, there's no physical abuse. In terms of emotional abuse, this child basically was her mom's best friend. She has not had a lot of control, in terms of what she's chosen to do or not do with her life. I guess you could say she's been smothered. With her, the source of her abusive behavior is just control, as opposed to a trauma in her life or some kind of stressful act."

Whether or not adults who were abused as children grow up to become child abusers probably depends in part on the intensity of their narcissism, which may in turn have to do with the nature and circumstances of their abuse — what form it took, how long it went on, and who the abuser was. Child abusers tend to be grossly narcissistic, enormously compulsive, and almost completely unempathic, but there are many lesser degrees of narcissism that leave individuals with some ability to empathize and to control their impulses. Moreover, powerful cultural and internal inhibitions must be overcome before having sex with a child, and it requires a very strong degree of narcissism to accomplish that task. And while narcissists do tend to be promiscuous and attracted to deviance, there are many sexual deviations to choose from besides sex with children.[5]

It is also true that a surprising number of childhood victims of sexual abuse become compulsive caretakers, who find work in nurseries or with youth groups or in some other capacity that brings them in contact with children, even as child therapists or child abuse counselors. This phenomenon of going to the other extreme, a process known as reaction-formation, is often their way of setting up an unconscious defense against their impulse to reenact their own abuse in the role of the abuser rather than the victim. But it is a fragile defense, one that Freud called "insecure and constantly threatened by the impulse which lurks in the unconscious." The danger that the defense will give way and allow the return of the repressed impulse to the conscious mind may explain why a number of youth leaders and child care workers who seem genuinely devoted to the welfare of children have also been found to be abusing them sexually.

Though it is admittedly rather rough-hewn, the narcissism theory may tell us something about the genesis of child sexual abuse by adults who were abused by their own parents. But what about those child abusers who were abused as children not by their parents, but by other relatives or adults outside their families? The question here may be posed as follows: How can the child of parents who are neither abusive nor seductive, not distant and not smothering — in other words, the child of capable and effective parents — be derailed in his transition from narcissistic infant to well-ordered adult through abuse visited upon him by an outsider? The answer may be that the parents of a child who is seriously abused by someone outside his home are not, by definition, capable and effective parents.

It is difficult to imagine the child of parents who are the least bit sensitive to his emotions being abused by anyone for very long. Younger children who are molested by an uncle or a teacher may not know that what's happening to them is wrong, but most of them send their parents signals that something unusual is going on, and it is the narcissistic or otherwise ineffectual parent who is least likely to be tuned in to his child's frequency. For older children, the perpetuation of sexual abuse by someone outside the family depends most of all on secrecy, and the child who can be persuaded to keep such a secret from his parents has already received the message that he is not much trusted or loved by them. Either his parents have told the child in so many words that he cannot come to them for help, or they're so wrapped up in themselves that they're unavailable to him, or they're so demanding of perfection and intolerant of failure that the child fears being blamed for his own abuse. The pedophile, whose principal source of ego reinforcement is the affection and adoration of children, can be a rich source of the praise and understanding that such a child finds lacking at home.

The older child who consents to being abused by an unrelated adult raises a final question: If such abuse is not accompanied by either force or coercion, and if, as is most often the case, the pedophile is someone the child likes and admires, how do such experiences contribute to the proclivity such children display for becoming abusive adults themselves? When pedophiles insist, as many do, that they love children and treat them with respect, they may be echoing the expressions of love and respect they were denied when they were young, and on some level they may even believe what they say. But the attention and affection they shower upon their victims are manipulative and inherently empty, and consciously or unconsciously the victim knows it. The child who is spurned by distant or demanding parents and who seeks emotional solace from a child molester is both denied genuine affection and smothered by a bogus substitute, which may be the worst of all possible combinations.

The accumulative theory of child abuse — the idea that abuse begets abuse — suggests that nearly all child abusers were abused in some way as children. But the retrospective surveys that show the majority of victims to be girls and their abusers mostly men present an important question: If women who are abused as children acquire the same sorts of narcissistically disordered personalities as men who were abused, why aren't more women abusing children sexually? The answer may be that they are. The notion that sexual abuse by women is virtually nonexistent is common even among some professionals, and the idea of women having sex with children, particularly their own, does seem to violate some fundamental law of nature. Women are nurses, teachers, and mothers — caretakers, not tormentors. They heal, they don't hurt. It's as difficult to imagine the neighbor lady down the street abusing the little boy she sits for as it is to imagine a mother having sex with her own son. But neighbor ladies do have sex with the children they care for, and mothers do have sex with their sons, possibly in far larger numbers than most people suspect.

Of the male victims questioned by the *Los Angeles Times*, 17 percent said they had been abused by adult women while they were boys. That translates to more than two million American men who had similar experiences as children, and another million boys who will be abused by women before they reach adulthood. Surprising as such figures are, the real number of male victims may be close to, or even equal to, the number of girls. The main reason for the discrepancy is that, even later in life, men are much more reluctant than women to admit having been abused, because it goes against the grain of their masculinity to acknowledge having been taken advantage of by anybody. Boys who are sexually abused by men are often afraid they'll be labeled homosexual, but there's not much room for male victims of any kind in a society that celebrates *Rocky* and *Rambo*.[6] It's also possible, of course, that none of the male victims lied when they told the *Times* they had not been abused by women. But if that's the case, how to explain the large number of male abusers who say they were abused as children?

The sexual abuse of boys by women is particularly difficult to uncover, because many boys who have sex with grown women aren't sure whether or not they've been abused. They may secretly feel exploited and used, but their culture tells them they're lucky that they "got some" from an experienced female. The patient and tender older woman who initiates a young boy into the mysteries of love and sex is a perennial theme in fiction. In the film *Summer of '42*, the story of a fourteen-year-old boy who is seduced by the young, bereaved wife of a serviceman killed in action, the seduction is presented to the boy as a special gift, a loving introduction to manhood, and there are many other movies and countless novels based on variations of the same scenario. Because of the resulting mythology, when sexually abusive relationships between women and young boys are reported to the authorities, action is not always taken. A Los Angeles man who discovered his fourteen-year-old son having sex with a thirty-five-year-old woman who lived down the street telephoned the police to demand that the woman be arrested. The officer who answered the telephone just laughed. "More power to him," the man was told. "He's just getting an early start in life."

Only after they become adults do some men acknowledge, even to themselves, that they were intimidated and frightened by a childhood sexual experience with an older woman. One of the few available estimates of the sexual abuse of boys is a retrospective survey conducted in Knoxville, Tennessee, and it illustrates the difficulty of getting men to talk about their childhood sexual experiences. When the Child and Family Service Agency of Knox County first ran an advertisement in the local newspaper asking to hear from men who had been sexually abused as children, it received just a few replies. But when the wording of the ad was changed from "sexual abuse" to "sexual experiences," more than a hundred men responded.

Many of the callers began by saying, "I wasn't really abused, but I thought you might like to know about this experience." Only 25 percent of the respondents said their abusers were men. All of the others had had sex with grown women while they were still children. Seven percent had been abused by their natural mothers, 15 percent by aunts, another 15 percent by their mothers' friends and neighbors, and the rest by their sisters, stepmothers, cousins, and teachers.

The average age of the victims at the time the abuse began was eleven — the youngest of them had been five, the oldest sixteen. In nearly every case, the women fondled the boys' genitals or exposed their breasts or genitals to them, but in more than three-quarters of the cases the women also performed oral sex on their victims. Sixty-two percent of the experiences involved intercourse. Thirty-six percent of the boys were abused by two women at the same time, and 23 percent said they were physically harmed in ways that ranged from slapping and spanking to ritualistic or sadistic behavior. In more than half the cases, the abusive relationships continued for more than a year.

One reason for the smaller incidence of reported sexual abuse by women may be that some of that abuse is never recognized for what it is. It's easy for mothers and other female caretakers to fondle and stimulate the children they care for, since it can be done under the guise of performing such motherly tasks as bathing and dressing. But no matter how many American women are abusing children sexually, no one suggests that the number of female abusers is ever likely to equal, or even approach, the number of sexually abusive men. If that's the case, what becomes of the rest of those women who were abused as children but who don't grow up to become abusers?

A remarkable number marry child abusers and become the mothers of sexually abused children. Researchers are unanimous in reporting that high percentages of the mothers of incest victims, 90 percent in one California study, were themselves the victims of sexual abuse. In many cases their mothers were also victims, and their mothers before them, which raises the possibility that child abuse may be passed from one generation to another like a hereditary disease. But the process by which such women find abusive men to marry puzzles many experts. "It might take us weeks to diagnose a man as an incestuous father," one therapist says, "but an 'incest mother' can go out and find herself an abusive husband in a matter of days. There's no way around it, because we've seen it happen over and over again. It's like they have letters painted on their foreheads that are invisible to everyone else."

One theory is that since people tend to marry others from the same social and economic backgrounds, sexually abused children have more access to one another while they are growing up. But this idea implies that sexual abuse is far more common among some social classes than others, and there is no evidence to support such an inference. Another possibility is that many girls who wish to escape from an incestuous relationship at home see early marriage as a quick exit and are thus more hasty than selective in their choice of partners. But the question is not why such women marry or when, but whom they marry. The answer may simply be that victims are attracted to victimizers.

While the female victim of sexual abuse may be every bit as narcissistic as her male counterpart, her narcissism takes a form that is not only much less grandiose, but much more negative and destructive. Like the male narcissist, such women live in constant fear of being found out for the frauds they think they really are. Many admit to a continuing fear that their children will be taken from them once they've been identified as "bad mothers." Such women say they feel isolated from everyone around them, particularly their husbands and their children. They also feel degraded, not worthy of being treated well by anyone, and when someone does treat them well they feel guilty, because deep inside they're convinced they don't deserve such treatment.

As with male narcissists, their exaggerated underestimation of themselves leaves them almost completely dependent on the approval of others for their sense of self-esteem; much more so than for most other women, it is their relationships with men that they depend on for reflected status and power. Before they marry they often are promiscuous, in a continually unsuccessful effort to reconfirm what their narcissistic self believes is their desirability and attractiveness. They may distrust men and dislike them, but men are still the most important people in their lives. Such women often are overweight and unkempt, and they tend to speak with tentative, frightened voices, but the grandiose part of their personalities is likely to lead them to see themselves as physically appealing.

In many ways the narcissistic victim and the narcissistic victimizer are a near-perfect match, since the male's need to be admired and the female's need to be desired make them ideal mates. She tacitly agrees to supply the approval he so badly requires, while his gross dependence on her support of his fragile ego satisfies her desperate urge to be needed. It's not that such men consciously look for someone to marry so they can have children to abuse; though this undoubtedly happens, the equation is more likely to be made at an unconscious level. Such a man is naturally partial to a woman who he senses won't stand in his way on any count, who isn't going to ask many questions about how he lives his life, and it's easy for him to pick up on women who seem to have an unhealthy degree of dependence on men.

Neither does the narcissistic woman go about consciously seeking an abusive mate. But because her sense of self-esteem is derived indirectly from the men in her life, she finds the narcissistic male's attitude of surface superiority appealing. Not only does she not threaten his fragile ego, she nurtures it, because his ego is as important to her as it is to him. If it's their collective fiction that he's the smartest and handsomest guy in the world, then by extension she's the wife of the smartest and handsomest guy in the world. At the same time, her husband's narcissistic tendency to dismiss everyone around him as inferior confirms her own opinion that she's not worth much as a human being. Her husband may be manipulative and deceitful, and he may not afford her much respect, but if she was sexually abused as a child, these are things she's been comfortable with for years.

FIVE

Families

THIS IS RACHEL'S STORY. "I really can't remember much about my past, but from what my father told me it started very, very young. I wasn't even in kindergarten, less than five. It happened in the car. We were on our way to the store, me and my dad and my two sisters, and he just pulled us to the side of the road and asked us to play with him, you know, his privates. It became an everyday thing. I never even thought of questioning my father. My father was right — that's all there was to it. He fondled my chest, and he put his dick right between my legs. He never actually went in. He liked me to be in his bed. He liked me to massage his back, and stuff like that. My father would ask me to give him head and to play with him and pretend I was his wife. I'd cook for him, I'd massage him, and then I would please him. I just did it. For a long time it didn't make me feel like anything. It was something I was so used to that it just became an everyday thing. When Daddy said this was our little secret, I never even thought of questioning my father.

"We had a great relationship. He was everything I wanted in a father. He provided whatever I needed. He was always there to talk to. Mom always had something else to do — church meetings, school projects, something. Whatever my dad was doing, working on the lawn, fixing the car, he'd always pay attention to me. He never shut me up, never. He went to work every day, brought home his paycheck. He checked my grades constantly. I had to have a B average. He'd let me go with my girlfriends, and I always had girlfriends over. He was understanding about certain things. If my mother said I couldn't do something, Dad said I could. I'd always go to my dad first. I remember one time when I was going to the mall with my friends, and I needed a couple of dollars. And he said to me, 'Well, you know what you can do.' I didn't care, I just did it, took the money, and ran. I used it. I could say, 'Daddy, I need school clothes,' something like that. My dad was always willing to give. He provided whatever I needed. My other sisters, they never got what I did. But there was always a price to pay. I never felt like I was in competition with my mother. I never thought my mom and dad had a sex life. Seriously. Every time we'd go into their room, my dad had his pajamas on, and my mom had hers on.

"When I was twelve, we really lost contact a lot. I was at the age where I wanted to go to school dances. I wanted to have a boyfriend. Everybody else had one. I had someone who liked me, but I couldn't have a boyfriend. The only thing he didn't understand was when I talked to him about my boyfriend. I was never allowed to have boyfriends. We had an Italian student come live with us for the summer, a girl. And she was never left alone, I made sure of that, because by then I knew what was happening to me, and I sure as hell didn't want that to happen to her. At some point I just realized that this was not the way to go. I asked him kindly not to touch me anymore, that it was wrong, because I had started learning that in school. I asked him twice to stop. He would, but then he'd start again. I started hating him while it was happening, when I realized it wasn't daddy-love anymore. The first person I opened up to was my best friend. I just couldn't hold it in anymore. She couldn't believe it. I made her swear that she wouldn't say anything. I didn't know where to go. I went to Barbara, my oldest sister, and I cried, and I told her the truth. She said, 'You're not the only one.' My sisters, I didn't know about them. She said it happened to her, it happened to Renee, and we'd have to tell Mom. Barbara was like our second mom. So I went to Renee, and I said, 'We have to do it now.' She said OK. The thing that made us finally tell was Tanya and Lorene. We didn't want it to ever happen to them.

"We just held each other's hands, and we went to my mom's room. We told my mom, and my mom called my dad in. My dad said, 'I knew this would happen sooner or later.' He says now that when he found out I had said something, all he could think was, It's finally over. We had this discussion, and she asked us what we wanted her to do. At the time I didn't want my family to break up. So I told my mom that if she said anything I'd deny it. She said, 'All right,' and she made my dad swear to her that it would never happen again. A year or so later, my mom was out of town. Renee and Barbara were at work. I was tired, and I went to bed. I thought my dad had really changed. I heard the phone ring, and I woke up. I went to the hallway, and my dad said he'd be right there. And I heard his pants go on. All I could think was, God, please don't let this happen. Lorene broke down. She said he had asked her — that if she wanted to, they would. My mom was out of town. She called, and I said, 'I have to tell you something — Dad asked Lorene to do it.' She said, 'I'll be right there.' She was home in an hour. Everything happened at once. My dad left, and then we called the cops.

"For a long time, I thought it was my fault. When I was smaller, everyone used to say how pretty, how beautiful I was. Because I was so close to my dad, I'd always hug him and kiss him. I wore pajamas that were knee-high. I always thought that that had turned my dad on. For a long time afterward, I had so many problems. I had men teachers I couldn't even speak to. I didn't want to be touched. My boyfriend and I were becoming more involved. He stayed with me through the whole thing. But just because he was a guy, I didn't want to be around him. At first there would be certain things that he would want that I had a real hard time with, like getting on top, because it reminded me of my father. It was hard at first. But it was like, as long as I redid that act I was clean again. I've had a couple of nightmares where I'm terrified. But usually I say this little prayer that always gets me through it: 'Let the blood of the Lord Jesus Christ flow through me and redeem all the evil.' And then I fall asleep, and the dreams don't come back."

This is Rachel's mother's story:

"I met Carl at the age of thirteen, in junior high school. First boyfriend, and I fell in love. He enjoyed walking with me. We didn't have a car anyway. He was tall and thin, not too good-looking. He's more handsome now than he was then. I wasn't out for looks. He was very honest with me from the beginning. He always saw other girls, but he didn't lie to me about it. I remember him saying one time when we were younger, 'A man's not a man if he turns it down.' In fact, he'd take them to the shows, and I'd give him my baby-sitting money. I'd iron his clothes for him. He wasn't a violent person. One time he beat me up. One slap he gave me, and that was it. He knew that was something I wouldn't tolerate, because my father beat up my mother constantly. I would put up with women in our lives, but I would never put up with beating me up. The two qualities I liked the most were, he was good to me and he was honest. To me, honesty is very important in a man. I loved him. I was never a possessive person. I figured, he can have ten girlfriends, that's OK with me, as long as I'm one of them. My kids, from day one, were very affectionate with their dad. They used to sit on their dad's lap and give him hugs. They loved kissing daddy. When we'd walk down the street, they'd grab daddy's hand. To me, that was the reality I wanted as a child. I always wanted that love and affection I never got. Even at that age, I was an adult. That was part of my survival. So I think that's why I was never a possessive mother. My younger sister was molested, but I wasn't. My father did touch Rachel, though, his own granddaughter. I hate my father for it, and yet I love my dad.

"They would have TV programs about how anybody can molest your children, it can be a member of the family. So I always protected my kids that way — telling them, 'I don't care if it's your daddy, don't let anybody touch any part of your body, you come and tell Momma right away.' Because of my dad. I still didn't trust men. It doesn't matter who it is. I thought, If my dad can do it, any man can. I always asked, because of the program I had seen. I guess because they loved me so much, they didn't tell me. That's the only thing I can think of. I think they were protecting me, really. They feared they would lose the family. I think they thought I wouldn't love them. When the time came, they looked at me, and they were real quiet. They sat at the end of the bed. I asked them what had happened. They didn't want to give any details, except that something had happened to them. I asked them, did he have sex with them? They said no, which he didn't with any of the kids. I told them, 'Dad's sick, Dad needs help, and I'm calling Dad in right now.' Carl already knew that Rachel was going to talk to me. She had told him it had to stop. He didn't run away. He stayed home. He waited for me to call him in the room.

"He didn't deny it. He said, 'Whatever they say.' He said he was sick. He couldn't explain it. He said, 'I can't tell you. I don't know why.' I was angry — how could he touch a part of my body? My children are my body, as far as I'm concerned. That was violating me. I cried and cried, until I couldn't cry anymore. That's when my love for Carl died. There's a part of me that will always love him. The real love that I had for him is there. The good love. But I think that I could kill him out of the hate that I have, if I didn't know how to control it. I fell apart. I literally was dying inside. It's like your world has ended. The person you trust more with your whole life has betrayed you. I trusted Carl totally. These were his daughters. I couldn't believe he could hurt them. My first thought was, Are my kids going to be OK? Because I've seen these programs about how kids turn into prostitutes and everything. None of them turned wild. My kids didn't wander the streets. Some kids destroy themselves. My kids did not become drug addicts. I knew I wasn't the only woman this ever happened to, but I never thought I'd be one of the women it happened to. Why me? Why did it happen to me? I was a good woman. I was an honest one. I raised his daughters clean. I kept the house up very, very well. Why touch my daughters? A lot of my friends, they were out there screwing around with other guys, friends that I knew. They were married and they were doing this. I had only one man in my life. There was nothing that he couldn't do to me.

"I didn't really have feelings in my sex life. I had already had five kids before I learned what it was to reach a climax. Sex to me was just being submissive to your husband, and that was it. I did it, and it was over with, and that's it. Once in a while he would put his arm around me and be kind to me. He was never violent with sex. I was always told you submit yourself to your husband, whatever he wants. He could have had it day and night. That's one part that bothers me a lot — that he could have had it anytime he wanted, and yet he molested the girls. I still can't understand that. I blamed myself for a long time. That I didn't pick it up. Maybe I didn't pick it up because my daughters always showed affection to their dad. They never showed the resentment or the hate they had for him, for what he'd done to them. They showed love and affection for him. He wouldn't let his daughters date. I thought it was an old-fashioned tradition, but he didn't want them near any other man. That any other man would get near his daughters, he couldn't handle that. We stayed together for the kids' sake, because they wanted Tanya and Lorene to have a dad. Rachel said she would deny it. She didn't want the law coming into it. I knew he'd get jail no matter what, and they didn't want that to happen to Tanya and Lorene, to lose their dad. So I told him, 'We're going to have to read some books.'

"I went to the library to do research on child abuse. But we didn't get anything out of it. I couldn't understand it. The words were too big. It was statistics, it wasn't real stories. He promised he wouldn't touch the girls ever again, and I believed him, one more time, trying to give him another chance in life. I think he was sincere. But after I found out about the molest, I put locks on their doors. I can see that sad face of his, trying to tell me he didn't do anything to Lorene. He said he had asked her, but he didn't touch her. To me it didn't matter. Then I didn't care if the law got involved in it or not. That's all I needed. My daughters come first. Carl was molested by his brother and by a stranger. What I can't understand is, he can remember the trauma — how could he traumatize somebody else? I thought I knew my husband pretty well."

This is Rachel's father's story:

"It started when I was a kid. With my brother. I was abused by my own brother. It was when we were alone. He's about three or four years older. I didn't give it much thought for a long time. After I grew up a lot of the things I was doing were kind of crazy, but I never knew why. Crazy things, like driving sixty miles an hour through a red light, trying to kill myself. All those years I just put it inside and left it there for a long time. When I was a kid, I never told anybody. I felt like telling my mother, but I didn't. I was still angry because it happened. When I was abusing my daughters, I didn't think about what had happened to me in the past. What started me to molest them is when they used to sit in my lap when I was watching TV. Sometimes we would have a cover over us. That was when I used to fondle them. They were still pretty young. They used to sit a lot in my lap. My penis would get hard. I used to turn them toward me and feel their little bodies close to me. Rachel didn't develop until a lot later. I didn't always know I was going to be sexually attracted to them. I didn't know when they were babies. It kind of just hit me, for no reason at all. They used to sleep with me when they were babies, and I used to fondle them, their little vaginas. But I never really thought much about it. As time went by, I got more aggressive.

"At first I thought it was nothing bad. I felt it was a good relationship between me and my daughters. They didn't seem to find anything wrong with it. I didn't find anything wrong with it either, at first. Matter of fact, I thought it was the right thing to do. Why go look for it somewhere else when you got it right there at the house? As for them liking it, I can say that Rachel enjoyed it a couple of times, when she was about thirteen. She enjoyed it with me. I don't know if she had an orgasm or not. That I don't know. I never did have intercourse with any of them. That was off-limits. I wanted them to get married in white. I can satisfy myself without going through that. I used to look at their little friends, but I would never take the chance of trying to molest somebody else. Because I didn't want them to get a bad idea about me, like, Here's Rachel's father trying to do this with me. But yeah, I used to look at them — young girls, good shapes, nice-looking. As the years went by, there were times I'd feel guilty. There were a lot of times I did feel good about it, and there were a lot of times I didn't feel good about it. I used to get sick about it. It would go into the bathroom, and I would want to puke. I thought I saw Satan in the same mirror with me. Then I knew it was wrong, yet I could not stop myself.

"Jean didn't have the slightest idea. I used to take a lot of risks at home, when she was there. I used to leave the doors unlocked. Sometimes she was in the next room. I felt I really wanted to get it over, get it out in the open. I didn't want to continue on, yet I couldn't stop myself. I couldn't go out and tell her, though. I remember one time Rachel and I had a talk. We were in the car, and she told me she wanted it to stop. I agreed with her, but I knew within myself I wasn't ready to let it go. I agreed with her just to make her feel good at the time. When it kept on, she said that she was going to tell her mother. I told her, 'Well, if that's what you want to do, go ahead and do it.' I didn't threaten her. I felt like I was going to lose them completely. I wanted them for myself. I wasn't ready to share them with anybody. I felt rejected by my own daughters, and I didn't know how to deal with it.

"The first time Jean found out about it, she didn't turn me in. We talked it over, and I promised her I would never do it again. She said, 'We're going to have to get you some kind of help, even if it's through books.' And that's what we tried. When they talked about it that night, I was pretty scared. I wasn't sure what to expect. I thought I would go to prison. I just said to myself, Well, I'm going to have to pay the consequences now. It was a relief that it came out. I spent a year in prison, at the county prison farm. I never talked to the other inmates about why I was there. They would ask, but I already had a story prepared. I told them I was in for assault and battery. When I got out, I had to look for another job. On the application, where it asks 'Have you ever been convicted?' I just told them no. It would be very hard to get a job otherwise. There's very few people that will give you a chance to work. It's my fault. I don't say it wasn't my fault. I don't feel good about it. I can't speak for them, but I know that I'll always love them. I know what I did was wrong. I wish a father would take a second look at himself before he starts this. If he gets any indication that he wants to, that's the time to get help. Don't wait until it's too late. I waited too long, and it got too easy."

*   *   *

It was not very many years ago that incest was thought to be principally confined to what Tennyson called "the crowded couch in the warrens of the poor," to urban ghettos or isolated rural families in the hills of southern Kentucky.[1] "When I started in 1971, it was supposed to be one case of incest in every million people," says Henry Giaretto, a San Jose, California, psychologist who founded one of the nation's first treatment programs for incest victims and their families.

"That year I had twenty-six cases. Now we're running more than a thousand new cases a year, in a metropolitan area of a million people. That's of epidemic proportions, isn't it?"

Giaretto is correct, but even to call incest an epidemic is to understate the case. A quarter of the female sexual abuse victims and 10 percent of the male victims who were surveyed by the *Los Angeles Times* said they had had sex with a family member — a father, mother, uncle, aunt, grandparent, brother, sister, or cousin — while they were children. Applied to the general population, such figures suggest that there are nearly eight million Americans over the age of eighteen — more than the entire population of New Jersey — who are the victims of childhood incest. If children today are being abused by family members at the same rate as their parents and grandparents claim to have been, the number of current incest victims is equal to the populations of Dallas and Philadelphia put together.

Though incest is not a small problem, it is still the least talked-about form of child sexual abuse. One reason is that, unlike sexual abuse in a day-care center or some other communal setting, incest simply doesn't make news. The majority of incestuous parents plead guilty before they ever get to trial, and most incest trials are pretty much alike. But the real reason for the lack of public discussion is the notion, still widely held, that what goes on inside the home and within the family ought somehow to be exempt from public scrutiny. Two years ago, when the U.S. Justice Department criticized local police and prosecutors for their reluctance to assign a high priority to incest cases, it felt compelled to remind them that incest and child molestation "are not matters of personal belief, or how to deal with children or keep order in the house. They are crimes. They are prohibited."

Not only is incest the least discussed, it is also the least reported form of child abuse. The principal reason is simply that so many of its victims never tell anyone what has happened to them, but there are other reasons. Because it has been commonly thought that most incestuous parents abused only one of their children, even when there were several children to choose from, until quite recently a child protection worker wasn't likely to ask about the victim's sister or brother — or, for that matter, about her uncle or her grandfather.

Parents and others who assume a child-tending role cannot avoid being intimate with the children they care for. Bathing and diapering inevitably involve contact with children's genitals, and hugging, kissing, and petting are things most young children want and need from the grown-ups who care for them. It's not only possible, but likely, that children who receive such attention from their mothers and fathers will become sexually stimulated — it's a rare mother who hasn't noticed her boy baby develop a tiny erection when his penis is being washed. Nor is it unusual for mothers who breast-feed their sons or fathers who bounce their daughters on their laps to find that they are becoming sexually aroused themselves.

But when do intimacy and affection become sexual abuse? It's appropriate for a father to bathe his infant daughter, but the father who continues to help his nine-year-old daughter with her bath while insisting that he is just being "fatherly" is not being honest with his daughter or himself. The father who accidentally glimpses his adolescent daughter's breasts and is distressed to find himself aroused by the sight is responding normally, but the father who pretends to blunder into her bedroom by mistake in hopes of catching her half naked is behaving abusively.

Because children are naturally inclined to experiment sexually with one another, it has long been assumed that sex between siblings, particularly between brothers and sisters, was the most common form of incest. But that assumption is challenged by the *Los Angeles Times* survey, which found that only 2 percent of the female victims, and only 1 percent of the males, had ever had sex with a brother or sister. Three percent of the female victims, on the other hand, said they had had a sexual experience with their fathers while they were children, and 14 percent with an uncle. Though sibling incest is not always consensual, particularly in the case of an older brother and his much younger sister, the betrayal it entails is relatively small compared to that when the abuser is an uncle, grandparent, or someone else who assumes the stature of a parent in the child's eyes.[2] But it is sex between parents and their children that does the most harm of all. Parents are supposed to be beneficent caretakers, but it's impossible to be caretaker and lover at the same time. The parent who has sex with his or her child commits the ultimate betrayal, a betrayal by the one the child loves and trusts the most.

Though it represents a common theme in pornography, sex between mothers and sons has been viewed by many as what Rosemary Dinnage calls "the unexplained nub of incest: most seductive, most dangerous, most rarely acted out."[3] Is mother-son incest really all that rare? Since 7 percent of the men questioned in the Knoxville study mentioned in chapter 3 said they had been sexually abused by their natural mothers, it is more likely that such relationships simply go unreported. But the Knoxville study was neither random nor broad in scope, and it does not provide a basis for any solid conclusions about the frequency of mother-son incest.

Reports of father-daughter incest are much more common. The *Los Angeles Times* survey suggests that more than 750,000 adult women, about the population of Baltimore, are victims of father-daughter incest, and that there are another quarter-million girls now alive who will have sex with their natural fathers before they reach the age of eighteen. But sexual relationships between fathers and daughters merit attention for reasons beyond their numbers. Because abuser and victim share the same roof, father-daughter incest is likely to consist of many more occurrences than that involving an uncle or someone else who lives outside the home. Because of the peculiar dynamics that seem to exist within families where it takes place, father-daughter incest often compounds the damage it does by going on for several years. Finally, because most father-daughter incest occurs within the framework of the family, it inevitably has an impact on other family members who are not directly involved, particularly the victim's mother.

In what sort of family does father-daughter incest happen? Since incestuous fathers come from every social and economic stratum, there is no such thing as a typical "incest family." Indeed, because they often achieve a kind of surface stability that many normal families lack, families where incest is taking place may look to the rest of the world like models of matrimonial and filial devotion. Behind closed doors, however, they're likely to be families in name only, with very little cooperation or sense of community, and not much communication among their members. What appears from the outside to be marital bliss is really a narcissistic symbiosis, a pas de deux in which each partner's ego feeds so voraciously on the other's that neither has any interest in rocking the boat. Not only do the father and mother have an unspoken agreement to validate one another, they may share a narcissistic need to be seen as a model family, and very often they're successful. As Rachel pointed out, it was her family, which hardly qualifies as a model of anything when seen from the inside, that was chosen by local school officials as home for an Italian exchange student.

Nearly all incest families center around the abuser, but not all incest families are alike, and neither are all incestuous fathers. Some are essentially pedophiles who begin abusing their children soon after they're born and keep at it for years, often extending their reach to include children who are not their own. As Carl himself admits, the only thing that kept him from approaching his daughter's friends was his fear that they would "get a bad idea about me." More common, and in some ways more difficult to comprehend, is the father who never considers having sex with a child until fairly late in his marriage.

When a father makes a sexual advance toward his child, it is almost always triggered by some traumatic event, and the most common "trauma triggers" are those that affect the abuser's relationship with his wife. It might be her death, or her extended illness, or a divorce, anything that makes her unavailable to him. A number of incestuous fathers begin abusing their children only after they have separated from their wives. But such men are so dependent on their wives for ego nourishment that anything that puts emotional distance between the two can become a traumatic event. Perhaps she takes a job, begins working longer hours, becomes involved in volunteer work or something else that occupies her outside the home. For the first time in their married lives, part of the attention she used to pay her husband is directed somewhere else. Her decision may have had nothing to do with her husband, may have been purely a matter of economic necessity, but her husband's narcissistic ego doesn't make allowances for good intentions. In his mind he's been rejected and abandoned, and he turns for relief and gratification to one of his children.

The same sort of trauma can be precipitated by problems with the father's other main source of self-esteem, his job. The severest of all ego blows is being fired or laid off, and there is some evidence that the incidence of incest may be linked to the rate of unemployment. In one Chicago neighborhood over the past several years, reports of child sexual abuse have risen and fallen in nearly perfect unison with the level of unemployment. In many families where the father is out of work, the mother is forced to take a job, leaving her husband to shop, clean, and take care of the children. Not only do many men find such work demeaning and humiliating, it gives them more time at home with the children. But the loss of a job is not necessary by any means. Even an unkind word from the boss can send the genuine narcissist in search of alternative sources of admiration and approval.

As trouble with his wife or his job pushes his fragile world nearer to collapse, the abusive father's first response is often to begin drinking heavily. Alcohol helps quench his craving for gratification, and it is an effective means of boosting self-esteem. But alcohol is also a powerful disinhibitor, and anything that lowers his natural inhibitions makes it easier to abuse his child. It cannot be coincidence that as many as 60 or 70 percent of incest victims say their fathers had been drinking at the time the incest first occurred. In recent years, as marijuana, cocaine, and even heroin have become more widely available and also more affordable, reports of narcotics abuse by fathers who molest their children have also begun to climb.

In most cases where incest begins at an early age, the incestuous father is likely to be a pedophile in disguise, a man who knows soon after his children are born, perhaps even before they're born, that eventually he's going to have sex with them. Such fathers don't act impulsively. For them the abuse isn't triggered by a narcissistic crisis, and there is time to arrange things in ways that are conducive to what they have in mind. They may actually begin grooming the child from an early age, establishing a relationship in which the child becomes comfortable with being intimately touched and caressed. Perhaps the child's father helps her with bathing and dressing, or with combing or braiding her hair. Perhaps the two of them play wrestling or tickling games, or maybe he rubs her back. Eventually the backrubs give way to rubbing her breasts and then her vagina. Without understanding what's happened to her, the child is involved.

Because narcissistic families are not very communicative, it's easy for the abusive father to isolate the child emotionally from those she might turn to for help. He may drive a wedge between the child and her mother, either by disparaging the mother openly or simply by emphasizing her lack of authority. The picture he paints in the child's eyes is of someone who is without much influence inside the family or out, of someone who cannot be turned to for help. Once the victim has been insulated from her mother in this fashion, incest can continue unimpeded for years. Because fathers who have carefully laid the groundwork for incest are looking for a long-term relationship, not a one-night stand, it is not surprising that the use of force by incest abusers is not common. One Boston study found that fewer than one incest victim in ten suffered any serious physical injury, and that only a third had been subjected to any force at all. The use of violence most often accompanies sexual intercourse, but even then it is not very frequent. Over half the victims surveyed by the *Los Angeles Times* said they had had intercourse with adults while they were children, but only a fifth said they had been forced to do so.

The question of force really begs the issue anyway, because it's a rare child who's going to tell her daddy no. The father's natural authority is usually strong enough to assuage whatever initial doubts the child has about the propriety of what he proposes, and she may not have any doubts in the first place. If the girl is an adolescent when the father's regressive tendencies are triggered, or if their relationship has been particularly strained, his initial advance may be met by an outright refusal and a threat to tell someone if it happens again. But if most incest victims do not initially resist, it is simply because they have no way of knowing that the incest is wrong. As Rachel pointed out, "I never even thought of questioning my father. My father was right — that's all there was to it."

Even to portray the incest victim as a reluctant participant is to overlook the possibility that there are likely to be aspects of the relationship she enjoys. As a by-product of the incest, she's receiving a great deal of attention from the abusive parent. He may be slipping into her bedroom three or four nights a week after her mother goes to sleep, taking her on trips without the rest of the family, or doing whatever else he needs to do to get her alone. To ensure her compliance he gives her special presents and permissions, all the while telling her he loves her more than her brothers and sisters, even more than her mother.

For young girls who love their daddies, such attention can be heady stuff, and while it is an exceedingly difficult idea for many people to grasp, there is also the possibility that the child is enjoying the sex. In Rhode Island not long ago, a Family Court Judge suggested that many children "really enjoy" having sex with an adult. "I have these cases all the time," the judge said, "and I never hear the girls complain until they get hurt or something." The judge missed the point, but even for young children sex can be highly pleasurable. Kinsey reported orgasms in boys as young as five months, but Freud was the first to recognize that small children, even infants, are capable of responding to sensuality. "No child," he wrote, "none, at least, who is mentally normal and still less one who is intellectually gifted — can avoid being occupied with the problems of sex in the years before puberty."

The incest victim may have another motive for becoming an accomplice in her own abuse. In the child's mind, once the incest has begun she's won the competition with her mother for her father's affections, and she often begins to take on aspects of her mother's persona. Though it is by no means universal, in many incest cases the victim actually exchanges roles with the parent of the same sex. This sort of role reversal can happen when a mother who abuses her son substitutes him physically and emotionally for his father. Most often it is the daughter abused by her father who trades places with her mother, becoming a "little mother" herself. Rachel puts it best when she says of her relationship with her father, "I was the wife. I'd cook for him, I'd massage him, and then I would please him."

More often than might be suspected, the mother of an incest victim cooperates in such an exchange. If the mother herself was abused as a child, she may be so uncertain of her motherly role and her maternal authority that she tacitly allows her daughter to assume some of the burden. In the most extreme cases, the mother's authority is usurped until she is practically her child's child, almost without standing in her own home. Deep inside she may be angry and jealous over the alienation of her husband's affections and the loss of her wifely prerogatives, but her passivity and insecurity, and her ego's dependence on her continuing association with her husband, prevent her from stepping forward to reclaim her authority.

Role reversal may also contribute to the duration of father-daughter incest, both by making it easier for the father to rationalize his relationship with a daughter who is now behaving more like his wife and by making it more difficult for the daughter to stop the abuse. As she assumes her mother's responsibility for keeping the family intact, in a very proprietary sense it now becomes her family. To report the incest would be not only to discard the quasi-maternal status that she may have come to enjoy, but perhaps to send her father to jail and tear the family apart. The incest victim also gains power from the reversal of roles, and she may eventually recognize that she has acquired a tremendous hold over her father — a word from her and he goes directly to jail. What began as a one-sided exploitation now becomes a mutual one. As Rachel says, "I used it, but there was always a price to pay."

How does the incestuous father explain his behavior to himself? If, like Carl, he is without much apparent empathy of any kind, he can justify what he's doing with the most superficial of explanations. Perhaps he tells himself that he's showing his daughter how much he loves her, or that he's helping her to "learn about sex." For the fixated pedophile-father, the rationalization doesn't matter very much, because he really doesn't feel very bad. For regressive fathers, self-justification is a more complicated matter, because the father who turns to his daughter in a fit of narcissistic desperation is much more likely to detest himself. The conflict this ambivalence creates between his narcissistic ego and his "real" one may cause him to break down in tears and apologize, even to beg his daughter not to let him touch her again. Sensing the genuineness of his torment, his daughter may offer her forgiveness. But as soon as her father's ego feels empty again, his remorse begins to fade, and the cycle of seduction, remorse, forgiveness, and seduction can repeat itself for years.

Some fathers may abuse a child once or twice and then, for reasons known only to themselves, stop forever. A few incestuous relationships go on until the father dies, or the daughter goes away to college or marries. A tiny number continue even after that. But no matter how old the child is when it begins, incest is most likely to come to an end during her early teenage years. When it does, it is nearly always the victim who wants out first. By the time the child becomes a teenager, she has almost certainly realized that her relationship with her father is not only illicit, but illegal. Everything about the incest is making her increasingly uncomfortable, but her discomfort may have less to do with her father than with boys her own age.

Now that she is thirteen or fourteen, her girlfriends are discovering boys, and as the incest victim listens to their adolescent natterings, she can no longer escape the fact that she's a species apart. Her friends are giggling about how they kissed a certain boy, while she's been having oral sex or intercourse with her father for years. As her resentment over her father's theft of her innocence grows, the incest victim's response is to tell him how she really feels about their relationship and to appeal to him to end it. If there are other children in the family, her father may simply let her go and turn, as Carl did, to one of her sisters. But if she is an only daughter, or if her siblings are not the right age, her father may do whatever he can to prevent the incest from ending.

He may seem sympathetic to her plight, and unless he's completely hardened to her, some of the sympathy may be genuine. But the narcissistic cravings that led him to his daughter in the first place continue to persist, and as the child's determination to break free continues to grow, her father tries to exert an increasing degree of control over her life. He regulates her friendships and associations, particularly those with boys, how much housework and homework she does, even what kinds of clothes she wears. He's trying to remind her of who's really in charge, but his controlling behavior only deepens his daughter's resistance, which in turn drives her father to new heights of anger and desperation. Usually the victim decides to fight back with one of the two weapons in her arsenal — either she runs away from home, or she blows the whistle on her father. But sometimes the incest ends in violence.

When thirteen-year-old Sarah Ann Rairdon disappeared during the four-mile walk from her rural Minnesota school to the house where she lived with her ten brothers and sisters, the people of Otter

Tail County organized a search party. In the weeks that followed, the Rairdons' friends and neighbors printed thousands of flyers with Sarah Ann's picture and mailed them to police departments around the country. They raised a reward of six thousand dollars for her safe return, and Sarah Ann's picture began appearing with those of other missing children on grocery bags across the state. Her father, John Rairdon, a thirty-eight-year-old tire repairman, even went on television to appeal to his daughter's abductor. "Let her go," he pleaded. "Spare her from any more harm."

When Sarah Ann's badly decomposed body was discovered in a pasture, Otter Tail County mourned as one. It wasn't until three months later that John Rairdon confessed to police that he had murdered his daughter. They had been having sex for almost five years, he said, on at least sixty occasions that he could recall. There hadn't been any problem until the last couple of months, when she began resisting his advances. The day before Sarah Ann died, she successfully fought her father off for the first time. The next day he picked her up while she was walking home from school, drove her to an abandoned farmhouse, and tried to have sex with her again. Again she fought, and in a narcissistic rage, John Rairdon stabbed her in the stomach with an awl he used to repair tires. He watched while his daughter bled to death, then hid her body in a barn until he could bury it later in the field.

John Rairdon recanted his murder confession a few months later, saying he felt so guilty about having abused Sarah Ann that he had confessed to a murder he hadn't committed. "I knew I'd go to prison for the sexual abuse," Rairdon said at his preliminary hearing. "The officers knew me well and persuaded me I was guilty of murder. I just had to figure it out so the deputies would buy it. I was convinced that I had killed her. They told me I had to give them the details, and I thought I would have to make up a story good enough for them to believe." The jury was not persuaded. Convicted of his daughter's murder, John Rairdon was sentenced to life behind bars. Sarah Ann's stepmother, Marilyn Rairdon, was also convicted — not of having participated in the abuse, but of having knowingly allowed it to take place. She got two years' probation.

Sometimes it is the abusive parent who meets with a violent end. In March of last year, Cheryl Pierson, a seventeen-year-old Long Island cheerleader, pleaded guilty to manslaughter charges after she admitted promising a classmate $1,000 to kill her father, who was later shot to death in front of his house. In her confession to authorities, the girl said that her father, a forty-two-year-old electrician, had been abusing her sexually for years, but that she had only decided to arrange his killing because she feared he was about to turn his attention to her eight-year-old sister. Some juries have acquitted battered wives who admitted killing their abusive husbands, but no jury has yet been asked to decide whether incest might be grounds for a verdict of justifiable homicide.

Cases like those of Sarah Ann Rairdon and Cheryl Pierson raise the question, among others, of how a prolonged sexual relationship between a father and daughter can escape detection. To put it as frankly as possible, how can the mother of a child who is having sex with her husband *not* know what's going on? Some do. Some mothers actually conspire with their husbands in the abuse of their own children, like the Arizona woman who tried to obtain birth-control pills for her two daughters by explaining to a Planned Parenthood worker that the girls were "sleeping with their daddy." But most incestuous fathers aren't so open with their wives, and the mothers of their victims are far more likely to see or hear something — a word, a glance, a touch that seems practiced rather than casual — that only hints at the possibility of incest. Because the implications are too terrible to contemplate, such mothers may go to extraordinary lengths to deny the obvious.

Nahman Greenberg, a Chicago psychoanalyst, tells of one family in which the father, a highly paid director of computer services for a large corporation, had abused his eldest daughter since she was three. "They graduated to sexual intercourse by the age of eleven," Greenberg says, "and by the age of thirteen they had entered into a contract, the father and daughter, that she would be his primary sexual mate. The mother was allowed to have sex with him once a month. The contract was the daughter's idea. She liked this arrangement. She really was in love with her father. Quote, unquote, in love. The daughter describes a scene in which she and her father are nude, sitting in a room, watching TV. The mother walks in, and they don't have enough time to dress. So the mother turns around and walks out, apologizing for walking in. It's incredible — she walked in on this scene, and she just walked out. The girl didn't believe it. The mother does not acknowledge that she knew what was going on. Absolutely ignorant, had no knowledge of it. When you try to reconstruct it for her, to point out how she missed it, it's 'But I didn't see it.' "

Most "incest mothers" insist they had no notion of what was taking place beneath their own roofs, and when incest is limited to one or two occurrences, there isn't much for a mother to suspect. Even if she senses that something is amiss and asks her child what the trouble is, she may be told some vague story about problems at school and let it go at that. But in longer-term incest cases, even though neither the father nor the child is advertising the fact that they're having sex, the relationship is likely to be surrounded by a heavy air of secrecy and illicitness. In defense of such mothers, even when a direct question is asked of a longer-term incest victim, the child will often insist that nothing is wrong. One mother, concerned about the increasingly cuddly relationship between her husband and her fourteen-year-old daughter, made a special effort to tape a television movie about incest so that she and the girl could watch it together. "After it was over," the woman recalled, "I asked her, 'Has there ever been a time when Daddy has tried to be more than your father and your friend?' She said no." A few weeks later, the girl confided to a neighbor that she and her father had been having sex regularly for several years.

More than protecting themselves or their fathers, some children withhold the truth in the belief that they are sparing their mothers the anguish such a disclosure would entail. But children who lie for whatever reason often send subtle countervailing signals. "There were always hints I tried to give my mother," one incest victim recalled. "Once every two years, maybe, she'd ask me if my father had ever tried anything with me. And I'd always say no. But I'd be real quiet about it. I'd change the subject. If my daughter did that to me, I'd ask her why she was so quiet." It is a mistake to assume that the mother who has suspicions and fails to act condones what's going on. She may be horrified by what she half suspects, but the chances are good that she also feels immobilized, trapped in a web of circumstance not of her own making and powerless to act. If she's an ineffectual woman and easily intimidated, she may even fear her husband's physical retaliation.

In many cases, however, the child holds back the truth for fear of not being believed by the mother, and such fears are often well founded. The child sees how her father treats her mother and, more to the point, how the mother allows herself to be treated. Sooner or later she comes to realize that her mother's interests lie in maintaining the status quo. When incest victims finally decide to tell someone, it's no accident that most of them choose a teacher, a school counselor, a neighbor, a girlfriend — anybody but their mothers.

Once the incest is out in the open, many mothers summon the courage to provide their children with the protection and support that they have needed all along, ordering the abusive husbands from the house and cooperating as best they can with the police, prosecutors, and social workers. But even an incest mother who is sympathetic toward her daughter may be unable to keep her conflicting loyalties from becoming apparent to the child. When the girl who watched the incest movie with her mother told a neighbor she was being abused by her father, the neighbor called police. Later that night, the girl's mother asked the child if her accusations were really true. "I said yeah," the girl recalled. "She believed me. Then she went straight to the jail to try and see my dad. It sort of made me upset. She keeps telling me that she's on my side, but sometimes I feel like that and sometimes I don't. She's been with him for years, and she just can't let go, I guess. She says she needs him. I know she cares a lot about me and my brother, but to think that she can't get along without him sort of makes me upset."

For some incest mothers, the impending loss of their husbands and the dissolution of their families may be more distressing than the disclosure of the incest. No matter what such a mother has suspected until then, to take the side of her daughter against her husband is to abandon her claim to the emotional and physical security their relationship provides. Unless he's willing to face the consequences, the husband usually makes it easy for his wife to take his side over that of their child. He denies the child's accusations, and the mother follows suit, agreeing that the child must be lying. If the mother's anger at her child seems genuine, part of it probably is anger at having been displaced by her daughter as the focus of her husband's affections. The rest is drawn from the damage to the narcissistic fantasy the mother has been weaving and embroidering for years, her pretense that she has a happy home and that she's been a good mother and wife.

If, despite the mother's protestations and those of her husband, the authorities continue to believe the child, her only hope of regaining what she stands to lose is to convince the child to change her story. "Look what you've done to our family," she says. "Everything was fine before you started telling these lies. Now all these strangers are poking around in our business. Your father is already in jail, and if he's convicted he'll have to go to prison. Then where will we get the money to live?" A mother whose loyalties are divided to any degree plays on the tremendous guilt and responsibility the child already feels, not just for having participated in the incest but for having reported it. If there are brothers and sisters who haven't been abused, they probably have grown to resent all the attention the victim has been receiving from their father, and now they join the chorus. The victim may be angry at her father, but part of her probably still loves him. What she wanted was for the incest to stop, not to become alienated from her family or to see her father in the penitentiary. As she comes face-to-face with the consequences of what she's done, the victim may begin to wish that she had kept quiet after all. It's too late for that, but she has another out. She can always tell the police that she lied.

The word *recantation* entered the popular American vocabulary in the summer of 1985, when a twenty-three-year-old New Hampshire housewife named Cathleen Crowell Webb said she had lied six years before when she accused a Chicago man named Gary Dotson of having raped her. She had made up the story, Webb said, because she feared she had become pregnant by her boyfriend. When Dotson appeared in a police lineup, she had picked him out at random. Because Webb's recantation contained a number of puzzling discrepancies, the judge who originally convicted Gary Dotson denied him a new trial. But by then public sentiment was so much in the young man's favor that Illinois governor Jim Thompson commuted his sentence to time served. For several weeks the Dotson case remained a staple of television interview programs and supermarket magazine covers, and it triggered a number of similar recantations by other adult victims of rape.

Though the fact was largely lost in the flurry of media attention, it is not unusual for adult rape victims to withdraw their initial allegations. While some recantations are no doubt the result of mistaken identity, rape crisis counselors believe that victims often change their stories because they fear testifying in public or retaliation from their attackers. Recantations by victims of child sexual abuse, particularly victims of incest, are more common still. When David Jones, a British child psychiatrist attached to Denver's Henry Kempe Center, surveyed three hundred sexual abuse cases, he discovered that one victim in eight eventually withdrew his or her accusations. Jones also found that such recantations were most likely to come about two weeks after the first allegation was made.

As prosecutors and judges become aware of the likelihood of recantations in incest cases, victims who change their stories are not always believed. A fourteen-year-old girl from Des Moines testified at her stepfather's trial that she had lied when she first said he abused her, explaining that she hated the man and wanted him out of the house. The judge refused to believe her, and the stepfather was convicted. The girl later withdrew her recantation, saying she had changed her story the first time at the behest of her mother. "I kept thinking that this guy did this to me, and my mom still loves him," she said. "Why can't she give me a little bit of that love? I figured maybe if I got him out of prison she'd love me. If I had known what I was getting into, as much as I wanted to satisfy my mother, I would never have gotten into this mess." Convicted of perjuring herself, the girl was sentenced to ninety days in jail.

The most celebrated recantation in a case of sexual abuse so far has been that of Amy, a twelve-year-old California girl who accused her stepfather, an Air Force surgeon, of having abused her sexually for several years. When Amy refused to take the witness stand against her abuser, the judge found her in contempt of court. After keeping Amy in solitary confinement for nine days at a juvenile detention center, the judge finally let her go, but on the condition that she have no contact with her stepfather. While children's-rights organizations railed against the judge for his heartlessness, Amy's mother told reporters how proud she was of her daughter's refusal to send her stepfather to jail. But the victim-witness coordinator for the local district attorney's office quoted Amy as having told her that she hated her stepfather and wanted him punished. Her mother, the girl said, had refused to let her come home if she testified against the man.

Open hostility, pressure to recant, divided loyalties that raise questions about the mother's ability to protect her child — all can have bearing upon the decision that must be made by child protection authorities of whether to take the incest victim from the home. The obvious solution to such a dilemma would seem to be to remove the abuser, not the victim. But when an incest mother chooses to side with her husband, nothing short of a court order can force him to leave. The result of such a step is that the child is left at home with a hostile mother, and even a court order does not guarantee that the mother will not allow her husband to return home surreptitiously.

Many victims solve the problem by running away, but in a significant number of cases the choice is to place the child in a foster home or children's shelter. More than a quarter of the victims in six thousand incest cases studied by David Finkelhor were placed in youth shelters or foster homes, a higher percentage of foster placements than for children who had been physically abused. Foster placement is supposed to be an emergency measure, reserved for cases where a child's physical safety is in jeopardy. But it is easy for children to get lost in the juvenile welfare system, and it is not unusual for the victims of incest to be shuffled from one temporary home to another for most of their childhoods.[4]

SIX

Pedophiles

I t is best when beginning sex with a kid to do it as part of a game. Sometimes a kid will make the first move, sometimes the adult. Sometimes the adult can create a situation where a kid can ask for sex or start sex if they want. Curiosity is a big factor; exploring somebody and having them explore you is another good way to start off. This can be a kind of show and tell. Just about everything that adults can do together an adult and a kid can do together. It's best to go slowly the first time — and it's more exciting that way too — but of course you have to be sensitive to size differences. Kids enjoy nonpenetrating sex the best. Most very young or small kids cannot and should not be penetrated by an adult. Having sex is having fun. If anyone is not able to relax, it won't be as enjoyable. Sex is play, not work. If you have sex with some that like it, they can tell those of their friends who may also be interested. Sometimes starting out sex is better if other kids are there doing it too. Group sex is a good way to experiment and experience all kinds of sex with all sorts of different partners. What better way to learn!

Thus begins a pamphlet entitled *How to Have Sex with Kids.* Though it had enjoyed a brisk underground circulation for several years, police were unaware of the pamphlet until 1983, when they found a copy in the apartment of a Houston jeweler convicted of sexually abusing a four-month-old boy. Further investigation revealed that the author, David Sonenschein, had "published" the document on copying machines in the offices of the Texas school district where he worked.[1] The police also discovered that Sonenschein was a member of the Texas-based Howard Nichols Society, an organization named after the fictional character who preyed on young girls in the television movie *Fallen Angel.* In public, the Nichols Society presents itself as a political-action organization, publicly disparaging a culture where "pictures of affirmative sex are condemned while photos of the Hiroshima cloud are printed in millions of children's schoolbooks." In private, as Sonenschein's pamphlet shows, the society takes a somewhat different tack.

The propensity of pedophiles to organize and proselytize illustrates one of the principal distinctions between those who abuse their own children sexually and those who abuse other people's children. Incestuous fathers are so secretive that it's difficult to imagine one of them composing an essay about how to have sex with a daughter or a son. Pedophiles, on the other hand, are "groupers" who actually seek one another out, to swap not only half-baked philosophies about having sex with children, but pictures of their victims and often the victims themselves. For those who devote their lives to the pursuit of sex with children, it's reassuring to consort with other outlaws. What pedophiles really seek from one another is validation, the knowledge that they're not alone.

The pedophile's grouping instinct also reflects his narcissism, because many have managed to convince themselves that they're at the forefront of a social and cultural revolution the rest of the world is blind to. They don't see themselves as child abusers at all, but as a politically oppressed minority of "child lovers" whose vocabulary doesn't include words like *sexual abuse*. To pedophiles it's "transgenerational sex," and they talk endlessly of their love for children and of children's affection for them. Because their devotion to children is so single-minded, they see themselves as vastly superior to other adults, particularly parents who don't have much time for their own children. Since it's usually the children of inattentive parents who become their victims, pedophiles insist that they're performing a service by filling the affection gap in children's lives. Though they may idealize children in the abstract and celebrate their "innocence" and "purity," the shallowness of the pedophiles' affection is betrayed by their private lingo, as in their description of a child who is new to having sex as "a kid with low mileage."

In recent years, a few bolder pedophiles in this country and abroad have set out to convince the rest of the world that sex with consenting children is fine. There was a considerable fuss in Great Britain a few years back when Parliament discovered the existence of something called the Paedophile Information Exchange, a small and selective group whose stated purpose was to "discuss strategies" for abolishing laws prohibiting consensual sex between adults and children. The Exchange even published two magazines for a brief time, one called *Maypie* and another named *Minor Problems*. According to Geoffrey Dickens, the member of Parliament who first disclosed the existence of PIE, its members included a former British ambassador to Canada and several members of the household staff at Buckingham Palace. Others identified later were an employee of the British Home Office, a scoutmaster, a public school teacher, and a vicar's son.

Largely because of its slogan — Sex by Year Eight or Else It's Too Late — the pedophile organization that has attracted the most attention in this country is the Rene Guyon Society. The group, which claims a membership of several thousand, is named after a French-born justice of the supreme court of Thailand who argued that much of what is wrong with contemporary civilization is traceable to its distorted view of sex. According to its own legend, the Guyon Society was founded in 1962 by seven couples who attended the same lecture on sexuality in the ballroom of a Los Angeles hotel. Whatever its true membership and origins, its only visible manifestations are a newsletter, a Beverly Hills post office box, and a self-appointed spokesman who gives his name as Tim O'Hara. "We were in the black civil rights movement originally," O'Hara says, "working with the ACLU and the NAACP. We were a bunch of high-principled activists, and we renamed ourselves the Guyon Society. We have no dues. It's not like the Elks Club. We advocate legalizing sex with children, but we do not practice it. We'd all be in jail, for one thing. No one can come into our society who has ever had sex with a child."

Though the Guyon Society has received a good deal of attention from the press, police suspect that its membership may not extend much beyond O'Hara himself. But there are a number of less well-known pedophile organizations that do boast a significant membership. One is the San Diego-based Childhood Sensuality Circle, founded by an eighty-four-year-old retired social worker, which seeks for children "the right to loving relationships." Joseph Henry, a convicted child molester who is a former member of the CSC, maintains that the group's "children's rights" stance is just a pose. "I can't stress enough," he says, "that that group and others, regardless of their publicly stated goals, are in practice little more than contact services for pedophiles. These groups serve as a reinforcement for pedophiles and a constant source for new friendships and, thus, a supply of new victims."[2] When the CSC's records were seized last year by the San Diego County sheriff's department, at least thirty of its members were found to have been arrested for child sexual abuse.[3]

Another pedophile organization in this country is NAMBLA, the

North American Man/Boy Love Association, which made headlines a few years ago when seven of its members pleaded guilty to sexually abusing numerous children, including several members of the same Cub Scout pack. Among those convicted were a Manhattan neurologist, an Ohio politician, and a California physicist. NAMBLA is dedicated to fighting for the rights of children to have sex, but a recent issue of its monthly bulletin acknowledged that its chances of success were not good. "Man-boy love faces almost universal condemnation in America," the editors admitted. "Whether we are open about our feelings or try to blend in quietly, we are all threatened to some degree. We need not panic, but we should be prudent." The NAMBLA bulletin also publishes letters from its members and supporters, including a number who are behind bars. "I am still an inmate," one man wrote, "and appreciate receiving your Bulletin each month. I am here for consensual love with two brothers, eleven and fifteen. I too believe that boys shouldn't be exploited or abused. They should have freedom to choose whomever they want as friends, no matter what age brackets."

While organizations like NAMBLA and the Guyon Society present themselves as advocates for "children's rights," the right in which they're primarily interested is the right of their members to have sex with children. Such groups insist that the only thing that's wrong with sex with children is that society says it's wrong, and they point to a handful of studies suggesting that some children who began having sex at an early age were unharmed by the experience.[4] Any psychological damage, they say, occurs only after the child discovers that he has violated a social taboo.[5] When the government of the Netherlands recently suggested lowering the age of consent from sixteen to twelve, pedophile organizations in this country wondered why twelve-year-old Dutch children might be able to handle sex with adults when twelve-year-old American children weren't.

How many pedophiles are there? There isn't any real way of knowing, but it's likely that they are far outnumbered by their victims. Because their pursuit of children is so single-minded, most pedophiles have sex with many children during their lifetimes — not just with two or three, but with dozens and even scores. One group of thirty child sexual abusers studied by researchers at the Oregon State Hospital admitted having had sex with a combined total of 847 children, an average of nearly thirty victims apiece — a remarkable figure considering that most of the men had not yet reached the age of forty.[6]

More is known about how pedophiles meet one another. One way is by advertising, and one of their favorite advertising mediums is a curious brand of publication known as the "swinger magazine." Slickly lithographed on glossy paper and filled with advertisements mailed in by readers, such magazines are available in almost any adult bookstore. Most of the ads are placed by couples in search of other couples, but a surprising number are placed by men, women, and couples in search of other adults who enjoy having sex with children. To the uninitiated, the pedophiles' ads look like the others, but those in the know distinguish the child molesters from the wife swappers by looking for special code phrases. One commonly used phrase is "family fun" or some variation, such as "The family that plays together stays together."

Over the past couple of years the signals have become more subtle, but some pedophiles are still amazingly indiscreet. One young man, who described himself as "very sensual, very oral, college-educated, and divorced," advertised for "young ladies who are aware of the teachings of the Rene Guyon Society and approve of same." In response to a letter from a stranger seeking more information, the man readily acknowledged that he had been "involved in this type of thing for many, many years. My range of contacts in the past covers ages six to sixteen, both sexes."

Such indiscretion involves a much greater risk now that police officers in several cities have begun answering such ads and even placing some of their own. One of the police officers' favorite targets is *Wonderland*, the newsletter of a Chicago-based organization called the Lewis Carroll Collectors Guild.[7] David Techter, who presides over the Guild from his Lincoln Park apartment, describes it as "a voluntary association of persons who believe that nudist materials are constitutionally protected expression, and whose collecting interests include preteen nudes." Each issue of *Wonderland* is illustrated with suggestive, though not technically pornographic, drawings of very young children, and filled with a hodgepodge of Techter's philosophy and "reviews" of pornographic publications. Next to Vladimir Nabokov, whose satiric novel *Lolita* has become the pedophile's bible, the patron saint of Techter's followers is David Hamilton, a British-born photographer whose portraits of early-teenage girls are available in legitimate bookstores across the United States. The notion that Hamilton's work is art and not pornography is encouraged by the pairing of his photographs with text from some distinguished writers, among them the French surrealist Alain Robbe-Grillet. Since state and federal laws do not prohibit the sale of nude photographs of children who are not engaging in sexual activities or posing in an otherwise "lascivious" way, Hamilton's work is not illegal. But whatever its attraction for lovers of art and photography, its greatest appeal may well be to lovers of children.

Despite its own philosophical pretensions, *Wonderland* is really a flea market for the buying and selling of pictures of young children. Some of the advertisements it contains are placed by dealers, like the Redmond, Washington, firm that offers one photo collection of prepubescent girls titled *Still Too Young* and another called *La Petite Parisienne*, but most come from private individuals. "I want to buy VHS videotapes of preteens and teens doing anything nude," wrote one New Hampshire man, who promised "confidentiality assured." A Tennessee woman sought "photos of girls in swimsuits, panties, short sleepware [*sic*], or shorts — back, front, side views." For fifty dollars apiece, a woman in California offered videotapes of "beautiful teenage girls in all their NATURAL beauty." Some of his readers may, as Techter claims, be nothing more than individuals "whose collecting interests include preteen nudes." But some are clearly pedophiles, like the Pennsylvania man who mailed pornographic photos of children to a *Wonderland* advertiser who turned out to be an undercover policeman. Only after the man's arrest on pornography charges did police discover that he was wanted in another state on nineteen separate charges of child sexual abuse.

In recent months, several police officers around the country have begun corresponding with advertisers in *Wonderland* and similar publications, hoping to entice them into an exchange of child pornography that will result in a conviction. A few investigators, using pen names, have even placed their own carefully worded ads. One of Techter's readers complained in a recent letter that "there was a tri-state bust for [alleged] pornography distribution, and I and several of your followers were netted by an undercover cop out of Los Angeles named William Dworin, AKA Paul Davis. Anyone in contact with this man best beware! I was hit with a ten-man SWAT team that got everything I owned. My *very* expensive lawyer swears he'll get me off with probation — I hope."

Finding and prosecuting pedophiles through the exchange of child pornography is an effective tactic, since it is an unusual pedophile who does not also photograph his victims. Virtually all the child pornography produced in this country since the 1978 passage of federal antipornography statutes comes from practicing pedophiles who have graduated from making pictures for their own use to swapping them with other pedophiles. Such behavior may seem odd — what does an adult who has access to real children want with pornographic photos? But such photographs are much more than a child substitute. Homemade pornography not only feeds the pedophile's fantasies, it becomes a permanent record of the children he has known. The victims themselves may not stay young forever, but in the pedophile's album the eight-year-old remains forever eight. Not only do pictures of smiling children validate his behavior; such photographs also have a more practical application. In attempting to break down the resistance of a prospective victim, the pedophile can produce documentary evidence that children have sex with adults.

Because he takes such pains to compile his photographic record, and because that record acquires such enormous importance in his life, the pornographic photos the pedophile has made become his most treasured possession. If there is anything to be said in behalf of child pornography, it is that such pictures are better than a signed confession. The FBI's Ken Lanning calls pornography "the single most valuable piece of evidence you can have in any sexual abuse case. I would rather have child pornography than fifty-seven eyewitnesses. No child molester will go to court when you legally seize his pornography collection." For those who do choose to stand trial, the chances of an acquittal are slim. When a downstate Illinois dentist who served as the village school-board president and the local soccer coach was charged with sexually abusing a ten-year-old girl, his friends and neighbors leapt to his defense. Such was the dentist's reputation that he might never have been convicted had the police not discovered hundreds of pornographic photos of children hidden in a crawl space beneath his house.

Those pedophiles who don't have any other recourse obtain their victims from child prostitution rings. One such ring, located in the village of Waterville, Maine, provided children as young as four to a tightly knit group of friends and relatives for up to thirty dollars apiece. The Waterville victims were recruited from the neighborhood, but in some cases it is the parents who put their own children up for prostitution. A study of nine East Coast prostitutes between the ages of eight and twelve found that all had been living at home and attending school, and that their families were not only aware of what they were doing, but condoned and even encouraged it.[8]

Joseph Henry, currently serving a long sentence for child sexual abuse at California's Patton State Hospital, admits having sexually abused at least twenty-two girls during his fifty-plus years. Most of them he met on his own, children he describes as "lonely and longing for attention." But at least three of Henry's victims were acquired through a California prostitution ring run by a man named John Duncan who placed a classified advertisement in a pedophile publication called *Better Life*. As Henry recalled later, "Duncan wanted assurance I was not a cop, or any other such person trying to entrap him. He also wanted to hear about my experiences, past or present. I wrote and said I wasn't a police officer. I also told him about Barbara, the first girl I molested, and how I got interested in little girls. We began a long correspondence. Duncan began telling me about two girls he was molesting at the time, Tammy and Lisa, ages eight and nine. He also sent me their nude photos. I was desperate for friendship, someone who understood my obsession with children. My letters to Duncan ran as long as nine typed pages. I would sign them 'A fellow little girl lover.' I wrote Duncan telling him I planned to travel to California in the summer and would like to attend a child sex orgy, and I would be very glad to pay for this privilege. I wrote him, 'I want to assure you that I can keep my mouth shut.' "

When Henry arrived in California, "Duncan brought Tammy and Lisa over to my motel. That day I could not have the children alone to myself, because Duncan had arranged for another member of the ring to molest them. Several days later, Duncan and I molested Tammy and Lisa in my motel room. Then we went to a nearby park, where I pushed the girls on some swings. A few days later, after paying Duncan the hundred dollars that we agreed would be given to Yvonne's father, I had this eight-year-old to myself for about six hours. I wasn't sure I could go through with actually paying someone to have sex with their daughter. It was obvious Yvonne had been rented to several other men. The first thing she said to me that night was, 'What would you like me to do?' When I was unable to take Yvonne home that night because I didn't have a car, Yvonne's father phoned my motel room and said that since I was keeping her overnight, it would cost me another hundred dollars. The next day, when her father came to pick her up, the first thing he said was, 'Did you cooperate?' "

After returning to New York, Henry wrote John Duncan a note thanking him "for taking me out of hell and giving me a brief taste of Heaven." Joseph Henry, John Duncan, Yvonne's father, and six other men who had abused the children in the Duncan ring, several of whom were from out of state and one from England, all went to prison. Henry says he hears that Yvonne, now eighteen, "will never be normal." [9]

If such "baby pro" rings, as they are known, are relatively rare, one reason may be that there are so many underage prostitutes working the streets of America's cities. They can be found in New York City's Times Square and Chicago's Uptown, along Miami's Biscayne Boulevard and the Las Vegas Strip, in Boston's Combat Zone and San Francisco's Tenderloin, and not all of them are girls. Los Angeles police say there may be five thousand male prostitutes in that city under the age of fourteen. Some are homosexuals, but many have sex with men only because it is men who pay to have sex with young boys. "I don't consider myself gay," said one sixteen-year-old boy. "I really didn't like to have sex with other men, because it made me feel cheap. Most of the men who picked me up were stupid middle-class guys. I did it so I wouldn't starve to death. You do what you have to do."

Child prostitution is no longer just a big-city problem. Prostitutes as young as eleven were recently discovered working out of an Indiana truck stop, and Cedar Rapids, Iowa, now has one police officer assigned full-time to juvenile prostitution. According to the police chief of Wichita, Kansas, the recent arrests of a dozen child prostitutes there only "scratched the surface of a very significant problem in our community." Because the subject is a guaranteed shocker, over the past couple of years there have been a number of articles and television documentaries on child prostitution. But there is nothing very new about child prostitutes — back in 1944, the FBI reported that the number of young girls servicing the GI trade had risen by 70 percent since Pearl Harbor[10] — and the emphasis on this most visible manifestation of pedophilia obscures the fact that many pedophiles never have to pay for sex with children.

As David Sonenschein points out in *How to Have Sex with Kids*, "the important thing about meeting kids is that it happens best when you meet in places or in doing things that interest both of you. Like in video game arcades, kids can tell if you're just in there cruising for sex or are there because you like to play the games. The same with sports and sporting events. You can meet kids anywhere you go that you're interested in going. You can get to know kids through your job. Friends are a good source — once you get to know a kid, you can meet their friends. If you take kids anywhere after you meet them, unless you know them pretty well it may be best to stay in familiar areas so that if the kids want to leave, or have to, they can. This will help them be more at ease with you."

One of the newest ways of finding children is through computerized "bulletin boards," arrangements through which anyone with a personal computer hooked up to a telephone can contact other computer owners by calling a central telephone number. The computer industry estimates that there are something like 2,500 of these bulletin boards in operation at any one time, but since they are mostly run from garages and spare bedrooms, it is impossible to keep an accurate count.

Because pedophiles are compulsive record keepers, some of them are as attracted to computers as they are to children. Many pedophiles keep meticulous notes about each of the children they abuse, recording what was done to whom and where, the child's reaction, and so on. The records compiled by one Tennessee man included the average number of sex acts per child (64.68), the average duration of each relationship (2.2 years), the average age of each victim (10.89 years), even the approximate number of sperm ejaculated by each boy.[11] Such records help to satisfy the pedophile's compulsive need for reaffirmation, since by reliving each experience over and over he can continually reassure himself that he is loved by children. Before the advent of the home computer, pedophiles kept their records in notebooks or on index cards. In the hands of the police, however, written records also amount to a confession. In recent years, pedophiles have discovered that computers are not only a vastly superior system of record keeping, but that they can be programmed to destroy everything on command. For the pedophile who already owns a computer for some other purpose, plugging into a computerized bulletin board is a simple matter. An even more recent electronic advance is the "teenage party line," computer-controlled telephone services that charge callers one dollar a minute to take part in a free-for-all conversation with up to seven other people. Over the hubbub of eight voices speaking at once, introductions are made and home telephone numbers exchanged. Explicit sexual suggestions and four-letter-words are common. Though the party line operators admonish callers that they must be eighteen to participate, many sound much younger and some quite a bit older.

Computers make it easier for pedophiles to contact strange children, but there were plenty of children available before there were computers. To listen to pedophiles, one would think finding a child to seduce was the easiest thing in the world. Phil, a forty-one-year-old truck driver, had his first sexual experience with another boy at the age of fourteen. Since then, as he told Lynn Emmerman of the *Chicago Tribune*, he has abused about 130 boys. "Everybody has a niche, something they're good at," Phil said. "Unfortunately, I'm very good at picking up kids. It's incredibly easy. I like to go where the level of income is not too high. Bowling alleys are good. I'm a very good bowler, the kind of person people watch. I've raced motorcycles and stock cars, flown airplanes and parachuted, all to meet kids. I've always met boys through the jobs I've had — running a karate school, driving an ice cream truck, selling motorcycles.

"One of the easiest ways to meet kids is through their parents. Now, I live with my mother, and I know kids' fathers and older brothers, so there's plenty of opportunity. I can introduce you to dozens of parents who think I'm Mr. Wonderful. I try to find kids who smoke dope. They're already keeping something from their parents. If you let a kid off a block from his home with a little reefer and a twenty-dollar bill in his pocket, he's not going to tell anybody what he just did. For me, the magic words are 'My folks are divorced.' [Most] of the boys I've had sex with came from single-parent families. The others had family troubles. A kid from a good, solid home wouldn't be with me in the first place.

"Usually the way I test kids is, I touch them on the knee. If they don't jump, I know I can go further. I take them out a time or two. Go-cart tracks and water slides are big. Invariably the kid says, 'When are you going to call me again?' First I build him up. I say, 'You're a really nice-looking kid, but the problem is, I'm gay.' The kid usually says, 'Well, it's OK. Don't worry about it.' I say, 'Well, one of these days I'm going to ask you to take your clothes off — don't get mad at me.' They just laugh. They don't think that will ever happen. It almost always does."

Phil's modus operandi says a lot about what sort of child becomes involved with a pedophile. Very young victims are not likely to have much in common with one another, since it's easy for a pedophile to use his status as an adult to convince a child who doesn't know any better that there's nothing wrong with having sex with him. For older children, entering into a sexual relationship with someone who is not a parent or relative is almost always a matter of conscious choice, and the children who make that choice appear to have some personality traits in common. As Phil suggests, the children most likely to become sexually involved with an unrelated adult are those with absent or indifferent parents, relatively unattractive children or those who think they're unattractive, children with negative self-images, poorer children, and children without many friends their own age.

Such children are prime candidates for the affection, attention, and understanding that are the pedophile's stock in trade. "If a seven-year-old loses his brand-new bike, his parents will probably yell at him," a police officer says. "A pedophile will try to help him find it. And if he can't find it, the pedophile will buy him a new one." The busy or indifferent parents of such children are often relieved that their children have developed a close association with another adult, and it is also such parents who are least likely to interfere. Joseph Henry was amazed to find that the parents of his many victims "didn't ask questions when I spent hours and hours with their children and gave them gifts. On several occasions when they became aware of what I was doing, they just told me to stay away from their children. Charges were never pressed in many cases, because the parents did not want to cause any trouble."[12]

As was the case with the four young sisters from a Houston suburb who were abused for years by a group of neighborhood men, it is not uncommon for children to be attracted by the material benefits a relationship with a pedophile can offer. In return for sex, the men gave the sisters food, candy, clothing, and makeup, even a trip to the local amusement park. "It was like prostitution, but they didn't know it," a police officer said. "They thought this was the way life was, the way to get nice things." A Little League coach from Santa Clara, California, who lavished his fifty victims with gifts, trips to the movies, and pizza admitted that "the burden of repaying the debt, plus the fact that most children are taught to obey adults, was usually sufficient to ensure their cooperation."

Not all relationships between children and pedophiles are mercantile ones, nor are all children who become involved with pedophiles lonely or needy. None of the dozen or so girls who ran afoul of Walter Holbrook was particularly plain-looking. None was from a broken home, none was failing in school, none was bereft of friends. And Walter Holbrook was hardly the sort of person to help a child look for a lost bicycle, much less buy her a new one. As Sandi tells the story, it was during the summer between her freshman and sophomore years in high school that she first met Walter Holbrook. They were introduced by Colleen, one of her classmates, who had taken a part-time job cleaning the California townhouse that Holbrook shared with a traveling salesman. Holbrook was in the market for a second housekeeper, and he promised the two girls ten dollars apiece for a couple of hours' work. But he proved to be a demanding customer, ordering the girls around like the retired Marine sergeant he was.

At first, neither girl knew quite what to make of their employer. When they arrived with their cleaning paraphernalia, Holbrook greeted them dressed in a pair of undershorts, explaining that a "skin disease" made wearing clothes uncomfortable. The cheap etchings of nude women that covered his walls also seemed out of place for such a fastidious character. But the girls just shrugged it off — as one policeman put it later, "they were fourteen going on forty-five." Before long, Holbrook's real intentions began to emerge. When the girls' work was done, Holbrook would call them into his bedroom to receive their money. After they had been paid, he would ask one girl or the other to rub his back with some of the vitamin E oil he kept on the nightstand by his bed. The massages, he said, helped to ease the pain of an old war wound. To Sandi and Colleen it didn't seem to matter; if Holbrook wanted a massage, that was fine with them. Nor did they appear to mind when, at Holbrook's suggestion, the massages progressed from his back to his front. "I can teach you things that will make you a better girlfriend," he told the girls.

Eventually Holbrook mentioned a way the girls could make more than the ten dollars he was paying them to clean his house. "He started telling us about people who were going to come over, and how we were going to have parties," Sandi said. "He said that we would be posing for pictures. He told us they were going to be sent overseas, and that there was no way they would be published in America." When Holbrook began taking pictures, he kept reminding the girls to smile, "so the pictures would look better and sell better." When the photo session was over, he paid Colleen and Sandi each twenty-five dollars. In the months that followed, there were more parties. To loosen things up, Holbrook might provide some wine or a little marijuana. Sometimes he would hand Sandi the camera and ask her to photograph him and Colleen. Once he paid the girls fifty dollars apiece.

When they asked where the photographs were going, Holbrook vaguely mentioned a woman friend named Betty who sold pictures of young girls through the mail. When their curiosity persisted, he suggested that they write Betty a letter telling her which sexual acts they were willing to perform and which they weren't. The two girls drew up a two-column list, the first headed "Do Want to Do," the second "Don't Want to Do." A few days later Holbrook showed the girls Betty's reply, written in red ink. "Great," it said. "Love you, B." Once, Holbrook asked Sandi and Colleen if they had any other friends who were interested in cleaning house. He was particularly looking for twelve-year-olds, Sandi recalled, "because they're flat-chested, and the younger girls would sell better."

Colleen and Sandi were not Walter Holbrook's only housekeepers. When police searched his townhouse, they found more than three hundred Polaroid pictures of a dozen other girls. The police later called him a "serial" abuser, and one officer remarked that he must have had the cleanest house in town. A few of the girls in the photographs were identified by Colleen and Sandi from among their schoolmates, but the rest remained a mystery. Just as Walter Holbrook's preliminary hearing was about to begin, he pleaded guilty, explaining that he didn't want to be "an asshole" by forcing Colleen, Sandi, and the other girls to testify in open court. He was sentenced to twenty-six years in prison, and if he lives to serve his full sentence — no certain thing for a child molester in prison — he will be seventy when he gets out.

The most perplexing question was why Sandi, Colleen, and the other girls had gotten involved with Walter Holbrook in the first place. Afterward Sandi was ashamed, but she couldn't really say why she had done it. For the money, certainly, but there had to be more to it than the money, or even the marijuana and the sex. "They must have been getting some sort of emotional support and attention they weren't getting at home," one policeman suggested. "There was also a sense of adventure and excitement." What he seemed to be saying was that the girls had just been bored.

As the Holbrook case makes clear, it is hardly necessary for pedophiles to kidnap children in order to abuse them sexually. And yet, a 1985 survey by the magazine *Good Housekeeping* found that the number-one concern of American parents was kidnapping. On its face, what came to be known as the "missing children" story appeared to be one of the most wrenching of the decade. "This," intoned Phil Donahue during one of the many programs he devoted to the subject, "is as painful as life gets." It was also an issue tailor-made for the news media, which set out with determination to answer the many questions such stories provoked: How many American children were missing from their homes? Had these children been kidnapped? For what purpose, and by whom?

The reports became increasingly chilling. One wire service dispatch, carried by hundreds of newspapers in mid-1984, reported that "countless thousands" of American children had fallen victim to "an ugly underworld of abuse, terror, and death." *USA Today* warned that strangers were stealing twenty thousand children from their parents every year. Even *The New York Times*, not noted for overstatement, reported that thousands of children were "killed annually by repeat murderers who prey sexually on children, and by adults involved in child prostitution and pornography." A number of articles, and at least one network television documentary, repeated rumors of a shadowy ring of wealthy pedophiles who arranged to have young children snatched off the streets and sold into sexual bondage.

No missing child received more attention than six-year-old Adam Walsh, who disappeared from a Hollywood, Florida, shopping center in July 1981 and whose severed head was found two weeks later floating in a canal eighty miles from his home. The story of Adam's disappearance and death became the basis for the television movie *Adam*, which has so far been shown three times on network TV. Adam's father, John Walsh, quit his job as a hotel executive to become a full-time advocate for the cause of missing and murdered children. Walsh made headlines when he told a congressional subcommittee that one and a half million American children were reported missing every year. "We don't have a clue as to what happened to fifty thousand of them," Walsh said. "No town is safe and no child is safe from the sick, sadistic molesters and killers who roam our country at random. This country is littered with mutilated, raped, strangled little children."

Once the issue of missing children became a certified national problem, nearly everyone was eager to help resolve it. One idea that quickly gained currency was that the missing children might be found if only people knew who they were. If their pictures were posted in public places, the reasoning went, whoever was taking the children could not keep them for long. The logic behind the picture campaign was dubious at best, since children's appearances change so rapidly. But logic was obscured by the urgency to act, and major corporations began tripping over one another to help out.

More than sixty supermarket chains announced plans to post photo displays in fifty-five hundred stores, where they would be seen by eighty million Americans each week. The same pictures began turning up on milk cartons, grocery bags, utility bills, and bank statements, on the sides of moving vans, in the back seats of taxicabs, even on the plastic bags used by dry cleaners. More than ninety local television stations around the country began showing photographs of missing children as a regular part of their evening newscasts. So did the Cable News Network and CBS, which featured one child each night in a ten-second prime-time spot. The pictures were obtained for a fee from an Ohio production company whose president declared that as many as 150,000 children were being abducted by strangers each year.

For the tens of millions of children who were not yet missing, there was Kiddie Alert, a radio transmitter that could be attached to a child and set to trigger an alarm if he or she wandered too far. Even at $129.95, the manufacturer said that more than fifteen hundred had been sold. Much cheaper, at $6.95, were Kid-Kuffs, nylon straps that could be used to link a child's wrist to a parent's waist. A company official suggested that "when the children are grown, you can use it as a dog leash." Schools and shopping malls began fingerprinting elementary school children for free; many of the malls that sponsored the programs reported large increases in gross sales on the days the service was offered.

Dentists began implanting microdots containing children's names and addresses inside their teeth as an aid to identifying tiny bodies. A few pedophiles even got in on the act by setting up a Florida company called Child Search, Inc., to seek "possible solutions to the problem of lost and missing children." The forty-eight-year-old machinist who was the organization's president turned out to be a convicted child molester. So did its treasurer. A member of the board of directors had been convicted of kidnapping his own child from the home of his former wife. The company's state-issued license was finally revoked, but only after the president had been convicted again, this time of indecent exposure. It turned out that the backgrounds of the men had never been checked by the Florida agency that issued their license.

The intensity of the effort to locate missing children made it inevitable that some would eventually be found. Following the third showing of *Adam*, in April 1985, NBC broadcast the pictures and descriptions of fifty-four missing children. President Reagan himself introduced the "Adam Roll Call," asking his viewers to "please watch carefully. Maybe your eyes can help bring them home." Afterward the National Center for Missing and Exploited Children, a private agency funded by the U.S. Justice Department, received more than twenty-six hundred telephone calls from viewers who thought they had seen one of the children pictured.

Of the five children that were eventually located, none had been abducted by a stranger. Two teenage sisters listed as missing for the past seven years, and an eight-year-old girl missing for a year, were found living with divorced fathers who had taken the children from their ex-wives. The two other children identified through the broadcast were living with their divorced mother in Texas. A judge ordered them returned to their father, a Los Angeles physician who had previously been granted full custody by the courts.

Considering the number of missing children who were turning up living with one of their parents, it might have made more sense to put the parents' pictures on the milk cartons. But not all the missing children had been taken by their parents. Like Adam Walsh, a handful had actually been abducted. Among them was three-year-old Tara Elizabeth Burke, taken from the backseat of her mother's car by Luis (Tree Frog) Johnson and his eighteen-year-old lover, Alex Cabarga. For most of the next year, Johnson, Cabarga, Tara Burke, and an eleven-year-old Vietnamese boy named Mac Lin cruised the streets of San Francisco's warehouse district in Johnson's cream-colored van. In exchange for food, Mac Lin said later, the children had been forced to have sex with the men and with each other.[13] But Tara Burke was an exception, since most of the few other children known to have fallen into the hands of pedophiles appeared to have done so voluntarily.

One was eleven-year-old Bobby Smith, whose picture had been included in the "Adam Roll Call" and who was also among the seventy or so children listed in the National Center's directory of abducted children. Bobby's whereabouts were discovered after police in Providence, Rhode Island, tried to stop a car with a loud muffler. During the chase that followed, the police discovered that the car was registered to a man named David Collins. Collins wasn't driving his car that day, but the registration bore his address. When the police went to his apartment, they found Bobby Smith. Collins was charged with kidnapping and sexual assault, but the testimony at his trial left some questions unanswered.

Collins and Bobby had met at a Long Beach, California, video arcade more than two years before, when Collins gave the boy a handful of quarters. A friendship developed, followed by a sexual relationship. According to Bobby's testimony in court, when Collins took him for a ride up the California coast to Santa Barbara, he told the man he didn't want to go back home. The pair kept driving north, beginning a twenty-one-month journey that led them through the Pacific Northwest, the Deep South, and finally to Providence. Collins found a job and Bobby enrolled in school; neighbors said later that the two had seemed like father and son. Bobby said he had not been forced to pose for the nude photos that were found in the apartment. Nor, he said, had he ever tried to escape, even after having seen his picture smiling back at him from the television screen. He had been free to come and go, even to call his parents if he had wanted to.

Asked why he hadn't, Bobby said he had been afraid — not afraid of David Collins, but of being found by his parents. "I was getting more and more scared," he said. "I was afraid that they were getting more and more close to finding me, and that I would be put in a home." On the basis of Bobby's testimony, the judge dropped most of the sexual assault charges against Collins, but he instructed the jury that the issue of Bobby Smith's consent was irrelevant to the charge of kidnapping. If the jurors found that Collins had not had lawful custody of the boy, the judge said, they had no choice but to convict him. They did.

When they are examined closely, the numbers of missing children, which at first seem so alarming, turn out to be impossibly high. In many cases the statistics have been inflated or exaggerated by those who have an emotional or financial interest in sustaining the hysteria, but there has also been a good deal of genuine confusion that can be traced to faulty record keeping. Before 1982, when President Reagan signed the Missing Children's Assistance Act, there were no reliable statistics at all. Although the FBI created its computerized "missing persons file" in 1975, local police departments were not required to record the names of missing children with the FBI. Under the missing children's act, however, parents could insist that the names of their missing sons or daughters be entered into the federal computer, and many did. Since 1982, the FBI has received on the order of 330,000 such reports a year. But most of those reports are erased almost as fast as they come in, since more than 90 percent of the children reported to police as missing are actually runaways who are found, or who return home, within days.

In some cities, a mother who calls the police every time her toddler wanders a few yards from home raises the number of missing children by one. Even if the child is discovered ten minutes later sitting on a neighbor's lawn, he remains on record as a "missing child," and if he does the same thing a week later, the number of children who are missing goes up another notch. At any given time, there are only about thirty thousand missing children who have been gone for more than a few weeks. Of these, FBI agents say they believe that 95 percent are teenagers who have run away from home, in many cases to escape sexual abuse, or "throwaways" who have been kicked out by their parents.

Nearly all the rest are believed to have been taken by one parent from another in a custody dispute, which leaves room for a very small number who have actually been abducted by strangers. The National Child Safety Council, a thoroughly reputable body, knows of no more than a hundred children who have probably been kidnapped, and in 1985 the FBI had open investigations of only sixty-eight cases of missing children that met the strict federal criteria for possible kidnapping — one fewer than the year before. Even if that number is multiplied ten times, it is still barely half the number of children who die each year in accidental drownings.

Lost in all the emotion is the fact that the monumental effort to track down missing children has yet to recover a single child abducted by a stranger. Also lost is the potential effect of the hysteria on children who are not missing. "It's causing unnecessary fright in children, morbid fears," warns Dr. Benjamin Spock. "I don't see it doing any good, and I'm sure it's doing a lot of harm. It's wrong to scare children." His colleague, the psychologist Lee Salk, tells of children who are so terrified by all the warnings about malevolent strangers that they refuse to leave their homes. "We are terrifying our children to the point where they are going to be afraid to talk to strangers," Salk says. "How can they make friends?"

In 1985, when the *Denver Post* won a Pulitzer Prize for a series of articles that shed the first real light on the true dimensions of the missing-children problem, it should have signaled the beginning of a public awareness that the problem had been vastly overstated. By then, however, the issue had become institutionalized. The fingerprinting continued apace, and so did the televised announcements.

The pedophiles must have found the missing-children campaign amusing, for many of them were beginning to realize that they didn't even need to hang around video arcades and bus stations in order to have sex with children. What they were discovering was that by becoming temporary caretakers of one kind or another, it was possible to get parents, including many of the same parents who were so frightened by the specter of kidnapping, to deliver their children to them.

SEVEN

Caretakers

FOR NEARLY two decades, parents in Minneapolis vied with one another to gain admission for their children to the prestigious Children's Theater Company and its affiliated school. Under the leadership of John Clark Donahue, the company's distinguished artistic director, the school had become a nationally acclaimed institution. One of the many magazine articles written over the years about Donahue and his methods lauded the man as a teacher given to "exploring feelings and emotions, not shying away from human relationships." Two years ago, the Twin Cities were stunned when Donahue pleaded guilty to having had sex with a number of his male students, including one he had abused during a performance, in an office overlooking the stage. Donahue later acknowledged having himself been abused as a child, and after he was sentenced to a year in prison, he wrote a letter to his students. "I was wrong to have engaged in any and all sexual activity with you," he said. "I was responsible for that activity, not you. I wish to sincerely apologize for my actions and assure you that you were correct in reporting me to the authorities." He promised the judge that when he was released from prison, he would help in the search for a solution to "this vast problem of child abuse."

There was nothing unique about John Clark Donahue. When the FBI studied the modi operandi of forty convicted pedophiles, it found that half had used their occupations as their principal way of meeting children. Many adults who work with children as part of their jobs or in their spare time do so only because they are committed to improving the welfare of children. But it cannot be a coincidence that pedophiles have turned up within the ranks of virtually every American youth organization, and in some cases several organizations at once, as was the case with the Connecticut minister who was also a Little League umpire and a scout leader on the side. John Donahue was a dedicated thespian, and no one suggested that his interest in the theater or in his school extended only to the young boys with whom he came in contact there. But pedophiles who lack Donahue's talent may take any job that permits them access to children. The number of Santa Clauses and clowns convicted of sexually abusing children is not small, but few pedophiles have displayed the imagination of the Dallas man caught posing as a woman, complete with wig, high heels, and makeup, in order to obtain jobs baby-sitting for the children he abused.

For much of the past decade, child protection workers have been struggling to convince the public that the greatest danger to children is not from the stranger who lurks outside the schoolyard, but from within their own homes and families. It may be true, however, that more children are abused outside their homes by grown-ups they know and trust than by members of their families. Twenty-three percent of the victims questioned by the *Los Angeles Times* said they had been abused by a parent or other close relative, while 33 percent said their abuser was an unrelated adult whom they knew. Even allowing for the fact that incest victims may be more reluctant than others to talk, it is possible that the greatest danger faced by children today is from unrelated adults they have been taught to obey.

One of the best ways of gaining access to children is to become a teacher. Some pedophiles are doubtless teachers first, eventually succumbing to a sexual attraction to children. But others are pedophiles first, only entering teaching as a way to be around children, and few American cities have been spared an accusation of child sexual abuse against such teachers. No city, however, has suffered so much recent anguish as Chicago, where at least nine educators, among them a former high school principal and a deputy school superintendent, have been accused or convicted of sexually abusing their pupils. One of the cases involved a veteran substitute teacher who was charged with abusing seven of his students, five girls and two boys, by prosecutors who said he used the school system "as a private hunting preserve." Two other Chicago teachers were charged with photographing their students and then selling the pictures to customers who included a former Catholic-school teacher, a retired public-school teacher, a lawyer for the Social Security Administration, and a nurse.

Another occupation attractive to pedophiles appears to be the priesthood. No faith is exempt, but more than a dozen Roman Catholic priests have been convicted of child sexual abuse over the past two years — four in Louisiana, three in Rhode Island, two in Illinois, and others in Portland, San Diego, Boise, Milwaukee, Los Angeles, and San Francisco — and many more have been accused; even *L'Osservatore Romano*, the Vatican newspaper, was moved to issue a call for action against the "horror, worry, and humiliation" of child sexual abuse. "To attribute a whole series of episodes such as these to an occasional outburst of maniacs or of sick people," the newspaper said, "would be to exorcise a problem whose dimensions are growing." Among the most notable was the case of the Reverend Gilbert Gauthe, the pastor of Saint John's Parish in Henry, Louisiana, who admitted abusing at least thirty-seven young boys, some of them altar boys, over a five-year period. The forty-one-year-old Gauthe said the abuse had occurred in his rectory, on overnight camping trips, even in the confessional. On the eve of his trial, the priest pleaded guilty to most of the charges against him and drew a sentence of twenty years' hard labor. "God in His infinite mercy may find forgiveness for your crimes," said the judge, "but the imperative of justice cannot." In the first such settlement in its history, the Roman Catholic Church agreed to pay five million dollars to nine of the families whose sons were among Gauthe's victims.

Not only do teachers and priests have access to children, they are authoritarian figures and, often, the objects of an adolescent hero-worship that eases the road to seduction. While not every pedophile can become a teacher or a priest, there are plenty of other jobs available. The number of scout leaders convicted of abusing their charges rivals the number of clergymen, and judges seem to become particularly incensed at those who use such a beloved institution as a way to have sex with children. When a longtime scoutmaster from Norfolk, Virginia, admitted abusing twenty members of his troop, he was sentenced to 151 years in prison, and two troop leaders in St. Johns, Michigan, received life sentences. "If you're asking for mercy," the judge told the men, "you came to the wrong place." Scouting does not provide pedophiles with access to boys only. In 1984, several Los Angeles police officers, all of them men, were discovered having sex with the underage female Explorer Scouts who took part in a "ride-along" program their department sponsored. Like the Catholic Church, over the past few years the Boy Scouts of America has had to pay millions of dollars to the parents of scouts who were abused by their leaders.

Apart from the fact that they ensure access to a steady stream of children, youth organizations provide places for pedophiles to congregate. Even those pedophiles who are not card-carrying members of NAMBLA or the Rene Guyon Society — and most are not — share the need for reinforcement and validation. In New Orleans a few years ago, a group of pedophiles actually formed their own Boy Scout troop and turned it into a sex-for-hire ring with customers across the country. The real purpose of Troop 137 was discovered only after one of the four leaders took pornographic photos of some of the scouts to a neighborhood Fotomat for developing. The scoutmaster, Richard Halverson, who worked during the day as a juvenile probation officer and was a foster father to two children, was sentenced to thirty years in prison. Three other men, including one who had been abused years before by his own scoutmaster, were also convicted.

When police searched Halverson's home, they found a letter from an Episcopal priest who ran Boy's Farm, a home for fatherless youths in Winchester, Tennessee. When police in Winchester searched the priest's house, they found a copy of an article in the Episcopal Church's national magazine praising Boy's Farm as "the farm that works." They also found pornographic photographs of several of the boys, including the priest's adopted son. The priest had been sending the pictures to his sponsors in return for tax-free contributions to the home's welfare fund. For larger contributions, meetings with the boys had been arranged.

Where a pedophile chooses to work depends on his preference in victims as much as on anything else. Abusers who are attracted to adolescent boys and girls are likely to become scoutmasters or coaches. For those whose attraction is to very young children, the day-care center is a nearly perfect milieu. One American child in ten is now cared for each day outside his home, whether in a day-care center, a nursery or Montessori school, or the home of a neighbor who looks after a few children each morning. There are no reliable statistics on the number of day-care centers where child sexual abuse has been reported or confirmed. Nobody even knows for sure how many day-care facilities there are, since so many of them are unlicensed. Executives of day-care trade associations try to minimize the problem by suggesting, without any basis in fact, that between 80 and 90 percent of all sexual abuse still takes place within the home.

While there is no reason to believe that the number of day-care centers where sexual abuse occurs is very large, there have been enough such cases that many insurance companies have canceled their coverage of day-care centers altogether, or raised premiums sufficiently to drive some centers out of business and others underground. Fred M.

Hechinger, the respected education writer for *The New York Times*, has maintained that "these incidents can no longer be viewed as aberrations," and a few rough statistics do exist. The California Department of Social Services has between two and three hundred investigations of day-care centers under way at any one time, the majority of which involve sexual abuse. Given that there are six thousand licensed day-care centers in that state, the number under investigation is relatively small. Looked at another way, it is far too large.

There is practically no American city of any size in which at least one day-care center has not become the target of a sexual abuse investigation, and in some cities there have been many more than one. But there could be no more improbable setting for such charges than the U.S. Military Academy at West Point, New York. The West Point child abuse case surfaced in the summer of 1985, when Walter Grote, a doctor attached to the Point's medical staff, announced that he was turning down a scheduled promotion to major. By all accounts, Grote had been an outstanding physician. His superiors used words like "excellent," "superb," and "extremely dedicated" to describe his performance, and his internal ratings were the highest possible. As Grote would explain later, he refused the promotion to protest what he considered an official cover-up of sexual abuse at a day-care center set up for the children of West Point's Army and civilian personnel.

According to Grote, the first indications of sexual abuse at West Point came when two boys who attended the center were seen by another doctor's wife engaging in anal sex behind her house. A few days later, another five-year-old boy at the same center attempted to have sex with a four-year-old girl while several other children looked on. In a letter to Secretary of the Army John Marsh, Jr., Grote maintained that "by the time I left West Point, I knew of approximately three dozen children who were ritualistically abused there," among them his own three-year-old daughter. Following Grote's refusal to accept the promotion, seventeen FBI agents were assigned to investigate the case, and they worked on it full-time for more than four months. By the time they were finished, the agents had conducted nearly a thousand interviews of parents, children, day-care workers, and others, enough to keep a federal grand jury busy for more than a year.

The grand jury failed to return indictments, and prosecutors said later that it had not been possible to identify any of the abusers from the testimony given by the children. The parents disagreed. "Many of the children clearly point the finger at several individuals," Grote said, and other parents said that at least four children had given graphic descriptions during videotaped interviews of having been sexually abused. Several, they said, were still suffering from nightmares. Rudy Giuliani, the United States attorney for the Southern District of New York, finally acknowledged that "there were indications that some children may have been abused at the West Point Child Development Center," and he recommended that West Point make "a program of therapy" available to the children.

There seemed to be a history of child abuse at West Point. In the fall of 1985, an employee of the Officers' Club was convicted of having sexually abused some boys on the Academy grounds. The man, a civilian, was on probation from a previous sexual abuse conviction. The year before, a senior commissioned officer at West Point, one of those Grote claimed was "implicated" in the day-care case, had been convicted of enticing two children to pose for pornographic pictures. When a West Point official said later that "the incident appeared alcohol-related," Walter Grote suggested that the official be assigned to "tour the country, reassuring mothers and fathers of children killed by drunk drivers that the consequences weren't so bad because they are 'alcohol-related.' "

The bitterness at West Point lingers on, but no child abuse investigation has created a bigger municipal scandal than the one that arose in New York City after three workers at a day-care center run by the Puerto Rican Association for Community Affairs were convicted of abusing twenty-one of the center's thirty children. Along with several hundred others, the center was funded and supervised by the city's Human Resources Administration. Investigators eventually uncovered thirty-nine cases in which children said they had been abused at six other city-funded centers, including one run by a Methodist church. In the wake of the scandal, Mayor Ed Koch sent letters to more than ten thousand city child-care workers in which he urged them to report any other instances of abuse. The head of the HRA was forced to resign after the Bronx district attorney accused the agency of obstructing his investigation by refusing to turn over records and tipping off some of the suspects.

Some parents whose children claimed to have been abused at the PRACA center vented their anger by throwing rocks at its windows. The anguish in the Bronx was replicated in Memphis, Tennessee, after a three-year-old girl who was being given a routine checkup by her family doctor mentioned that she had been touched in the same place by her preschool teacher. Not sure what to make of the child's comment, the doctor reported it to the police. When child protection workers arrived, the child named three other children the teacher had also touched. Those children named other children, and those children named still others. "It was like dropping pebbles in a pond," one observer said. A fifty-four-year-old housewife and mother who worked part-time at the Georgian Hills Early Childhood Center, a church-run preschool in the heart of a conservative, solidly Baptist neighborhood, was charged with abusing nineteen children at the center, all of them under the age of five. Police later arrested the woman's law-student son and the pastor of the Georgian Hills Baptist Church, with which the day-care center was affiliated. When all of the indictments were added up, the number of victims totaled twenty-six, and doctors said many had physical symptoms consistent with having been sexually abused. By the summer of 1987, none of the defendants had yet gone to trial.

As was the case in most states, allegations of child sexual abuse in nurseries and preschools were not new to Tennessee. In the months before the Georgian Hills case surfaced, the state had closed a half-dozen other day-care centers because of suspected sexual abuse by staff members. But as the Georgian Hills children continued to talk, their stories ranged far beyond sexual abuse, and even their recollections of having been photographed nude were fast becoming standard. Some of the children told of having been taken to the Memphis airport, put aboard a small plane, and flown across the Mississippi River to a town in Arkansas, where they were abused by strangers. The strangers, they said, had worn masks and robes and carried black candles, and they had slaughtered gerbils and hamsters while the children watched. One of the strangers had even killed a child. Such stories might have been dismissed as childish fabrications, except for the fact that the same stories were being told by other children around the country, including more than a dozen children in Bakersfield, California, a hundred miles north of Los Angeles and two thousand miles from Memphis.

It was in Bakersfield, a fast-growing city at the southern end of California's Central Valley, that two married couples had been convicted the year before of having ritualistically abused their own and each other's children over a period of several years. The children in that case also told of having been taken by their parents to a motel and rented out to strangers by the hour. The ringleader in the earlier case appeared to have been one of the women, Deborah McCuan, a

Bluebird troop leader who also ran a licensed day-care center out of her ranch-style house. At her trial, McCuan testified that she had been sexually abused as a child. Following the longest criminal proceeding in Kern County history, the McCuans and their codefendants, Scott and Brenda Kniffen, were sentenced to a collective total of more than a thousand years in prison. A week after the sentences were handed down, the Kniffens were charged with having abused another nine-year-old girl while they were out on bail. Deborah McCuan's parents, charged in the same case with thirty-three counts of abuse of their grandchildren and the Kniffens' children, jumped bail and disappeared.

The current Bakersfield case seemed to be unrelated to the McCuans and the Kniffens, and it was also much more improbable. The children in this case were accusing *seventy-seven* adults of sexually abusing them. The abusers had worn robes and masks and chanted prayers to Satan. The rituals involved swords, knives, black candles, mysterious potions, dead animals, blood, urine, feces, and the sacrificial murders of at least twenty-seven other children. Some of the children were saying they had watched dead children being cooked and eaten and had been warned that they would meet the same fate unless they kept quiet. The local sheriff told reporters he was "absolutely convinced" that the children had witnessed the things they recounted, including the killing of babies. "It would be very easy to sweep all this under the rug and say, 'The kid made it up,' " said the sheriff's top deputy. "We don't take that attitude. We understand the initial human reaction of, I don't want to believe it, make it go away. But there are cases like this popping up all across the United States."

So there were. Another was in Mendocino County, California, north of San Francisco, where several children who attended a preschool run by fundamentalist Christians told police that they had been tied to crosses and made to chant, "Baby Jesus is dead," while being abused. That investigation began after a mother discovered her four-year-old daughter "acting out things in her sleep, stripping herself, putting her hands above her head like she were tied or handcuffed, spreading her legs on the bed, screaming in terror, begging someone not to hurt her." The nightmares, the mother said, "were like pornographic movies."

Mendocino County, a stunningly beautiful patch of green on the California coast that was once home to Charles Manson and the Reverend Jim Jones, has a long history of cult activity. But the same could not be said of Carson City, Nevada, where a woman, her nephew, and her son were charged with abusing, photographing, and torturing more than a dozen children they met through their baby-sitting service. Several of the children in that case said the trio had killed chickens, cats, and even a calf in their presence, and then used their blood and parts of their dismembered bodies in the abuse. As of the summer of 1987, the case had not yet gone to trial.

In one form or another, the ancient practice of devil worship has been around at least as long as Christianity. But modern Satanism can be traced to an occult revival in the last century led by a wealthy English magician and poet named Aleister Crowley, who is said to have been the inspiration for Somerset Maugham's novel *The Magician*. Crowley's hedonistic doctrine found its share of followers in America, some of whom erected a temple in his honor in the Palomar Mountains of California. Perhaps not entirely by coincidence, California is also the headquarters of the two modern-day satanic churches known to be active in this country. The oldest and largest, with a claimed membership of ten thousand, is the Church of Satan, founded in San Francisco two decades ago by Anton Szandor LaVey, a one-time circus performer who shaves his head, uses a tombstone for a coffee table, and claims to have performed the first satanic wedding ceremony in the United States while using a naked woman for an altar. The number-two satanic cult is the Temple of Set, also located in San Francisco and established a few years ago by an Army colonel who resigned as one of LaVey's top lieutenants in a dispute over the future direction of the Church of Satan.

It is not difficult to understand the attraction that Satanism, at least as interpreted by Anton LaVey, holds for those who cannot find comfort within the confines of ordinary religion. LaVey's doctrine is both hedonistic and libertarian, a self-centered and highly narcissistic creed that raises selfishness and revenge to the level of a sacrament while cloaking the whole mélange in intricate rituals and mystical symbols. Much of its appeal doubtless derives from the fact that Satanism and the occult have always been closely entwined with sexuality. A fundamental satanic tenet is the right of practitioners to abundant and guilt-free sex of nearly every description. In his *Satanic Bible*, LaVey accords his followers the freedom "to indulge your sexual desires with as many others as you feel are necessary to satisfy your particular needs." He also approves of the use of human sacrifice, but only "to dispose of a totally obnoxious and deserving individual."

Whatever else they are, are Satanists child abusers and child murderers too? Not, at least, on paper. The *Satanic Bible* declares that "under no circumstances would a Satanist sacrifice any animal or baby," and it forbids "rape, child molesting, or the sexual defilement of animals, or any other form of sexual activity which entails the participation of those who are unwilling or whose innocence or naïveté would allow them to be intimidated or misguided into doing something against their wishes." Like the Christian version, however, the *Satanic Bible* is open to a multitude of interpretations, and there is no reason to believe that all of LaVey's followers adhere to his prohibitions. In northern Arkansas, the number 666 and a five-pointed star, both universally recognized as satanic symbols, were found painted on rocks in a field where several cows had been slaughtered. In Santa Cruz, California, ninety miles south of San Francisco, the same symbols were left on the front door of a Greek Orthodox church where a priest was murdered.

Whenever authorities in this country have followed up rumors of satanic child abuse, they have come up empty-handed. In Oakland, California, not long ago, police got a tip that a local satanic sect was preparing to sacrifice a child. As they arrived at the appointed place, the officers heard screams coming from inside the building, but when they broke down the door they found a group of men and women who were about to kill a cat. Sheriff's deputies in Toledo, Ohio, bulldozed a suburban field after being told that a local satanic cult had buried the bodies of seventy-five children there. Various satanic artifacts were found, but no bodies. "There's a real problem in terms of investigating this thing," says a California police officer. "You can't get into it without being part of it. And you can't be part of it without doing things that you and I would consider unspeakable."

The only children's bodies recovered in California in recent memory were found in the summer of 1985, in shallow graves dug near a cabin in the Sierra Nevada mountains. The cabin belonged to thirty-nine-year-old Leonard Lake, who popped a cyanide capsule into his mouth after he was caught shoplifting in a south San Francisco hardware store. In the days that followed Lake's death, investigators literally unearthed the horror that had been his life — the mass graves he had filled with the bodies of two dozen friends, neighbors, and their children.

Near the cabin was a cinder-block "torture chamber," where Lake had sexually tormented a number of the women while video cameras captured it all on tape. The videotapes and the bodies were real, but the rest of the evidence was circumstantial. Lake, a self-styled survivalist, had told neighbors that he belonged to a San Francisco "death cult" that practiced ritual murder. He had once lived in Mendocino County and had known the woman who ran the fundamentalist preschool where children claimed to have been tied to crosses. One of Lake's neighbors recalled that he had tried to date her twelve-year-old daughter. When police found pictures of nude and partially nude girls inside his cinder-block chamber, Lake's ex-wife explained that her former husband had had a "fascination with virginity."

The secret of whatever Leonard Lake was about died with him. Not so with Richard Ramirez, the Los Angeles "Nightstalker," who was charged with having raped and murdered at least fourteen women in their beds, and of having kidnapped and sexually abused several young girls as well. At the scene of some of the slayings, Ramirez left a crudely drawn pentagram, the five-pointed "Devil's star"; one of the few women who survived an attack by Ramirez said he had worn a baseball cap with the letters AC/DC on the front. After his arrest, a high school classmate said Ramirez had been obsessed with Satanism ever since he heard *Highway to Hell*, an album by the rock band that calls itself AC/DC. His favorite song from the album, the classmate said, was called "Night Prowler." Anton LaVey recalled that Ramirez had once stopped him on a San Francisco street to say hello, and police said footprints found at the scene of some of the slayings matched those outside an East Los Angeles house used as a meeting place by a satanic cult. As he left the courtroom after being arraigned, Ramirez raised his fist to the judge and shouted, "Hail, Satan."

Leonard Lake and Richard Ramirez may have been committed Satanists, or merely pathological killers who used satanic doctrine to concoct a rationale for torture, rape, and murder. But some of those who have studied the Bakersfield and Memphis cases and others like them are at least open to the possibility of a connection between Satanism and the sexual abuse of children. "The only thing I know about it is that it exists," says a Denver pediatrician. "We've seen at least two families here where there was an enormous amount of acting out of Satanistic activities and where the children were also sexually abused. How widespread it is, I don't know. I think that whatever's going on has been going on underground, and that every now and then something bubbles up." A San Francisco child psychiatrist who treats sexually abused children agrees. "I've heard enough and seen enough," he says, "to think that it's something I don't want to be identified as knowing that much about. It does appear to be real and to exist. It appears to be pretty organized. Nobody's found enough physical evidence yet in any of these cases to really confront society. People aren't ready for it. There's so much disbelief just around molestation itself that when you add that to it, it becomes totally unbelievable, and juries won't convict."

In most cities where cases of ritualistic abuse have arisen, the police have taken such stories seriously, but most of the investigations have not made much progress. When prosecutors in the Mendocino case announced that they weren't going to trial, one of them explained that "all we really have is the testimony of very young kids who probably couldn't qualify as competent witnesses." Two of the Bakersfield children independently pointed out the same "evil church" where they said some of the ritualistic rites had taken place, but once the children were inside the church, they said they had made a mistake. When the police excavated the fields and dredged the lakes where the children said the bodies of the murdered children were, nothing was found — no bodies, no bones, no shreds of flesh. A search of one defendant's home turned up only some adult pornography; another defendant's home produced evidence of human blood on the living room carpet, but nothing else. "I'm not naive," said an attorney for several of the Bakersfield defendants. "I think that probably some of these kids have been molested in some way. By whom and when, I don't know. But the satanic aspect of it, that's where they lose me."

The absence of physical evidence to back up the bizarre assertions was giving prosecutors nightmares, but not all of the ritualistic child abuse cases were being lost. In Des Moines, five members of a "witches' coven" were convicted of hundreds of counts of sexually abusing teenage boys. In Richmond, Virginia, one person was convicted in a sexual abuse case where police recovered candles and other ritualistic paraphernalia. In El Paso, Texas, across the Rio Grande from Mexico, a young prosecutor named Deborah Kanof won a conviction of a thirty-five-year-old mother who had been charged with abusing eight children at the East Valley YWCA. Some of the victims in that case said they had been taken from the "Y" to a nearby house, where they were made to have sex with the teacher while men dressed in masks and werewolf costumes looked on. The woman got life in prison plus 311 years, the longest sentence for child sexual abuse in Texas history.

In other cases in other cities, the story had a different ending. Several children in Sacramento, California, were telling not only of slaughtered animals and adults who wore robes and masks, but of being forced by adults in the neighborhood to participate in mock marriage ceremonies that were followed by pretend honeymoons. Some of them mentioned three young children, dressed in ragged clothes, who had been stabbed to death during one of the abusive rituals. Despite a medical diagnosis that some of the children in the case had been sexually abused, the judge dismissed the charges against all five defendants, saying he had found it impossible to separate those portions of the children's testimony that might be true from those that were not.

The prosecutor in the case protested the judge's dismissal, but to no avail. "I don't see where these kids would be able to come up with the consistent detail they come up with," he said, "if not from their own experience. Four of these children have described one specific incident where three other children were killed. If I worked night and day, I could not coach these kids into saying something like that. It's very difficult to place things in a child's mind when they haven't experienced something directly. Four of the children had physical findings consistent with kids who have been sexually abused — anal scarring in three of them, venereal warts on one of them, a notch in the hymen in one, which is highly significant in sexual cases. When it's all four kids from the same family, it's highly significant. We also had two kids in Texas who were saying the same thing, kids who had lived in the neighborhood at the time this occurred. Those kids hadn't seen anyone in the family for over two years. Their stories tracked very well. Some of the bizarre things that occurred, some of the threats, being taken to another house, the ritualistic activity, it was all consistent."

The Sacramento case never went to trial, but in other cases that did, prosecutors were discovering the difficulty of convincing juries to put aside whatever children had to say about black masses and dead babies and to concentrate on the question of whether they had been sexually abused. When a nine-year-old girl in a small town across the bay from San Francisco said she had been abused by her father and others under circumstances nearly identical to those described in Sacramento, the child therapist who examined the girl had no doubt she was telling the truth. "This happened in her father's home," the therapist said. "She was able to recite for me what she called their Egyptian names, to sing for me the chants and songs they sang. She described every conceivable sex act you can imagine. She described their playing with live snakes. She talked about how young women in their teens were sacrificed. Her description of how the guts pop out when you slit open a live abdomen does justice to a Vietnam war veteran."

Though he was certain that the child had been sexually abused, the prosecutor in the case was not convinced that all of the accompanying stories were true. "They were as detailed as they were, I hesitate to use the word, unbelievable," he said, "because to at least some degree I believed them, although I had questions about some of it. I question how much of it was exaggeration or misunderstanding, and how much of it was fact. There's no doubt in my mind that she was a participant in satanic worship, but she also described at one point how her father put his hand around her hand holding a knife and how the two of them plunged the knife into the chest of an infant. There was some question in my mind about whether that was an actual sacrifice or possibly a simulated sacrifice, and that's what I said to the jury. I argued that this case wasn't about devil worship, that it was about child molestation, and that whether they believed or disbelieved the child about the satanic stuff, there should be no question that she was a victim of child molest." Unable to separate the two questions, the jury found itself hopelessly divided, and a mistrial was declared.

As cases involving the same allegations of ritualistic abuse popped up in Pennsylvania, New Jersey, Florida, Iowa, Michigan, and Texas, the police officers, prosecutors, and psychologists from around the country who had been assigned the task of unraveling them began talking and meeting informally, first among themselves and then with experts in child behavior. They were looking for an explanation that made sense, especially one that made sense to juries. Unless such an explanation was found, those adults who abused children sexually under bizarre circumstances would continue to go free, but there was a more compelling reason than that. The ritualistic cases were a tiny proportion of sexual abuse cases nationwide, but they were receiving a great deal of attention from the news media. The danger was that those who read and heard such preposterous-sounding accounts might begin to think that all children who claimed to have been sexually abused, whether by Satanists or not, were lying.

When the investigators and therapists compared notes, some common themes began to emerge. Among the most important was that many of the children involved in the ritualistic cases had physical symptoms of sexual abuse, which meant that even if they hadn't been abused by witches and devils, they had been abused by someone. The descriptions the children gave of the rituals and chants were also remarkably similar, and many reported being forced to drink some sort of liquid that made them feel strange. Almost all described the ceremonial killings of small animals, and several the murders of other children, usually babies. Another similarity was that most of the children had talked about being sexually abused before they began talking about ritualism or dead babies — sometimes months before.

One theory was that the masks, the chanting, the potions, the dead animals, and all the rest might be nothing more than a ruse designed by child abusers to discredit their victims' stories. By the mid-1980s, any child who claimed to have been sexually abused was being taken very seriously indeed. But would a child who claimed to have been abused by someone wearing a devil's mask and holding a dead cat be taken quite as seriously? A second theory was that the rituals, particularly the animal sacrifices, were an attempt to frighten the children into silence. "It doesn't take an absolute genius to scare a child," one police officer said. "That's the simplest thing an adult can do. Saying, 'I'm the Devil, and I'm going to do this to you if you don't keep quiet,' that sort of thing. But I don't know." Or perhaps the masks were merely a way some abusers had of disguising their identities from their victims.

Some of the psychiatrists offered a more sophisticated explanation, drawn from the theory of the collective unconscious set forth by Carl Gustav Jung, the Swiss psychiatrist who founded the school of psychoanalysis that bears his name. According to Jung, there are fundamental myths about good and evil that are so common to human beings in every age and place that they cannot have been passed along from one generation to the next, but must have arisen spontaneously, from some sort of unconscious memory that is inherited by everyone. But if the tales of devil worship were the voice of the children's collective unconscious speaking, then why weren't all abused children talking about such things?

Was it possible that the children's unconscious minds were simply covering a terrifying core of real abuse with a protective overlay of devils and demons? Perhaps those who abused them somehow took on the black-masked personas of the devils of contemporary children's fiction, of characters like Darth Vader and Skeletor. Or perhaps it was an unconscious attempt to comprehend an inexplicable experience by placing it in a familiar context of good and evil. As for the dead animals and babies, perhaps the children equated being raped and tormented with death and murder. It was also possible, of course, that the children were simply making the stories up. But if what they were saying was make-believe, then why didn't their stories include such obvious impossibilities as dragons and flying saucers? And if they were lying, the question remained of how children in cities hundreds and even thousands of miles apart, children who had never met one another, were able to tell nearly identical lies — of why children in Sacramento, California, and West Point, New York, were talking about having taken part in mock marriage ceremonies.

If such reports were true, on the other hand, it meant that a certain number of abusers — how many no one could say — were not having sex with children for any of the usual reasons. The ritualistic abusers themselves might or might not have been abused as children. They might not even be sexually attracted to children. In contrast to the predilections of garden-variety child molesters, what appeared to excite these people most was terrifying and torturing the children they abused. Far from being child lovers, they were child haters.

The greatest obstacle to the successful prosecution of such cases was that none of the adults accused by the children had pleaded guilty. If only one defendant in a ritualistic case would admit his guilt and acknowledge the truth of the children's stories, it might be possible to get a handle on whatever was going on. Defendants in other child abuse cases were pleading guilty in great numbers, but all of those involved in the ritualistic cases still continued to insist that the stories of abuse and ritualism alike were lies, planted in the children's heads by the police, the prosecutors, and the therapists.

The first crack in the wall of silence appeared when a four-year-old Miami boy emerged from his family's bathroom and asked his mother to kiss his penis. Horrified, the woman asked him what he was talking about. "Ileana" had kissed his penis, the boy explained, and now he wanted his mother to do the same. Ileana was the eighteen-year-old wife of an interior designer and real-estate investor named Frank Fuster. In addition to their other businesses, the Fusters operated a child-care center from their home in the fashionable Miami neighborhood of Country Walk, and there the boy spent much of the day.

Ileana Fuster was a demure young woman, even shy, but her husband was a most unlikely baby-sitter. Frank Fuster, who had come to Miami from Cuba at the age of twelve, had killed another motorist in the middle of a bridge in an argument over which one of them had the right of way. A few years later, he had been convicted of sexually abusing a nine-year-old girl while driving her home from a children's birthday party. Since a convicted child abuser can hardly expect to obtain a day-care license, the Country Walk Baby-Sitting Service didn't have one, but it hadn't seemed to matter. The parents of the two dozen children for whom Ileana Fuster cared each day, among them an Eastern Airlines flight attendant and two Miami police officers, had never asked to see their license. "Everything seemed in order," the father of one of the children said later. "The house was very neat. They were very well-mannered people. They had it very organized, down to the health cards for us to fill out for our daughter before they would accept us." Only after the Fusters had been charged did some parents recall that one thing about the Country Walk Baby-Sitting Service had struck them as odd: there hadn't been any toys for the children to play with.

The investigators working on the Fuster case eventually concluded that more than a dozen children, all between the ages of three and six, had been sexually abused by the couple, and when eight of the alleged victims took the witness stand at the Fusters' trial, the stories they told began to sound familiar. The children said they had been forced to drink a liquid called "demon slime." They said the abuse had taken the form of games, such as the "ca-ca game" and the "pee-pee game," that involved excrement and urine. Frank and Ileana had worn scary-looking masks, and Frank had videotaped some of the games. Sometimes the couple had had sex with one another in the children's presence; the children had even seen Ileana put pennies up her husband's anus. Animals were killed, including some "bluebirds" that Frank Fuster stomped to death on the kitchen floor. Sometimes Frank had held a knife to the children's throats, threatening to kill them and their parents if they told anyone what really went on at the Country Walk Baby-Sitting Service.

Like the defense lawyers in the other ritualistic cases, the Fusters' attorneys argued from the start that the children were making the whole thing up — dead bluebirds on the kitchen floor and putting pennies up somebody's anus were the kind of fanciful ideas only a child could come up with. Ileana Fuster's lawyer went further, accusing the children's therapists of using "a more subtle form of coercion than the North Vietnamese did to our prisoners of war." As the children's bizarre testimony continued, the "Country Walk case" seemed headed for acquittal. Then came the break the prosecution had been hoping for. For reasons known only to her, Ileana Fuster pleaded guilty and agreed to testify against her husband.

With her deep-set eyes and long, braided hair, the young woman looked like a child herself as she took the witness stand to tell the strange story of her relationship with Frank Fuster. She had left her home in Honduras to join her mother in Miami, and she was barely sixteen when she met Fuster at a flea market. Six days later, he forced her into a closet in his bedroom, where he beat and raped her. It was then that she knew they would be married. It wasn't that she loved Frank Fuster, but she had no choice. "I was embarrassed, because I knew that nobody had ever seen my body," Ileana Fuster said. Ileana found out about her husband's sexual attraction to children only after he suggested that they begin taking in children to supplement his income.

As Ileana acknowledged her own part in the abuse, she also confirmed what the children had been saying. Her husband had indeed forced her to undress in front of the children, and ordered her to perform oral sex on them. Sometimes he wore a white sheet and a green mask, and when he did, he made her wear one too. The "demon slime" had been a combination of urine, Gatorade, and tranquilizers. Fuster had had sex with her in front of the children, and had even raped her in their presence with a crucifix and an electric drill. To frighten the children into silence, he had killed some blue parakeets in their kitchen. The "bluebirds" that had so puzzled the police hadn't been bluebirds at all, but "blue birds." The "pennies" she had put up his anus had been suppositories wrapped in copper-colored foil. As for what had happened to the videotapes, the masks, and the rest of Fuster's accoutrements, her husband had told her that somebody had removed them from their home the night before his arrest. Convicted of multiple accounts of child sexual abuse, Frank Fuster was sentenced to six consecutive life terms in prison.

EIGHT

McMartin

JORDAN, MINNESOTA, and Manhattan Beach, California, are about as unalike as two towns can be. Both are suburbs of bigger cities, but the seaside village of Manhattan Beach is what market researchers call an upper-quintile community. Manhattan Beach has its share of middle-class families, but most of them arrived before the California real-estate boom, which lifted the price of a two-bedroom bungalow well past a quarter-million dollars. Those who have moved in since the boom are largely aerospace engineers, lawyers, and other young professionals who can afford the cost of living there, but most of the new arrivals still need two incomes to gain a toehold. With so many working couples, the demand for day-care in Manhattan Beach is unusually brisk, and for those parents who could afford the tuition, Virginia McMartin's Pre-School seemed the most desirable of depositories for their children. Each day began with the children saluting the American flag. There were the requisite birthday parties and field trips, and the children often brought home some drawing or project they had made in class. Each December, their parents received a Christmas card with a group photo showing toddlers dressed in designer togs surrounded by their beaming teachers.

Those parents who bothered to look beneath the school's well-scrubbed surface found only further reassurance, in the form of glowing reports from state child-care inspectors that described the school as unusually well run, well staffed, and well equipped. But the ultimate in reassurance was Virginia McMartin herself, the school's seventy-seven-year-old founder and the matriarch of an established Manhattan Beach family. In the two decades since she had opened the school's doors, McMartin had received every award for civic service the city had to bestow. In a place where things change so fast that a year can be a long time, the McMartin school was about as close to an institution as it was possible to get.

Only in retrospect would many of the McMartin parents come to believe that they had overlooked some important clues. One was the rule that they were not to visit the school at all for the first six weeks their child was enrolled, and to visit later only after making an appointment well in advance. Parents who planned to pick their children up early in the day were required to give the teachers advance notice, and nap time was never to be interrupted. Similar rules apply at many preschools, but some of the McMartin parents also remembered that their children had sometimes come home wearing another child's clothing, or without the underwear they had worn that morning. "It just blew right past me," one father said. "All of us lead very busy lives." Another father, a lawyer, confessed to being puzzled about why his son cried when he was dropped off at the school each morning. "I said, 'You've got to be able to articulate it for me,' " the father said, "but he couldn't articulate it."

The first indications that something was amiss at the McMartin school trace back to the fall of 1983, around the same time that Officer Larry Norring was putting the handcuffs on Jim Rud up in Jordan. A few of the McMartin mothers had become vaguely uncomfortable with the way "Mr. Ray," one of the teachers at the school, behaved around their daughters. After talking among themselves, they got up the courage to have a word with Virginia McMartin's daughter, Peggy McMartin Buckey, who managed the school's day-to-day operations. "You know," one of them told her, "when we come to pick up the girls, they're crawling all over Ray. He's sitting there in his bathing suit, and they're hanging on his arms and legs, and it just doesn't seem appropriate."

"Mr. Ray" was Raymond Buckey, a twenty-six-year-old college dropout whose principal interests in life appeared to be lifting weights and gobbling health food. Buckey didn't have any particular qualifications for taking care of young children, but he did have excellent connections. Virginia McMartin was his grandmother, and Peggy Buckey was his mother. Not accustomed to having her son's motives questioned by those whose children she had seen fit to accept as students, Peggy brushed their concerns aside. A few weeks later, a two-year-old boy came home from the school with blood on his anus. His mother, a woman named Judy Johnson, went to the Manhattan Beach police, where officers encouraged her to have her son examined. When Johnson took the boy to a local hospital, she was redirected to the emergency room at UCLA; the doctors there informed her that her child had been sodomized. Johnson promptly withdrew her son from the McMartin school and returned to the Manhattan Beach police to file a complaint.

Manhattan Beach lies within Los Angeles County, but it is incorporated as an independent city, and criminal investigations there are the province of the small and rather relaxed Manhattan Beach police department, whose dozen or so detectives spend most of their time chasing narcotics violators and searching for stolen sports cars. Prosecuting those crimes, however, is the responsibility of the Los Angeles County district attorney's office — with more than six hundred lawyers on its staff, the largest legal office of any kind in the world. Prosecutors who draw a case within the Los Angeles city limits have the advantage of working with the Los Angeles police and its squadrons of crack investigators. But when a crime occurs in one of the many Los Angeles suburbs, it is usually the local police department that prepares the case for prosecution. The disparities among police agencies is particularly apparent in child sexual abuse cases. With detectives such as Bill Dworin among its members, the LAPD's Sexually Exploited Child Unit is widely considered the most experienced in the country. But most of the outlying police departments have few officers who can match the LAPD's expertise, and when Jean Matusinka heard about the Ray Buckey case, her first reaction was to ask herself why the McMartin school had to be in Manhattan Beach.

Matusinka, who headed the district attorney's child abuse unit, had been prosecuting child molesters for years, and she knew which police departments could make a case better and which could make it worse. But the Manhattan Beach police were on the case, and for better or for worse they were giving it their best effort. If Ray Buckey had abused one child at the McMartin school, the police reasoned, there might be other victims. But there were more than a hundred children enrolled at the school, and knocking on a hundred doors, or even making a hundred telephone calls, was more than the department's resources would allow. To Harry Kuhlmeyer, the chief of police, the most efficient solution seemed to be sending a letter to all the McMartin parents, advising them that Ray Buckey was under investigation and inviting them to report any suspicions that their own children had been abused. The letter asked the parents to keep the investigation confidential, but it didn't remain confidential for long. "If you're a parent," one recipient said later, "you get this thing and you go, 'My God, what's going on here?' When you think that because you tell people not to tell anybody, they're not going to run right down to the school, that's pretty naive." The mass mailing, Chief Kuhlmeyer said later, "may not have been the best idea in the world. But we wanted to get the news out and we didn't have the resources to go down and knock at everybody's door."

Forty-eight hours after the letters were mailed, there weren't many people in Manhattan Beach who didn't know that Ray Buckey was suspected of molesting children, including Ray Buckey and his family. A warrant was issued for Buckey's arrest, and he was taken into custody. But when the police searched his house, they found nothing to corroborate the allegations. Because Jean Matusinka was reluctant to rest her entire case on the testimony of a two-year-old child, the charges against Buckey were dropped. The investigation, however, remained open. Most of the parents who received the letter from the police had asked their children whether "Mr. Ray" had done anything to them. A few said that he had, and while many said he had not, they seemed oddly reluctant to discuss the matter further.

In ones and twos, children who had answered yes or whose parents doubted their denials were taken to the Manhattan Beach police for further questioning, and very soon the police were in over their heads. One of Jean Matusinka's colleagues described them as unsophisticated officers who failed to recognize the potential scope of the case at the beginning, and who were too proud to ask for outside help when its enormity finally became clear. The Los Angeles County sheriff's department had thousands of deputies at its disposal, including several who were highly trained in working with sexually abused children, and the nine detectives of the LAPD's Sexually Exploited Child Unit were fifteen minutes away up the San Diego freeway. But neither the LAPD nor the sheriff's department could lift a finger without a formal request for assistance from Chief Kuhlmeyer, and when Matusinka and another prosecutor implored the chief to call for reinforcements, he replied that his department could handle it. "That's just not true," Chief Kuhlmeyer says. "That happened later on, and it didn't happen the way they're saying it. But we did not formally request outside help until the latter part of October [of 1984], and I've got to take the responsibility for that." The Manhattan Beach detectives did seek outside advice, however. "The good news is, they called us right at the beginning," one Los Angeles detective said. "They said, 'Look, we don't know anything about this.' We gave them all our best advice. The bad news is, they didn't take any of it."

For many McMartin parents, particularly those who didn't trust their children's denials, their experience with the Manhattan Beach police was unsettling. Neither of the two detectives assigned to the Buckey investigation seemed particularly skilled at talking to children, especially children who said they had been sexually abused. Especially after the debacle of the police department's letter, Matusinka was reluctant to let the case stand or fall on the strength of the police investigation alone. In the course of her job, she had gotten to know practically everybody across the country who had anything to do with child abuse, including a woman at the National Center on Child Abuse and Neglect whose name was Kee MacFarlane.

MacFarlane had recently lost her job at NCCAN, a victim of the Reagan Administration's budget cutbacks in social services, and had moved to Los Angeles for what she hoped would be a pleasant sabbatical in the sunshine. She had some writing she wanted to finish, and she was thinking about studying for her doctorate in social work. She had also signed on as a consultant to the Children's Institute International, an agency that cared for abused and neglected children and which happened to be a favorite charity among the area's wealthy Republican women, including one who now lived in the White House. The institute's staff had begun to see increasing numbers of sexual abuse victims, and its directors were eager to develop the capability to treat such children. Kee MacFarlane had agreed to help design the program.

When Matusinka called MacFarlane to ask if she had time to talk to "a couple of kids from Manhattan Beach," MacFarlane reluctantly said yes. She hadn't intended to do any clinical work in California, and she hadn't applied for certification as a counselor there. But the Children's Institute itself was certified, and rather than say no, MacFarlane agreed to see the children. Despite everything else, she admitted later, she was curious to see just how big the Buckey case might turn out to be. The Manhattan Beach police might be able to keep outside law enforcement agencies from becoming involved in the McMartin case, but they couldn't very well tell the McMartin parents what to do with their children. When Jean Matusinka suggested that some of the McMartin parents call Kee MacFarlane, they did. "We don't like what the cops are doing with our kids," they told her. "Will you talk to them for us?"

At the beginning, the questions she asked the children were only about Ray Buckey. "In the first dozen or so interviews I never asked about any of the women," MacFarlane said later. "The prosecutors told me there was this guy they suspected, and could I find out? So I only asked about him." It wasn't until some of the children began to talk about having been abused in their classrooms that MacFarlane began to wonder whether the other teachers at the school had been aware of what was going on. "I got to thinking, it would have been pretty hard not to know this stuff was happening," MacFarlane said, "and I started saying things like, 'Well, where was Miss Peggy?' And they'd say, 'Oh, she was right there.' " MacFarlane assembled a small task force of friends and fellow social workers, including her roommate, to help with the interviews. The Manhattan Beach detectives weren't pleased, but if the children were talking to the social workers instead of to them, they had no choice except to relay their questions through MacFarlane and her group.

The role of go-between was not one the social workers relished. They might know something about children, but none of them had any training in how to question a witness or in the admissibility of criminal evidence. "The boundaries," MacFarlane admitted later, "got very blurred. The police brought me mug shots and photographs, and we showed those to the children. That's not something the institute had ever done before, and I don't think it was a good idea." MacFarlane was also troubled by some of the children's reactions to the photos. "I came to this real quick realization that kids are terrible at that kind of thing," she said. "They'll say, 'Oh, there's Uncle Bill,' and of course it isn't Uncle Bill. They were just picking out people who looked scary to them. I felt very uncomfortable with it. We never should have done it."

After months of playing therapist with one hand and policeman with the other, the social workers appealed to California attorney general John Van de Kamp to assign more investigators to the case. "We laid it on the line," MacFarlane said later. "We felt like we were way over our heads." But it was not until October 1984, more than sixteen months after Ray Buckey had first come under suspicion, that the Los Angeles County sheriff, Sherman Block, and Bob Philibosian, the district attorney, paid a visit to Chief Kuhlmeyer in Manhattan Beach. No one present that day will discuss what was said, or by whom, but a month later a special task force of twenty-five sheriff's deputies, headed by Lt. Dick Willey, entered the case from its temporary headquarters in an abandoned lifeguard station.

By then the trail was growing cold, but it had once been quite hot. As the children who had traipsed up the front steps of the Children's Institute began to number in the dozens, and then in the hundreds, the waiting time for interviews had grown to three months. Many of the children had been attending the school when Ray Buckey was arrested, but others hadn't gone there for several years. Some barely acknowledged that something might have happened to them at the school, and many kept insisting they had not been abused by anybody. But a few more children were talking every week, and they were telling a real horror story. Their teachers, they said, had tied them up and drugged them with various kinds of "medicine" — shots, little pink pills, and mysterious liquids that one child described as "making me feel like I was asleep even when I was awake." They had been raped and sodomized by Ray Buckey, and fondled and penetrated with pencils and other sharp foreign objects by some of the other teachers. Much of the abuse had taken the form of games. There had been the naked movie star game, the cowboy game, the doctor game, the alligator game, the tickle game, and the horsey game.

Among the most worrisome questions raised by the children's disclosures was why they had kept such secrets from their parents, in some cases for several years. The answer, according to the children, was that every so often one of the gerbils, turtles, or rabbits the school kept as pets had been killed in front of them, an example of what would happen to their parents if they ever "told." Some children told the interviewers that they had even been coached by their teachers about how to cope with the nightmares that resulted from the abuse. "They told us the monsters would come in the night and try to eat us," the children said, "and the way you make the monsters go away is, you sit up in bed and say, 'I promise I'll never tell anybody what happened to me.' And the monsters will go away."

The younger children's stories were chilling, but those told by a few of the older children, most of them boys who had been gone from the school for a few years, could only be called grotesque. The boys said they had been forced to drink rabbit's blood in an Episcopal church near their school, and they talked of having been abused by strangers wearing black robes and carrying black candles. Several told of visits to a local cemetery, where they were forced by Ray Buckey to help exhume bodies that Buckey then hacked up with knives. That story sounded slightly less improbable after the investigators found the children's descriptions of the cemetery's grounds and buildings to be accurate down to the placement of clocks and chairs.

The authorities' suspicions that there might be some satanic aspect to the McMartin case deepened after police who searched the house of an unemployed handyman identified by the children as one of their abusers found a pair of rabbit's ears, a black cloak, and a black candle. At the time of the search, the handyman was facing sexual abuse charges in connection with a baby-sitting service he operated with another man and a woman from a motel in nearby Torrance. The McMartin children had recognized his picture in the newspaper as that of an abuser they knew only as the "Wolf Man," but the charges against the handyman were never substantiated. He was found dead of an apparent drug overdose on the eve of his trial.

Clandestine satanic ceremonies at an Episcopal church, especially a church that was one of the few liberal strongholds in a rather conservative community? Surely not possible, the police thought. They had second thoughts when the state closed a day-care center operated by the church after a half-dozen children there were found by doctors to have been sexually abused. In the months after the McMartin indictments were handed down, five other preschools not more than a few miles away also became the targets of sexual abuse investigations. One, the Manhattan Ranch School, was closed by the state after three McMartin children said they had been taken there and abused by strangers. When Los Angeles County sheriff's deputies began trying to unravel the connections, they found "substantial numbers" of children at each school who showed medical evidence of abuse. There wasn't any solid evidence of a multischool conspiracy, but neither was there any good explanation for the fact that children who didn't know one another were telling about having been taken in the same cars to the same houses, where they were abused by strangers. When stories began appearing in the Los Angeles newspapers about an apparently unrelated pedophile ring in Sacramento, 350 miles away, children from one of the South Bay schools said they recognized one of the Sacramento defendants from his picture. "I don't know what it is," said one of the consulting psychiatrists in the McMartin case, "but something is going on."

The day-care conspiracy theory first gained prominence in 1984, when Kee MacFarlane made a nationally televised appearance before a congressional subcommittee. She began her testimony by emphasizing that despite the mounting reports of abuse, most preschools and day-care centers were "healthy, responsible, and developmentally appropriate places for young children." What bothered her, she said, were similarities in the accounts given by children who had been abused at schools in several different cities. "I believe that we're dealing with an organized operation of child predators designed to prevent detection," MacFarlane said. "The preschool, in such a case, serves as a ruse for a larger, unthinkable network of crimes against children. If such an operation involves child pornography or the selling of children, as is frequently alleged, it may have greater financial, legal, and community resources at its disposal than those attempting to expose it."

MacFarlane acknowledged that "the proposition that a totally unknown number of preschools and other child-care institutions could be serving such purposes is formidable, but many of the cases could only have existed under these conspiratorial circumstances. I don't know if what we're dealing with can be called organized crime, or if there is an entity that uses schools as procurement places. But I do know that hundreds of children are alleging that they were pornographically photographed during their entire time at preschools, that they were taken far away to do so, sometimes so far away that they were taken on planes." Pressed for evidence, MacFarlane mentioned a rhyme she had heard recited by many of the McMartin children in describing the naked movie star game. "What you say is what you are," it went. "You're a naked movie star." She went on: "Some time later, I heard the exact same rhyme recited by a parent in another state where an arrest was made. I asked, 'Where did you hear that?' and the answer was, 'From my child.'" Though MacFarlane didn't say so, the out-of-state case in question was a Montessori school in Reno, where the children were also telling their therapists that, like the children in Memphis, they had been taken on short airplane trips to places they did not recognize. (The proprietor of the Montessori school has yet to come to trial.)

In March 1984, a Los Angeles County grand jury indicted Ray Buckey, his mother, grandmother, and sister, and three other women who had taught at the McMartin school. The seven defendants included virtually everyone who had worked there for the past several years, and when the charges were added up they totaled 115 separate counts. Many of those who saw the defendants' pictures in the newspapers or on television found it difficult to connect them with the prosecutors' descriptions of what had happened at the school. The most improbable of all was Virginia McMartin, who at her arraignment insisted on wearing the fuzzy teddy-bear pin that had become her trademark. With her gray hair and glasses, McMartin's daughter, Peggy McMartin Buckey, looked like everybody's favorite aunt. It would have been difficult to distinguish Ray Buckey and his twenty-eight-year-old sister, Peggy Ann, from the other young people who lived in Manhattan Beach. The last three defendants, Betty Raidor, Mary Ann Jackson, and Babette Spitler, appeared equally benign.

Even one member of the prosecution team admitted later that "some of them look like people I would really like, if it weren't for all the children I've talked to."

As it was being reported in excruciating detail across the country, the McMartin sexual abuse case was billed as the largest on record anywhere. Of the 400 children interviewed by MacFarlane and her colleagues at the Children's Institute, 350 eventually said they had been abused by somebody at the McMartin school, and because the school had been in operation for nearly twenty years, the potential scope of the case was much bigger than that. Men and women in their late teens and early twenties were calling the prosecutors to say that something had happened to them at the school many years before. "The numbers are just unbelievable," one of the prosecutors said. "I think we don't even know how large the number is."

She was talking about the number of victims, but she might have been referring to the number of suspects. Only Virginia McMartin and the six teachers had been formally charged, but the children who had looked at Kee MacFarlane's mug shots had picked out at least three dozen other people, some of them friends of the McMartins and the Buckeys, others prominent Manhattan Beach residents, still others with no apparent connection to the school or the community.

Most of the children said they had been abused inside the school itself, but one told of being abused in the storeroom of a Manhattan Beach grocery store where Ray Buckey once worked as a bag boy. Another recalled being forced to have sex inside a van while it was going through a local carwash. Shortly after he came under investigation, a doctor whose home had been pointed out by some of the children as one of the places they had been taken checked himself into a sanitarium for a long-term "alcohol cure." The police were never able to corroborate the children's stories of a "wild ride" to the doctor's home in a van with a half-dead baby bouncing around inside.

As the case expanded, Jean Matusinka and her staff, perhaps the most experienced prosecutors in the country at trying cases of child sexual abuse, managed somehow to stay abreast of its twists and turns. Matusinka herself had interviewed each of the eighteen children who testified before the grand jury that indicted the seven defendants. Those children had also been examined by Astrid Heger, a pediatrician who had joined Kee MacFarlane's task force. Heger quickly accumulated a number of color slides showing what she said were vaginal and anal scars that could only have been caused by the penetration of large foreign objects. But as had also been true in Jordan, the medical evidence and the children's testimony amounted to the prosecution's entire case.

Like the Jordan children, the McMartin children said they had been photographed while being abused, but the police who searched the McMartin defendants' houses never found a single photograph. Despite a ten-thousand-dollar reward posted by a group of McMartin parents and an appeal placed by a Los Angeles television station in the pedophile publication *Wonderland*, no photos of the McMartin children ever turned up. Nor was any of the McMartin defendants going to testify against another. When the lawyer for one of the defendants offered a guilty plea by his client to a reduced charge in return for her testimony against the others, Bob Philibosian, the district attorney, rejected the overture. All the defendants were culpable people, Philibosian said, and all should be tried and convicted. His decision to accept no pleas of guilty was one the McMartin prosecutors would come to regret.

Even without much in the way of corroborating evidence, Jean Matusinka thought she had a winnable case. It wasn't airtight, but the eighteen children who had appeared before the grand jury had made convincing witnesses, and the medical evidence seemed compelling. A few days after the indictments were returned, Matusinka was stunned when Philibosian told her he was reassigning the case. He tried to justify his decision on the grounds that Matusinka's child abuse unit already had a full caseload, but the lawyers on her staff didn't agree. "Philibosian's thinking was that any good prosecutor could handle any case," one of them said later. "That's probably true in any area other than child abuse. Anyone can handle a murder, for example. But to do child abuse cases, you need to know how to talk to parents and children."

The new lead prosecutor was Lael Rubin, an aggressive trial lawyer who thought well on her feet and was equally adept at handling the media. Among her most recent victories had been securing a guilty plea from Catherine Wilson, a Los Angeles woman known as the "kiddie porn queen." But as Rubin herself acknowledged, her experience in the area of child abuse was limited to a couple of incest cases early in her prosecutorial career. As her two principal assistants, Rubin chose two lawyers who had even less experience in the field than she. One, Glenn Stevens, was a young trial attorney known for his self-confidence and aggressiveness, which was perhaps why he was not particularly well liked by his colleagues. The third prosecutor, Christine Johnston, had a reputation as a careful researcher, if not as a particularly talented trial lawyer.

With seven defendants, 115 counts, and a reservoir of 350 possible victims, the McMartin case was already enormous. But Philibosian, a hardrock conservative whose fast-draw approach to law enforcement was more popular among police officers than civil libertarians, didn't think it was big enough. Each of the counts in the grand jury indictment had been based on a specific allegation by a child who had testified behind closed doors, but there were still many uncharged counts that could be filed on the basis of subsequent statements by children who hadn't talked to the grand jury. When Philibosian said he wanted to add the rest of the charges, Lael Rubin agreed. "We as prosecutors," she said later, "have a duty to charge crimes that accurately reflect the magnitude of what has taken place."

In May 1984, the district attorney's office filed an expanded complaint that more than tripled the number of counts against the defendants, from 115 to 354, and more than doubled the number of child witnesses, from the original eighteen to forty-one. By then, considerable tension had developed between the new prosecution team and the old. "The McMartin prosecutors don't ask our advice, or welcome it for that matter," groused one member of the old team, who thought the expanded complaint was a serious error. "You can't charge too many counts," he said. "If you're talking about 150 or two hundred counts involving thirty or forty children, you have to be very careful. Little children have no time sense. It's very difficult for them to separate counts."

Philibosian, whose constituency was the downtown Los Angeles establishment, was then in the midst of a tough reelection battle against the city attorney, a liberal named Ira Reiner from the west side of town. Reiner was the favorite in the race, and there was more than a little muttering from Matusinka's staff about grandstanding in the face of a tough election. The expanded complaint did produce a whole new series of alarming headlines, but Philibosian lost the election anyway. Though it would not become apparent for months, the real problem the prosecutors faced was that they knew relatively little about the twenty-three new witnesses the expanded complaint had added to their case. Rubin and her team had met with a few of the children, but one of those present at the meetings thought they hadn't gone all that well. "They'd had no experience with child witnesses," the person said. "They'd never worked with kids. So we sat down together on the floor and I said, 'This is Lael, this is Glenn.' We had a little session where all I was really doing was facilitating the child's ability to talk to the DAs."

In hopes that the McMartin children might avoid the sort of repeated questioning that had marred the Jordan case, the Children's Institute was careful to preserve each of the initial interviews on videotape. Whenever someone wanted to know what a particular child had said about a particular defendant, all that was necessary was to watch the tape. But in their rush to draw up the expanded complaint, the prosecutors themselves hadn't had time to look at more than a few of the hundreds of tapes. Even then, what they saw was sketchy, because most of the tapes had been made early in the case, at a time when many of the children were still reluctant to talk. A few days before the expanded complaint was filed, MacFarlane offered to give Rubin her personal assessment of which children would make the best witnesses. When Rubin said that would be helpful, MacFarlane tried to remember which children had impressed her the most. She gave Rubin a list of names, but she wasn't sure it was the right list. After so many children, it was difficult to remember them all.

Some grand juries are little more than rubber stamps. Others can be more aggressive in seeking the truth than the prosecutors themselves. Most fall somewhere in between. But whatever their nature, grand juries are expensive, and many prosecutors save them for their most important cases, filing the less important ones in the form of a complaint. A few years ago, the California legislature, concerned that defendants who had been charged in a complaint were being denied an element of due process enjoyed by those indicted by a grand jury, passed a law mandating that anyone charged by complaint was entitled to a preliminary hearing before a judge. The hearing would be a pro forma proceeding at which the prosecution would present the bare bones of its case. The defendant, if he wished, could put on a brief affirmative defense. If the judge thought there was a reasonable suspicion that the defendant might be guilty, he would order a trial. If not, the case would be dismissed.

If the preliminary hearing seemed like a relatively inexpensive, efficient, and equitable means of ensuring greater justice, that was before the California Supreme Court decided that defendants who had been indicted by a grand jury were now being discriminated against. A preliminary hearing, the court said, gave a defendant some important rights that were not available to those charged in a grand jury indictment, such as the right to cross-examine witnesses and the right to a public hearing. Henceforth, everyone indicted by a grand jury would also be entitled to ask for a preliminary hearing. A "prelim" wouldn't be mandatory, but if a defendant wanted one, then the prosecution had to comply. Virginia McMartin and Peggy Ann Buckey waived their right to a hearing, choosing instead to stand trial on the strength of the grand jury indictment alone. But the prosecutors didn't agree. If they had to mount a preliminary hearing to accommodate the other five defendants, they said, then all seven defendants would have a preliminary hearing.

Aviva Bobb, the judge assigned to preside at the hearing, had never heard a child sexual abuse case. In fact, Bobb hadn't heard many felony cases of any kind in the three years she had been on the bench — drunk driving and other misdemeanors were more up her alley. Nor was Judge Bobb noted for her legal acumen; behind her back, lawyers called her "Judge Boob." In a rare interview, Bobb told the *Los Angeles Times* that she couldn't remember why she had wanted to become a lawyer, but that she liked being a judge and "deciding" things. The first thing for Judge Bobb to decide was what form the McMartin case should take. Should each of the seven defendants have a separate hearing, or should they be joined together into one giant hearing? Bobb's principal concern was which course would be easier on the children. As one prosecutor paraphrased her thinking, "Do you put the children through one big horrendous experience, or do you put them through seven slightly less horrendous experiences?" Bobb decided that one big horrendous experience was best, since it would theoretically reduce the number of times each child had to appear in court. The defense lawyers disagreed, but Lael Rubin had no objection. "We thought it was essential for pursuing the strongest case possible to have them all joined," she said.

Many preliminary hearings last for a day or less, and even in the most serious criminal case it is unusual for one to continue for more than a week. The McMartin hearing would run for twenty months, the longest judicial proceeding in California history and, at a cost of more than six million dollars, easily the most expensive. By the time it was over, forty-three thousand pages of transcribed testimony would fill more than five hundred volumes. Had the subject at hand been less grisly, the hearing would have been a fine satire of justice, worthy of Kafka or at least Gilbert and Sullivan. What it turned out to be was a monumental strategic error on the part of the prosecution.

There were a number of older children, some as old as fifteen and sixteen, who had once attended the McMartin school and who were now telling investigators essentially the same stories as the five-, six-, and seven-year-olds. But because the statute of limitations for sexual abuse cases in California is six years, none of the older children would be able to testify. The oldest of the scheduled witnesses, a ten-year-old boy, was barely inside the statute, and even so he would be testifying about events that had taken place when he was four. In theory at least, the best witnesses would be the youngest children, those whose experiences were freshest in their minds. But because they were so young, the prosecutors were concerned that they would also be least able to withstand the rigors of testifying.

When Lael Rubin asked Judge Bobb to allow the children to testify over closed-circuit television, it was in hopes of sparing them the anguish of having to take the witness stand just a few feet away from where the seven defendants were seated. But when the state court of appeals ruled that televised testimony was unconstitutional because it had not been explicitly provided for under state law, Bobb denied the request and ordered the children to testify in person. The compromise she offered was to close her courtroom to spectators and reporters, who would watch the proceedings over closed-circuit TV from an adjacent courtroom. The children would still have to testify in front of some two dozen adults, including the defendants they said had threatened their lives and the lives of their parents. When the children were asked who they thought might be able to protect them, they all had the same answer. "We got ahold of Mr. T and asked him if he would come and talk to the children, to try to reassure them a little bit," said one of those involved in the case. "He said, 'Fine.' He also said, 'If they was my kids, you wouldn't need to have no trial.' " Mr. T did spend time with a few of the witnesses, but as they climbed the steps to the witness stand most of the children were still plainly frightened.

While staying within her role as an impartial fact finder, Bobb tried her best to allay the children's fears. "Good morning," she would tell each new witness brightly. "I am Judge Bobb. I'd like to introduce you to some of the people in the courtroom, and then I'm going to ask you to tell the truth, and the lawyers will start asking you some questions." For the next few minutes, Bobb would point out the court reporter, the clerk, and the bailiffs, and explain what each of them did.

A few of the young witnesses did rather well, such as the girl who said she had been deputized by Ray Buckey to act as a lookout for approaching parents. "I was outside swinging on the swing," the girl recalled. "Inside was Ray and some children. They had their clothes off. Ray was molesting and abusing the children. For little girls, he was sticking his penis in their vaginas and his fingers in their behind, and for little boys he put his penis in their butt. I'd run in and tell Ray the child's mother was coming. He'd put the children in the bathroom and tell the mother, 'Go in the little yard and they'll be there.' He got the child dressed, peeked out the door, and said he had found the child in the classroom."

But most of the children who testified seemed overwhelmed, sometimes pausing for a full minute, or even two, before answering a question. For many children, however, the biggest trauma proved to be not the courtroom or even the defendants, but the defendants' seven lawyers. The McMartin defense team was not an overly distinguished group. Several had attended rather obscure law schools, some of them at night, but they made up for their lack of legal erudition with their tenacity and contentiousness. When they declared at the outset of the hearing that their clients were unequivocally innocent, it sounded like an echo from the Jordan case. Maybe some of the McMartin children had been sexually abused, the lawyers said, and maybe they hadn't. But it wasn't their clients who had done the abusing, and if the children were saying it was, then the children were lying. One of the lawyers' favorite tactics was objecting to nearly every question put to the children by Rubin and the other prosecutors; if there had been an award for the most objections raised, it would have gone to Ray Buckey's lawyer, Dan Davis. The following exchange was all too typical:

> *Rubin:* When you were a littler girl, did you go to the McMartin school?
> *Davis:* Objection, Your Honor. She's leading the witness.
> *Judge Bobb:* Objection overruled.
> *Rubin:* Can you tell us who your teachers were?
> *Davis:* Objection, vague.
> *Rubin:* Do you see Ray here in court today?
> *Witness:* Yes.
> *Rubin:* What is he wearing?
> *Davis:* Objection, calls for a conclusion.
> *Judge Bobb:* Overruled.
> *Witness:* A shirt.
> *Rubin:* Is the shirt a light color or a dark color?
> *Davis:* Objection, leading question.
> *Judge Bobb:* Overruled.
> *Rubin:* Do you see anybody else here in court who was at the school when you were there who was not a teacher?
> *Davis:* Objection, the "else" makes it vague.
> *Judge Bobb:* Overruled.
> *Rubin:* When you were at McMartin, did you ever have to play a game where you had to take your clothes off?

Davis: Objection, leading.
Judge Bobb: Overruled.

And so it went, hour after hour, day after day, week after week. Judge Bobb seemed tentative in her handling of the defense lawyers, and occasionally rattled by them. "There's this incredible dynamic that goes on in court with seven lawyers versus one," one observer said. "When one of them makes an objection, the other six join in — they're on their feet jumping up and down, their hands are up, they're yelling. Just the psychological weight of that on the judge has to be a factor. She can shut them all up by sustaining what they want." But Bobb's patience with the defense was not endless. When Dan Davis objected that a child's answer to a question by Lael Rubin about the date of her birthday was hearsay, because the child had no firsthand knowledge of when she was born, the judge told Davis to shut up. "I'll just assume you have a continuing objection," she said acidly. Davis tried to keep quiet, but he couldn't. Bobb fined him five hundred dollars for contempt.

When Lael Rubin or one of the other prosecutors was finally able to finish, the seven defense lawyers would begin questioning the child in turn. The first witness, a seven-year-old boy, sat on the stand for a week while he was cross-examined on the minutiae of his allegations. The second witness, the ten-year-old, testified for sixteen days. "Children cannot survive extensive cross-examination, period," said one of Jean Matusinka's assistants. "And if you have multiple defendants, the problem of cross-examination is exacerbated. If you have seven attorneys, it's not seven times worse, it's two hundred and fifty times worse. It goes up exponentially." Outside the courtroom, Davis and the other defense lawyers conceded that their strategy of searching for discrepancies in the children's testimony through repeated questioning was regrettable, but they defended it as necessary to show how the children had been "programmed" by the prosecution.

Whatever the defense lawyers' rationale, no detail went unquestioned. A boy who said he had been sodomized by Ray Buckey with a pen was asked what color the pen was. Davis was also quick to point out that several of the children hadn't admitted to being abused until after they were interviewed by Kee MacFarlane and her social workers, and he thought it significant that some of the witnesses used terms, such as "oral sex" and "pubic hair," that were not part of an ordinary child's vocabulary. When the seventh witness, an eight-year-old girl, testified that Ray Buckey had "put his penis in my vagina," Davis didn't lose a second. "You don't know what you mean by the word 'penis,' do you?" he shot back. "No," the girl admitted. "Did anyone ever tell you what a penis looks like?" he asked. She said that no one had. "I'm convinced this child didn't know what the sex organ was," Davis said later. "She used the word the adults told her to use." Kee MacFarlane had a different explanation. "She knows what a penis and a vagina are," she said. "It's just that she's at an age where she's horribly embarrassed by all of this. She just about died during the medical exam. I expected her to fold up on the stand. Those words didn't come from here, because we never used adult terminology with the kids. If they called it a google, we called it a google."

The prosecutors rejected the brainwashing allegations by pointing out, as had their counterparts in Jordan, that most of the children had accused only a few of the defendants. If the children had been brainwashed, the prosecutors said, then it hadn't been a very good job of brainwashing, or else why weren't all the children naming all seven defendants as their abusers? The defense lawyers were not persuaded, and according to them the head brainwasher was Kee MacFarlane herself. "She could get a six-month-old infant to say he's been abused," one of the defense lawyers said. In fact, MacFarlane had a certain childlike quality about her, and she was very good with children. She liked being around them, even those with problems, and they seemed to like her. "I think this is an ideal job," she said once. "They actually pay me to get down on the floor and play with kids all day."

The defense showed MacFarlane no mercy. When she took the witness stand to testify for the prosecution, one of the first things she was asked on cross-examination was whether she herself had been abused as a child. When she declined to answer on the ground that her childhood experiences were irrelevant to the issue at hand, Judge Bobb allowed her refusal to be interpreted as an acknowledgment that she had been abused. The first thing MacFarlane did after leaving the courtroom was to telephone her father and explain what had happened, before he heard about it on the evening news. He laughed and told her not to worry, but the attacks on MacFarlane continued.

When the defense pointed out that she was not a psychologist, MacFarlane replied that she had never claimed to be one. When rumors began circulating that she didn't even hold a degree in social work, the University of Maryland confirmed that MacFarlane was among its graduates. The most ludicrous attack of all came toward the end of the hearing, when one of the defense lawyers demanded that

MacFarlane be charged with a crime for withholding information from the authorities, because she hadn't filed the child abuse reports required by the state on the children she'd interviewed. "I thought that law was for when you took a case to the police," MacFarlane said later. "I didn't think it was for when the police brought a case to you."

What could not have been foreseen when the McMartin investigation began was that the videotaped interviews, which had seemed like such a good idea at the time, would provide the strongest ammunition for the defense's claims of brainwashing by the prosecution. A few of the tapes were models of therapeutic technique, but others were seriously flawed by questions that were unnecessarily leading and suggestive. One tape showed an interviewer assuring a reticent child that many of the other McMartin children had already told her "yucky secrets," and that all of the McMartin teachers were "sick in the head." When another child was asked whether "Mr. Ray" had ever touched her, she vigorously shook her head. Only when the questioning persisted did the child agree that Ray Buckey had indeed touched her genitals. When a third child continued to insist that nobody at the McMartin school had abused her, the two interviewers told the girl that they themselves had been sexually abused as children, and that she would feel much better if she told someone about what had happened.

Some of the tapes reflected what seemed to be fundamental errors of procedure. MacFarlane and the other interviewers rarely began a session by asking directly, "Did anything happen to you?" Instead, the child would be given a McMartin class picture and asked to point to the children he knew. When a child was pointed out who had already been interviewed, the interviewer might say, "He told us what happened at the school," thereby establishing the premise that abuse had occurred. Whether the children were interviewed a short time after they claimed to have been abused or months and even years after the fact, virtually the same techniques had been used with all of them. In hopes of easing what the interviewers perceived as the children's embarrassment at talking about such a sensitive subject, they were allowed to respond to questions by using hand puppets. Rather than answer yes or no, a child would simply move the puppet's head up and down or sideways.

"If you really look at what brainwashing is, this isn't brainwashing," Kee MacFarlane said later. "I just don't believe that we have this incredible power to influence children, that children are incredibly more susceptible than we've ever considered, and that they will not only acquiesce to what we're saying but will go on to elaborate on it in great detail." But even MacFarlane didn't defend all the techniques she and her colleagues had used. "There are parts of tapes that certainly look like children were led into saying things," she admitted later. "I think we need to look a lot more closely at children's susceptibility and the way questions are asked. Where I think you get in trouble is when they say, 'Somebody touched me,' and you say, 'I know it was Mr. Ray. All the kids told me it was Mr. Ray, and you can tell me it was Mr. Ray. It was Mr. Ray, wasn't it?' That's a leading question, that's asking for a specific answer. Things that are in the therapeutic interest of children are not always in the legal interest, and that's where we've all got to get a lot better."

As the McMartin hearing went forward, it took on an increasingly fantastic tone. The ninth witness, a boy, said that children at the school had been beaten regularly with a ten-foot-long bullwhip and taken to the Episcopal church, where they were "slapped by a priest" if they refused to pray to "three or four gods." When the defense lawyers showed the boy some pictures and asked him to pick out his abusers, he selected photos of the Los Angeles city attorney and Chuck Norris, the movie actor. The embarrassed prosecutors said later that the boy had been mistaken in his recollections, but after he stepped down they decided not to call any of the other children who were likely to testify about satanic rituals or bizarre events.

The decision may have been wise from a strategic standpoint, but it cost the prosecution a number of its scheduled witnesses, and with the witness list diminishing rapidly, it was a loss they could ill afford. As the parents whose children hadn't yet testified watched the early witnesses squirming on the stand, they were beginning to have second thoughts about putting their own children through such an ordeal. Some of the parents told Lael Rubin that their children would not appear at all, that they were withdrawing from the case. The rest said theirs would testify only over the sort of closed-circuit television setup Judge Bobb had refused to approve.

The McMartin parents had been lobbying the California legislature to enact a statute authorizing televised testimony, but when the bill was finally passed, Judge Bobb again denied the prosecution's request. Only after she was reversed by another judge were the television cameras and monitors set up in her courtroom, but by that time only one child's parents were willing to allow him to testify. The boy was the fourteenth scheduled witness in the case, and now he would be the last. Now that twenty-seven of the forty-one scheduled witnesses would never appear in court, Judge Bobb had no choice except to dismiss more than half of the charges against the seven defendants.

What had begun as the child abuse case of the century was rapidly dwindling, and the pieces that remained were much flimsier than anyone could have envisioned when the preliminary hearing began. None of the children who testified had been dissuaded from their insistence that they had been sexually abused at the school. As in the Jordan case, many of their accounts included the sort of anatomical and physiological details that it is difficult for young children to contrive. But the witnesses had been vague about times and places, and their testimony contained more than its share of discrepancies and contradictions.

Some of the contradictions were more serious than others. A nine-year-old boy who told of having been taken from the school to a private house where he was abused by strangers said at first that he had been driven to the house in a red convertible. Later he said it had been a green and white van. When the defense lawyers asked a seven-year-old whether some of his allegations were "stories" he had told so that the prosecutors "wouldn't be sad," he agreed that they were. But the most serious contradictions concerned who had done the abusing. One girl testified for the prosecution that Ray Buckey had photographed her and other children nude; on cross-examination she said that he had not. "When you say Ray did take pictures and he did not take pictures, are those both true?" Dan Davis asked. "Yes," the girl replied.

An eight-year-old girl who had named three of the McMartin teachers as those who had abused her said later she could not remember who her abusers were. Another girl identified the woman who had abused her as Peggy McMartin Buckey, then changed her mind. When a fourth witness was asked which of her teachers had abused her, she mentioned someone named "Miss Lo." Asked whether Miss Lo was in the courtroom, the girl nodded and pointed to one of the defendants. The woman she pointed to was Mary Ann Jackson. Miss Lo, it turned out, had been dead for several years.

The question raised by the children's testimony wasn't so much whether they were lying as whether they were testifying accurately. "With multiple defendants there is always a risk of implicating innocent people," said one prosecutor who was watching the case closely. "It's easy for those kids to remember that they were abused. Maybe they were even abused by four or five people. But there is a possibility — a danger, I think — of children starting to think that everybody they came in contact with when they were there was part of all this."

The contradictions, one defense lawyer said, were "killing the prosecution." But just how badly wasn't clear until the *Los Angeles Times* reported that two of the three prosecutors in the case had decided that there wasn't enough evidence against four of the seven defendants to bring them to trial. The only defendants who deserved to be bound over, the two prosecutors were said to have concluded, were Ray Buckey, his mother, Peggy, and Betty Raidor. The article didn't identify the two prosecutors by name, but Lael Rubin wasn't one of them, which left only Glenn Stevens and Christine Johnson.

The prosecution had barely rested its case, and now two-thirds of the district attorney's team was jumping off the boat, or at least had one leg over the railing. Fortunately, the next move didn't belong to the prosecutors; it was up to Judge Bobb to decide whether they had demonstrated enough probable cause for her to order the defendants to stand trial. Before that could happen, the defense lawyers, who had read the *Times* article with great glee, invoked their right to present an "affirmative defense" — in effect, to put on a hearing of their own by calling witnesses to rebut the children's testimony. The affirmative defense, which lasted for nearly three months, was exhaustive but not persuasive. On January 9, 1986, Judge Bobb ordered all seven defendants to stand trial. The children's testimony, she said, had been "very credible."

Because the prosecution's case had been pared away to its bare bones, there weren't many counts remaining against most of the defendants. Ray Buckey faced the largest number, with eighty-two. But his mother, Peggy McMartin Buckey, was now only charged with twenty-four counts, and his sister, Peggy Ann, with eight. Betty Raidor faced ten counts, and Mary Ann Jackson and Babette Spitler four each. Virginia McMartin, who had celebrated her seventy-eighth birthday during the hearing, faced but a single count, the common charge of conspiracy.

Merely because Judge Bobb thought all the defendants ought to stand trial, it didn't mean the prosecutors had to try them all. Ira Reiner, the new district attorney, had inherited the case from Bob Philibosian, and during his first few months in office he had seen large parts of it dissolve. The district attorney's job, Reiner said, was to decide not whether there was enough evidence to bring defendants to trial — Judge Bobb had already done that — but whether there was enough to convict them. It was his moral and ethical obligation, Reiner said, not to force the McMartin defendants to undergo the additional expense and anguish of standing trial if he didn't think he could win a conviction.

Reiner wasn't willing to trust such a momentous decision to his own judgment. He summoned the three McMartin prosecutors and several of his top assistants, and during one very long weekend they combed through the mountain of evidence produced by the preliminary hearing. When Reiner finally asked each of those present for their recommendations, Glenn Stevens said he thought that only the cases against Ray Buckey and his mother were strong enough to guarantee a conviction. Chris Johnston was even more cautious: only Ray Buckey should be tried, she said. Lael Rubin agreed that the cases against Ray Buckey and his mother were the most persuasive, but she thought she could convict Betty Raidor as well.

On January 17, 1986, in an announcement reminiscent of Kathleen Morris's press conference in Jordan, Reiner said that the charges against everyone except Ray and Peggy McMartin Buckey were being dismissed. The evidence against the Buckeys, Reiner said, was "very strong," even "compelling," but that against the five other defendants was weak. If Reiner's decision was a compromise, it was one that pleased nobody. Ray Buckey and his mother were furious, since they thought the charges against them should have been dropped along with the others. The other five defendants were equally furious — the hearing had cost them nearly two years of their lives and most of their savings, and now they were being denied the chance for a trial that might have cleared their names. Their five lawyers were equally angry. During the last weeks of the hearing they had begun to smell blood, and they had been looking forward, as one of them put it, to "kicking some derriere."

Angriest of all were the McMartin parents, including those parents who had declined to let their children testify. If the district attorney thought Ray and Peggy Buckey were guilty, then how could the others, who must at least have known what was going on at the school, be innocent? Ira Reiner, struggling to be as sensitive to their feelings as to his own reputation and to the public outcry his decision had provoked, tried his best to assuage them in private. "He made it very clear to us that he did not think these people were innocent," one parent said. "He said he just didn't have sufficient evidence to get a conviction, and that it hurt him greatly to have to let them go." But all the explanations in the world didn't help. "Ira Reiner is politically dead," one mother fumed, and she began organizing a drive to get the state attorney general to take over the case.

When asked later what had gone wrong, everyone had a different explanation. The worst mistake, Judge Bobb thought, had been joining the seven cases into one; she didn't seem to remember that it had been her decision in the first place. Ira Reiner kept repeating that he had inherited the McMartin case from his predecessor, and that once the preliminary hearing was under way, he had been powerless to stop it. What Reiner didn't seem to remember was that he could have dismissed the charges at any point during the hearing.

There were other explanations, but as what was left of the McMartin case ground its way through the criminal justice system, it was impossible not to see that many of the mistakes that had first been made in rustic Jordan, Minnesota, had been replicated in sophisticated Los Angeles County, and for many of the same reasons: the refusal of a tiny police department to ask for outside help, the use of social workers and child therapists to conduct crucial interviews with children, the resorting by some of those interviewers to leading or suggestive questions that would later give weight to charges of brainwashing, and the hasty and inadequate research done by a prosecution team always on the edge of being overwhelmed by its case.

Claiming that their reputations had been destroyed, the five former McMartin defendants filed a twenty-million-dollar lawsuit against the city of Manhattan Beach, the county of Los Angeles, Bob Philibosian, the Children's Institute, Kee MacFarlane, even against Wayne Satz, the local television reporter who had broken the McMartin story and whose coverage of the case had been the most aggressive of any local journalist. "All I want back is what I had stolen from me," Virginia McMartin told a news conference. "I want to be able to live my life the way I want."

As the McMartin case was collapsing under its own weight, the related sexual abuse investigations in the Manhattan Beach area were also falling apart. The sheriff's department task force that had been set up to look into the McMartin case had also interviewed scores of children from the half-dozen other local preschools that had fallen under suspicion. An eighteen-year-old playground aide at one of the schools had been indicted and tried, but when the jury could not agree on a verdict, prosecutors decided not to charge him again. By then the children at that school had been interviewed so many times and by so many different people that their stories were hopelessly confused. "I haven't got anybody I can put on the stand that hasn't contradicted themselves," one weary investigator said.

By the spring of 1986 the related investigations had officially been closed, but the McMartin case was still sputtering. Dan Davis, who was billing the county $116 an hour to continue his representation of Ray Buckey, asked the court to dismiss the 101 counts remaining against his client. Dean Gits, the lawyer representing Peggy McMartin Buckey, concurred in the motion for dismissal. Judge Bobb had retired to the sidelines, and the dismissal motion was heard by another judge, a man named William Pounders. Davis offered the court a number of grounds for throwing out what remained of the case, including the suggestion that Lael Rubin had been having an affair with another superior-court judge and might thus have influenced the collective judiciary against the McMartin defendants. Rubin denied that she had had such an affair, and when Davis was unable to come up with any proof, it simply confirmed the reputation he had among those who had been following the case: Ray Buckey's attorney would stop at nothing to see his client acquitted.

The most sensational of Davis's arguments involved prosecutor Glenn Stevens, who had been fired by Ira Reiner in January 1986 for having expressed his concerns about the case to the *Los Angeles Times*. After leaving the district attorney's office, Stevens had signed on, for an undisclosed fee, as a consultant to Abby Mann, a Hollywood movie writer who was trying to put together a television docudrama about the McMartin case. With his wife, Myra, Mann interviewed Stevens for more than thirty hours, and the tape-recorded interviews contained a good deal of inside information about the prosecution's preparation of the case. While working for the district attorney, Stevens had voted in favor of prosecuting Ray Buckey and his mother. Now, according to the tapes, he no longer believed that either one of them was guilty. What seemed to bother Stevens most was the fact that the massive police investigation hadn't turned up any solid corroboration of the children's stories. In the absence of corroboration, it seemed, he had stopped believing the children.

The McMartin parents were furious at Stevens's turnabout. "I put my child in his hands," one mother said. "He told us he believed us, and he has sold us out for thirty pieces of silver." In the interviews, Stevens painted Lael Rubin as blinded to reality by her ambition to follow in Jean Matusinka's footsteps and to become a judge, and he dismissed Kee MacFarlane as naive. "If you can criticize her for anything," he said, "it would be that she didn't really stop and take a look at exactly where we were and what was going on here, and really compare and contrast. Which is the same criticism you can heap on the DA's office." As for the docudrama, Stevens told the Manns, "You want this thing to generate a lot of controversy. That's when it becomes real sexy." If Ray Buckey and his mother were acquitted, Stevens said, "We'll be sitting on top of the world."

By far the most explosive part of the tapes was Stevens's revelation that the prosecution had been concerned that Judy Johnson, the mother of the two-year-old boy who had started the Ray Buckey investigation, was of unsound mind. When Abby Mann, acting on "advice of counsel," turned the Stevens tapes over to the defense, Dan Davis and Dean Gits were delighted. That the prosecutors had had concerns about Johnson's sanity was clear, not just from Stevens's recollections but from a number of confidential memorandums subsequently discovered by the defense in Lael Rubin's files. The memorandums showed that the woman had accused a number of people besides Ray Buckey of having abused her son, among them her former husband, the employees of a Los Angeles health club, an AWOL Marine whose name she didn't know, and a member of the Los Angeles school board. She had told the prosecutors that Ray Buckey could fly, and that he and the other McMartin teachers had put staples in her son's ears and scissors in his eyes.

Lael Rubin and her new coprosecutor, Roger Gunson, agreed that Johnson had been a deeply troubled woman. But they pointed out that her mental problems hadn't become evident until after the case was nearly a year old, and that in any event her emotional instability had no bearing on whether her child had been sexually abused — the doctors at UCLA had confirmed that. The problem for the prosecutors was that they had never communicated their concerns about Johnson to the defendants' lawyers, as the rules of discovery required them to do. Judge Pounders had thrown out all of the defense's other arguments for a dismissal, but he agreed to take testimony on the question of whether Davis and Gits had been unfairly denied a vital prosecution document. Now a third proceeding, an "evidentiary hearing," would be sandwiched in between the preliminary hearing and what promised to be an equally lengthy trial.

When Glenn Stevens was called as a witness at the evidentiary hearing, he began by taking the Fifth Amendment. For a prosecutor to convey privileged information about the prosecution's strategy to the defense might be a crime, and it was also potential grounds for disbarment. Asked a pro forma question about whether he had been assigned to the McMartin case while he was a member of the district attorney's office, Stevens refused to answer. But when Stevens was granted immunity from prosecution and finally began to talk, his statements under oath were much softer than those in the tapes. It was true, he said, that the prosecution hadn't given the defense any of the memos that bore on Judy Johnson's sanity. But he couldn't say that the material had knowingly been withheld, because he had simply assumed that Rubin or someone else had turned it over. Stevens also admitted that he hadn't thought the woman was unbalanced when the case began, and that she had probably "flipped out" over what she believed had happened to her child. It had been his view, Stevens said, that Johnson was "just another witness" for the prosecution, "and not as crucial as she seems to have become."

Though there were many other children and many other parents involved in the McMartin case, the defense was determined to make Judy Johnson a crucial witness, the fulcrum on which the forthcoming prosecution would depend. If Johnson took the stand and repeated the bizarre assertions she had made to the prosecutors in private, her testimony would likely sink the case. If she didn't, and if Gits and Davis questioned her about the memos, it would look as if she were covering something up. When Judy Johnson was found dead in her Manhattan Beach home, nobody quite knew what to think. But Judge Pounders ruled that the woman's death was not enough to derail the proceedings, and after a couple of suspense-filled weeks the coroner announced that she had died of natural causes, apparently from an alcohol-related liver failure. The mother who had started the McMartin case more than three years before appeared to have drunk herself to death.

It was in the midst of the hearing that Ray Buckey appeared in court to plead for bail. "I never in my life threatened a child, nor can I comprehend how anyone could," he told Judge Pounders, but Buckey insisted that he wanted a trial. "I do believe that this case should and must go to trial," he said. "The truth must be known and understood, the truth of my innocence and my mother's innocence and the truth of the wrong that has been done to the seven teachers and to the innocent families of the children. To say I don't fear for my future in the trial is a lie. But the one thing I don't fear, Your Honor, is the truth of my innocence and my mother's innocence. To put it simply, the truth will set me free."

Ray Buckey's request for bail was denied, and Judge Pounders ruled that the evidence against Ray and his mother was sufficiently compelling that both should stand trial. Many of the children's statements, Pounders said, appeared to be "spontaneous" and had "the ring of truth." He concluded: "The district attorney should proceed against these two defendants . . . these defendants are in a distinctly different situation than the other five." The defense's motion to dismiss the charges, the judge said, was denied.

NINE
Lawyers

A S IT HAD BEEN by the Jordan case for much of 1984, the topic of child sexual abuse in America was dominated during most of 1985 and 1986 by questions about what had happened at the McMartin preschool.

On Monday, July 13, 1987, nearly four years and six million dollars after Ray Buckey had first been arrested in Manhattan Beach in the fall of 1983, the McMartin trial finally got under way. It had taken three months to pick the jury of seven men and five women from a pool of several dozen potential jurors. Thirteen of the fourteen children the Buckeys were charged with having abused were scheduled to appear as witnesses; the children, all of them now between the ages of eight and twelve, would be testifying about things that had happened when they were three, four, and five. Some observers were predicting that the trial might last two years.

In her opening speech, Lael Rubin stated that following his second arrest in March of 1984, Ray Buckey had shared a jail cell with a convicted burglar who would testify that Ray had admitted sodomizing a two-and-a-half-year-old child and having sex with other children, taking photographs of some of them and threatening others to ensure their silence.

Dean Gits, Peggy McMartin Buckey's attorney, countered Rubin's disclosure with his own theory of the case. "These events never happened," Gits said. The McMartin preschool, far from having been the "hotbed of child molestation" portrayed by the prosecutors, had "functioned as a loving preschool for a period in excess of twenty years." Gits also pointed out that despite the searches of twenty-one homes, seven businesses, thirty-seven cars, three motorcycles, and a barn, despite interviews with more than six hundred people, forty-nine photo lineups, and an archeological dig, the McMartin prosecutors had not found a shred of evidence to corroborate the children's stories.

But somehow it was all a bit anticlimactic, and even the question of whether Ray Buckey and his mother were guilty or innocent seemed almost immaterial. Guilty or not, it wasn't likely that anybody would ever again entrust the McMartins or the Buckeys with their children. What mattered far more than their guilt or innocence was whether it was even *possible* to prosecute relatively large numbers of defendants accused of abusing relatively large numbers of children.

While McMartin was receiving most of the attention, six new charges of felony sexual abuse were being filed in Los Angeles County every day. Prosecutors in Indianapolis had a hundred sexual abuse cases pending, triple the number two years before, and those in Wichita had more than a hundred. In Tucson there were three hundred cases waiting to go to court, in Seattle 350. Dane County, Wisconsin, was reporting ninety-four cases of incest in 1985, up from twelve the year before. Even tiny Hillsborough County, New Hampshire, was prosecuting two hundred sexual abuse cases a year. "Something has happened within the last two years," said Mike Fondi, a district judge in the Nevada capital of Carson City, population thirty-five thousand. "I can't believe the number of these cases that I get nowadays — not just incest, but child molestation and child abuse. I have more of those cases set for trial than any other kind of criminal case on my calendar."

Cases like McMartin and Jordan, the so-called macro cases, in which there were several defendants and many children, were filled with potential pitfalls. With so many witnesses to the same purported events, there was no way their stories were going to track perfectly. When defense attorneys, acting well within the bounds of courtroom procedure and rules of evidence, zeroed in on the imperfections, it was easy for them to raise serious questions about the children's credibility. The macro cases were few and far between, but in every state and city, growing numbers of children were claiming to have been sexually abused. In many states, especially those that placed a high premium on ensuring defendants' rights, many of the same problems that plagued the macro sexual abuse cases were making ordinary cases difficult to win.

Merely establishing that a child had been abused was not enough, since the prosecutor also had to prove who had done the abusing. Even then, it was usually necessary to show that the defendant intended to "arouse or gratify" his own lust or passion or that of the child. Other crimes, such as murder, also hinge on questions of intent. But in other kinds of cases there is often corroborating evidence that makes the defendant's intention clear, such as eyewitnesses who can tell what they saw and heard, or physical evidence like a bullet or a fingerprint. Because most child abusers operate in secret, in sexual abuse cases there are practically never any disinterested witnesses.

With other kinds of crimes, police working undercover can sometimes watch the criminal act take place. But the surveillance of a suspected child abuser raises a moral dilemma, as was discovered by a policeman investigating a physical therapist suspected of abusing crippled children in a small Northern California town. In hopes of garnering firsthand evidence, the officer watched through a hole in the man's office wall while he performed oral sex on a four-year-old cerebral palsy victim. Only after the therapist had finished did the officer emerge and place him under arrest. Though the suspect was convicted, the officer was fired for not having prevented the abuse from taking place.

In most sexual abuse cases, the only corroborating evidence likely to exist is medical. But medical evidence is not that common, and it is almost always open to interpretation. Oral sex may leave no symptoms at all unless the abuser has a venereal disease, and genital fondling is usually impossible to prove. Vaginal and anal intercourse sometimes result in scarred hymens and stretched sphincters as well, but even these are not conclusive. There may be other reasons for a scarred hymenal opening; according to one study, an enlarged vagina in young girls indicates sexual abuse in only three out of four cases.[1] Except for pregnancy, venereal diseases like gonorrhea or chlamydia are among the most reliable evidence that a child has been abused, since they are nearly impossible to acquire except through sexual contact. But even venereal disease adds up at best to circumstantial evidence, because it carries no name tag. It may be possible to prove that the child in question had sex with somebody, but not with whom.[2]

Like ballistics tests and fingerprints, medical evidence is only as good as the physician who assembles it. Findings taken by hurried, inexperienced, or indifferent doctors in busy clinics or hospital emergency rooms often turn out to be worthless in court. "I know this one doctor who does all the things I consider to be classic mistakes," says Ken Freeman, a veteran Los Angeles prosecutor. "Without understanding children, without understanding how to take a history, without even understanding how to examine children, he attempts to stick his finger in the vagina of every child that is brought to him. And if he can stick it in, he says, 'Vagina will admit finger — no other evidence of sexual abuse.' And if he can't stick it in, he says, 'Vagina would not admit finger — no evidence of sexual abuse.'

"Cases are being dismissed left and right because of his poor examinations. In this one case I had, his examination was totally inconsistent with what the child described as happening. The case was going to be rejected by the DA's office. I interviewed her, and she was so compelling in her description of what occurred that I couldn't believe the examination was accurate. So I went ahead and filed the case. Before we had a preliminary hearing, I decided to have the child reexamined by another doctor. This kid had gross signs of sexual abuse. She was only ten, but she had the vagina of a sexually active woman."

Even when conclusive medical evidence does exist, sexual abuse cases end up resting on the testimony of the children involved. When those children are too young to testify, there is likely to be no case at all. Though there are exceptions, it is a rule of thumb that most children under five are not capable of giving evidence in court. Even if they are, the chances are better than good that their testimony will work to the advantage of the defense rather than the prosecution. "The last time I had a four-year-old on the stand, it took me less than forty-five minutes to break her down," one of the defense lawyers in the Country Walk case was quoted as saying.[3] Many abusers have figured out what prosecutors already know, that it's open season on very young children; about half of all sexual abuse victims, including nearly all of those in preschool and day-care cases, are under five. Unless there is abundant and conclusive corroborating evidence, and unless the victim is unusually precocious, even the most dedicated prosecutor will rarely consider trying a case in which the principal witness is a very young child.

"So often, we'll have a parent who has a two-year-old who in some way or another has communicated something," says Ted Dewolf, who heads the child day-care licensing division of the Michigan Department of Social Services. "We'll talk with other parents and with other children to try to get some kind of corroborative information, but oftentimes it's just not there. If we're really concerned, if it appears as though something might have happened, we might bring in a psychologist or a therapist who might be a little more effective in interviewing that child, and there may be some conclusions from that. But in many cases the problem is simply the age of the child. Many of the prosecutors around the state just won't deal with it if the child's not going to make a good witness."

A California prosecutor who took a chance on a three-year-old incest victim, the youngest child ever to testify in that state, thought he had made the right move when the boy took the witness stand at his father's preliminary hearing and confidently told the judge how he had been abused by his father. But when the father's lawyer took over the questioning, the child denied that anything had happened. "He did pretty poorly," admitted the psychiatrist who had helped prepare the boy to testify, and who then had to explain to the court why a three-year-old might say one thing one minute and another the next. The boy's father was ultimately convicted, but only because of the judge's willingness to accept the psychiatrist's explanation.

Most distressing was the case of three-year-old Janine, whose parents had been divorced for about a year when the teachers at her day-care center first noticed something unusual about her behavior. Janine was spending alternate weeks with her divorced father and mother, and it was during her times with her father that she seemed to become a different child, tugging violently at her hair, using sexually explicit language, even regressing in her toilet training. When the teachers mentioned the behavior to her mother, the woman put it down to her daughter's distress over the divorce. The mother, a lawyer, simply found it inconceivable that her former husband, also a lawyer, was capable of abusing their daughter.

When Janine mumbled something about her daddy and her vagina, however, the teachers called the state child protection agency. At the urging of the agency, her mother took the girl to a child therapist, who concluded that the girl had been sexually abused by her father. A doctor's examination showed that the girl's hymen was broken and her vagina enlarged. But when her mother demanded that the district attorney bring charges against her former husband, the prosecutors replied that because Janine was too young to testify, they had nothing to take to trial. When the mother tried to terminate the joint-custody agreement that had been a condition of her divorce, the court refused, pointing out that the father had never been charged with a crime. Janine, now eight, still spends one night a week with her father and his new wife. "He still calls my daughter a liar," her mother says. "He says it didn't happen. It gets so confusing for her. I just keep telling her, 'You know it happened, because you were there.'"

When is a child old enough to testify? The question is ultimately up to the court, because there is no statutory age limit for courtroom witnesses. Before children can testify in most states, however, they must convince the judge that they are competent witnesses, which means that they know the difference between the truth and a lie. The practice of testing a child's familiarity with the concept of truth dates back more than two centuries, to a ruling by a British jurist that whether or not young witnesses could give testimony depended on their awareness of "the danger and impiety of falsehood." From that decision has derived the modern-day competency hearing, a separate mini-trial that takes place before the regular one, and in which prosecutors, defense lawyers, and the judge take turns asking questions of the prospective witness.

If the judge decides that the child is capable of testifying truthfully, the trial proceeds. If not, the charges are dismissed. Most competency hearings begin with questions about the difference between truth and falsehood and the meaning of a sworn oath, but the divergent interests of the prosecution and the defense soon become clear. Because the prosecutors wish to show that the child is capable of testifying truthfully, they naturally tailor their questions with that goal in mind. The defense, on the other hand, tries to make the child out to be incompetent by asking questions like "Do you believe in Santa Claus?" or "What's the difference between right and wrong?" Not only are right and wrong difficult concepts even for adults, but most children do not have much experience in abstract thinking. "You ask a seven-year-old, 'Are you in school?' " one lawyer says. "And the child will say no. Well, you know darn well they're in school. You know they're in the second grade. What's wrong here? What's wrong is that the child is not in school at this moment. She's sitting right here in the courtroom."

Cases where the witnesses are very young present the greatest difficulty for prosecutors, but even with older witnesses there is a multitude of obstacles to be overcome. In helping juries assess guilt and innocence in ordinary criminal cases, prosecutors and defense lawyers have traditionally relied on disinterested experts to testify that a particular bullet was fired from a particular gun, or that a particular fingerprint was left by a particular individual. A major barrier in child abuse cases is the reluctance of many judges to allow the admission of expert testimony by psychologists and psychiatrists who can fill in the gaps in the jury's knowledge of child psychology and sexual abuse.

When such witnesses have been permitted, they have most often been helpful to the prosecution. A social worker who was permitted to take the stand as an expert witness at the trial of a Mount Vernon, New

York, woman who ran a day-care center in her home explained to the jury such things as the post-traumatic stress syndrome, and why many children wait for several days, or even weeks, before reporting that they have been abused. The jury found the woman guilty of two counts of child endangerment and convicted one of her employees of eleven counts of child rape. (The trial, which went on for more than four months, involved so much graphic testimony that the jurors asked the judge to exempt them from all future calls for jury duty. He did.)

Anyone can appear as an expert courtroom witness, as long as the judge in the case believes that the person's experience and training give sufficient weight to his opinions. But many judges refuse to permit expert testimony in child abuse cases on the grounds that there is no clearly defined field of expertise. Where, they ask, does it reside? With the police officer? The social worker? The psychologist? The family counselor? The sociologist? The professionals, who argue the same question among themselves, have yet to come up with an answer.

Another obstacle to the successful prosecution of child abusers is the ability of the defendant's lawyer to delay the trial for months, in some cases even for years, by filing a blizzard of motions seeking discovery of the prosecution's evidence, depositions of the victims, changes of venue, and whatever else the lawyer can think of. Such delaying tactics are a common feature of the criminal justice system, but in sexual abuse cases they exact a special cost. As the case drags on through continuance after continuance, the victim's family often becomes so frustrated and so concerned about the continuing impact of the ordeal on their child that it withdraws from the prosecution altogether. Even if the victim and his family stay the course, by the time the trial begins, chances are that the child will be called upon to testify about something that happened a year or two before. Because children's memories fade much faster than those of grown-ups, often the only choice is to dismiss the case.

If the case finally does come to trial, the defense's strategy changes from delay to attack. No matter what the charges against their client, most defense lawyers believe that the best defense is a good offense, and in sexual abuse cases the best offense consists of attacking the credibility of the prosecution's star witness, the child victim. As with Jordan and McMartin, the defendant's lawyer may declare that the child has been "brainwashed" by a policeman, a therapist, a social worker, or someone else associated with the prosecution. Or he may argue that the child's allegations are the result of the "hysteria" that surrounds the issue of child abuse. Or he may accuse the prosecutors of conducting a "witch hunt" aimed at destroying his client. Whichever course he chooses, the lawyer has a single, overriding goal — to show that the child, for reasons of his own or at the behest of some adult, has made up the allegations.

If such a contest seems like a gross mismatch, it usually is — an intelligent, well-educated trial lawyer with years of experience in questioning hostile witnesses pitted against a child who is easily confused about time, place, and the sequence of events, who tells different parts of the same story at different times, and who links things in his mind that may not be connected. "Didn't you tell the police this happened in the bedroom?" the defense attorney may ask. "Now you're saying it happened in the bathroom." Perhaps the door between the bedroom and the bathroom was open; perhaps the abuser took the child from the bedroom into the bathroom. In the child's mind the abuse occurred in the bedroom and the bathroom, but to the adults on the jury, who have learned to equate consistency with truthfulness, it begins to sound as though he is making the story up.

A defense attorney doesn't have to be brutal, or even particularly devious, to tie a child witness up in knots. Most of them are not brutal at all, since browbeating a child on the witness stand is not likely to win points with the jury. If the lawyer is smart, his questions are gentle and patient, even kindly. "Now, Susie," the lawyer may begin, "tell me. Have you ever told a lie? Do you have a special word you use for a lie? Have you ever told any little lies? A big lie? What's the difference between a big lie and a little lie? What's the biggest lie you ever told? Have you ever told a lie where your mother didn't find out? If your best friend said please don't tell your mother about something, would you lie for your best friend? Did you ever do this? Did you get caught?" The answers to such questions are preordained. Not only are all children capable of lying, all children do lie, since lying is a natural part of being surrounded by adults who dispense punishment for infractions of their rules. But once it has been established that the child is capable of lying, the first seeds of doubt have been planted in the jurors' minds.

As recently as a year or two ago, lawyers who would even consider representing a defendant in a sexual abuse case either advised their clients to plead guilty before trial or offered at best a half-hearted defense. In the aftermath of Jordan and McMartin, however, many lawyers have reached the conclusion that child sexual abuse cases are "defensible," by which they mean that children can be intimidated and confused into withholding information, giving incorrect answers, or seeming untruthful when in fact they are not. Defending those accused of child abuse is now such a common practice that lawyers' organizations are even offering seminars on the fine points of how to confuse children and bamboozle jurors.

At one California seminar, a lawyer began by declaring that "children are insidious liars, and they're practiced liars. They are the best. They can lie at the drop of a hat." In order to effectively discredit a child, the lawyer went on, "you want to know about the child's history. You want to know about people who don't like the child. You want to know what those people have to say about the child — subpoena the school records. Then insist upon your right of confrontation, insist that you must be able to cross-examine this child in an adversarial atmosphere. That's what a trial is all about. I find that children do not have real good memories, and to show that these children do not have real good memories, I ask them about specific occurrences in their life, such as their birthday, Valentine's Day, and so forth. I ask them where they were and what they did on that day, and I try to show that they really don't know any of these things. Give wings to the child's imagination, if it's a young child especially. Be prepared to show through your cross-examination that the child has a vivid imagination, that it's very suggestible. Be prepared to lead the child into a situation that could not possibly occur. What you want to project is the feeling that this particular child cannot be trusted to tell the truth."

Another lawyer at the same seminar offered his colleagues advice on how to deal with the jury. "Get them to realize the tremendous task you have," he said. "It is imperative to humanize the defendant. Don't be afraid to pat the defendant on the back. Prepare the defendant for their scrutiny, and have his family and friends nearby. Reeducate the jurors. Remember, we are dealing with a media blitz on this subject." In the event that the jury appeared to believe the child anyway, a third lawyer said, all was not lost. A possible defense is simply the assertion that the defendant was intoxicated when the abuse took place. Another is to argue that a good-faith mistake has been made about the victim's age, as in the time-honored plea, "Well, Judge, she said she was eighteen . . ." A third is the "out-of-character defense" — to insist that, no matter what the child says, the defendant is not the sort of person who would ever harm a child.

When the California Public Defenders Association held a similar gathering in Los Angeles, the featured speaker was Brad Brunion, the lawyer who had represented Virginia McMartin, and who began his talk with a little joke. When a public defender is assigned a sexual abuse case, he said, "you look in your in-basket and go, 'Ick, what is this?' But if you're in private practice, there's a much more pristine approach. You wait until the check clears." Then Brunion offered his idea of a last-ditch defense. "Obviously, if you've got sexual intercourse, it's hard to say he didn't intend to gratify his lust, passion, etcetera," he said. "But if you have marginal-type acts like fondling, then you can put it into a context where it could be innocent. Changing the kid's wet pants can be a defense, if you've got nothing else."

Despite all the attention being paid by lawyers to the defense of those accused of child abuse, most child abusers never go to trial. In many cities it is not unusual for 90 or even 95 percent to plead guilty, and almost nowhere is the figure lower than 70 percent.[4] Assuming that a man or woman who is falsely accused of sexually abusing a child is more likely than not to fight the charges in court, such statistics say something about whether most children who claim to have been abused are telling the truth. In the aftermath of Jordan and McMartin, however, increasing numbers of defendants are choosing to take their chances with a jury, and many of those juries are becoming increasingly reluctant to convict.

Given the prevalence of child sexual abuse, a jury may contain at least one member who shares the defendant's sexual attraction to children, as happened in a sexual abuse case where the jurors were divided eleven to one in favor of conviction. "The jury is deliberating," the prosecutor said. "They're not coming back with a verdict. The case was pretty strong at trial, but still no verdict. So one day I get a phone call from the judge. He says, 'We have a note here that you need to consider.' I go to the courtroom. There is a note from the jury foreman, and the note says the following: 'Is it misconduct that one of the people on the jury says he feels that what the defendant did was no big deal because he regularly has sex with eleven- and twelve-year-old girls?'

"I look at that and I say, 'Oh, my God.' We have a hearing in chambers. The defense says that even if it's true it doesn't make any difference, because that doesn't necessarily mean the guy is a bad juror. When he said that, even the judge couldn't restrain himself from laughing. Then we called in the jury foreman. He says, 'Well, one day Joe was late to deliberations, and he said the reason he was late was that he had had some experience with a girl that day.' It turns out that in the neighborhood Joe lives in there are a lot of little girls who, if he gives them marijuana, will allow him to do anything he wants.

The next day the jury comes back with a note saying they're hopelessly deadlocked. I said, 'Your Honor, I think if we get rid of this juror we'll get a verdict.' He wouldn't do it. After the jury was excused I talked to all the jurors, and I heard the same story about Joe from other people."

Most jurors are not child molesters, but many still have an instinctive need to feel that intelligent, successful people like themselves wouldn't abuse a child. They may empathize with the children involved, but they identify with the adults. "The whole trouble," says Ken Freeman, "is that we are so frightened for our children and so horrified that these crimes exist that we'd rather think they don't." An Arizona prosecutor agrees. "I don't understand what juries want," she says. "You don't have fingerprints, you don't have a videotape of the crime. What it really boils down to is, given the word of a child versus the word of an adult, they're going to believe the adult." Her frustration, shared by many of her colleagues, is highlighted by recent research at the University of Denver in which adult jurors at a mock trial were asked to evaluate the relative credibility of testimony by children and adults. Though they later had trouble explaining why, the jurors found all the children to be less credible than the adults.

The question of whether children lie about being sexually abused is central, and it is difficult to find a prosecutor or judge who does not recall at least one case in which he thought the child was lying. But it is also their nearly universal opinion that children very rarely lie about sexual abuse and that young children almost never lie, and such opinions are supported by some empirical evidence. When researchers at a Boston hospital reviewed more than a hundred sexual abuse cases from the first accusation to the final disposition, they found that only 4 percent of the allegations were ultimately proven to be untrue. When sexual abuse claims by three hundred Denver children were studied in comparable detail, fewer than 2 percent turned out to have been fabricated.

In both studies, nearly all the false allegations had come from older teenage girls, and most prosecutors agree that the greatest likelihood of fabrication exists when a girl of fourteen or fifteen claims to have been abused, particularly by a stepfather, a mother's boyfriend, a teacher, or some other unrelated adult with whom her relationship is already strained. The specter of the malicious teenager who points her finger for revenge is disturbing, but such fabrications are not only few in number, they are usually easy to detect. Most children are awkward liars to begin with, and a child who can sustain a false accusation over weeks of interviews with police and prosecutors is probably seriously disturbed. Pathological liars are easy to spot, because they lie about everything.

If older children rarely lie about sexual abuse, it seems that younger children almost never do. It's not that they're incapable of lying — where is the child who hasn't made up a story about an invisible playmate or a talking pet? But most little children aren't malicious, and neither are the lies they tell. Their childish instinct is usually to trust everything and love everybody; it's simply not in their nature to make a malevolent, unprovoked accusation against an adult, especially one they know. Even those few children who might be so inclined are unable to lie convincingly about things with which they're unfamiliar. A teenage girl who makes a false accusation may have some firsthand knowledge of sex, and even if she doesn't she probably knows something about the mechanics involved. Younger children who don't have any firsthand knowledge cannot fool anyone for very long.

One idea that has been in vogue among defense lawyers is that all a child need do to acquire an encyclopedic knowledge of sodomy and intercourse is switch on the television when nobody's home and tune to the "porno channel." If such a channel exists, it is difficult to find. The closest thing to hard-core pornography on cable television is an occasional movie known as a "hard R," containing simulated sex. With the advent of videocassette recorders, adults can view the hardest-core pornographic films in their homes, and a few children may gain access to these in an unattended moment. But children who have seen graphic depictions of sexual intercourse can only describe sex from a visual perspective, and there is a vast difference between what sex looks like and what it feels like. A child who has glimpsed an erect penis on television cannot convincingly describe how it felt inside her mouth or her vagina, nor does a child who has merely watched an ejaculation know that semen tastes of salt.

Though false accusations in sexual abuse cases appear to be rare, most of those that are lodged come not from children but from adults, usually adults who have a vendetta of some sort against the person they're accusing. When young children lie, it is almost always because they have been coached by such an adult, often by a parent involved in a child-custody battle. As the divorce rate continues to rise, such fabrications appear to be rising along with it, but they are even easier to detect than lies told by teenagers. A child who has been taught to tell a story by rote can tell it in only one way. As soon as he is asked about extraneous details — "What color shirt did you say he was wearing?

Was it raining outside? Where was your dog while this was happening?" — he becomes hopelessly bogged down.

"I've had a couple of cases where a child would come in and go through this canned account of what happened," says a Minneapolis therapist. "But then you ask the child to slow down or something, and the kid gets all mixed up and has to go back to the very beginning, to make sure that the story gets straight. Anybody who has worked with sexually abused kids to any extent has a sense of when you can believe that this is a child's own account of what's happened and when this is something the child has been programmed to say."

To say that children rarely lie is not to say that they always tell the truth, only that most of them believe they're telling the truth. Children are more susceptible to confusion than adults, particularly when their questioner is consciously attempting to confuse them. But even when they're being questioned by a sympathetic therapist or prosecutor, some children will add improbable details to their stories. Children are highly suggestible, and most of them have learned that the way to get along in the world is to try to please everybody who's bigger than they are. That's one of the qualities that makes them vulnerable to being abused in the first place, but it means there is a danger that a child may supply the answers he thinks his questioner wants to hear.

Suggestibility becomes a particular problem when children testify a long time after the event. An eight-year-old who is recalling something that happened when he was four is much more amenable to suggestion than a child who is describing the events of the past week. Ironically, one of the special courtroom rules intended to make testifying easier on children, a rule that allows children to be asked the sort of leading questions that are forbidden for adult witnesses on direct examination, also makes it easier for the defense to create the impression that a child is being untruthful.

"What, if anything, did you do then?" is an example of a neutral question. Posed in a leading manner, the question becomes, "Did you run out of the house?" But when the question is really a statement of fact — "You ran out of the house, didn't you?" — it is clearly suggestive. A lawyer who says to an adult witness, "You ran out of the house, didn't you?" will surely be met with an objection from the other side. In the belief that children need to be helped along in their testimony, most courts allow both prosecution and defense to ask questions on direct examination that are leading. But the line between leading a witness and suggesting an answer is a fine one, and when the defense lawyer asks of Susie, "Isn't it true that your father was at work while this was happening?" Susie's childish desire to please him by agreeing may prompt her to say yes when the answer is really no.

The problem of suggestibility is raised long before the case comes to trial, and it may be exacerbated by the special status that is accorded some victims of sexual abuse. The moment the suspicion arises that a child has been abused, he is likely to become the object of a great deal of attention and concern. He finds himself surrounded by policemen, social workers, and other solicitous adults who are sensitive to his every mood and who hang on his every word. Like most sexual abuse victims, he probably feels profoundly ashamed, even humiliated, but he also feels important, valued, and needed. Above all else he feels powerful, and within his family and among his classmates he may even briefly become a kind of celebrity.

There is a danger that, in order to hold on to the unaccustomed attention, some children may embroider their accounts of having been abused. As with children who lie outright, such embroidery is sometimes easy to recognize. When a four-year-old Arkansas boy said he had been abused in a rowboat on a lake during a nursery school outing, police thought the story sounded plausible. But when the child said the rowboat had sunk and that he and his abuser had swum ashore, they reminded the boy that he didn't know how to swim. In cases where there is a single victim and a single abuser, the problem of suggestibility is minimal. When there is a single set of assertions from a single victim, they can easily be cross-checked against one another. The danger reaches its peak in "macro" sexual abuse cases, where there are several possible abusers and many victims telling complicated stories about many different instances of abuse.

Even in cases where many children have been abused by many adults, it is unlikely that every available child has been abused by every possible abuser. Most pedophiles tend to target children who are withdrawn and passive and less likely to resist, and they also have their favorites. One danger in macro abuse cases is that a child who is among those not abused at a day-care center or in some other communal setting will claim that he was abused. Though the child's initial instinct may be to tell the truth, he finds himself surrounded by adults who continue to ask him if he is sure that nothing happened. Those children who were abused, moreover, seem to be accorded some special status. Under repeated questioning, the child's suggestibility and his wish to please his questioners may combine to produce a bandwagon effect in which he finally says, "Me too."

If the result is that a defendant who abused ten children is charged with abusing eleven, the extra charge by itself is an injustice but probably not a major one — in for a penny, in for a pound. But what happens when the eleventh "victim" takes the witness stand to testify against the abuser? Because the story he tells isn't based on experience, he's an easy target for the defendant's lawyers, and when his story unravels during cross-examination, the jury can't help but wonder about the credibility of the ten other witnesses.

A corollary danger in such cases is that a child who has been abused may continue to add to his story until he is no longer useful as a witness. One California policeman recalled the case of a young girl who showed clear medical evidence of abuse, but whose story "just kept getting more and more fantastic, until she was talking about her teacher and her whole class standing out in the middle of the street naked. Our investigator said, 'Hey, wait a minute. I've been believing you up to now, but I think you're making this up.' At which point she admitted that maybe that part wasn't true, but that the part about the abuse was true. How in the hell do I put a kid like that on the witness stand?"

The greatest danger in macro cases, however, is that the child who exaggerates or lies — who introduces bizarre or otherwise improbable elements into his testimony that have not been mentioned by the other children — will cast serious doubt on the credibility of all the children, with the result that the entire case is dismissed as a fabrication on the part of the children.

In arguing that children have been "programmed" to testify against their clients, defense lawyers in sexual abuse cases often receive some unintended help from the victims' parents. If parents believe their child's story, they are understandably beside themselves. Though much of their anger is directed at their child's abuser, they probably reserve some of it for themselves, since they're the ones who hired the baby-sitter, or put their child in the day-care center, or unintentionally contributed in some other way to the abuse. It is not unusual for such parents to try to assuage their guilt by helping the police with their investigation. Because the child spends more time with his parents than with anyone else, there are many opportunities for the parents to go over the story again and again, to continue asking questions about how often the abuse occurred, what form it took, and who else was involved. Sometimes the parents' determination to "get" their child's abuser becomes a vendetta that consumes their lives.

The unfortunate result of parental involvement is often that the official investigation is muddled beyond repair. When another child at her daughter's preschool reported having been abused by a teacher, one worried mother took matters into her own hands. "I got out a Care Bear book that she'd gotten for Christmas," the woman recalled, "and I pretended to start reading her the story. But I didn't really read the story. I made up something to the effect that there were these two little girls, and they used to run and play together and have lots of fun. And then this bigger girl tried to become their friend, but the big girl was really only pretending to be nice, and she ended up hurting the little girls. And after about ten pages my daughter goes, 'Just like Marcia did to me and Tawny, huh, Mommy?' "

Sensing that she had a receptive audience, the child went on to name a dozen other children who had been similarly abused. Several other mothers were conducting the same sort of interrogation, and they formed a "support group" that met once a week to compare notes. When one of the mothers reported that her child had seen a rabbit killed by one of the teachers, all of the other mothers asked their children about the rabbit. Those children who said they hadn't seen any rabbit were reminded that someone had seen one, and before long five or six children were talking about dead rabbits. By the time the case got to the prosecutors, the children's stories had become so cross-fertilized that no charges could be brought.

Though prosecutors agree that intervention by parents is becoming a serious problem, defense allegations of "brainwashing" are less often made against parents than against the child therapists who have become a fixture of nearly every sexual abuse case. To listen to some defense lawyers, one would think the therapists were modern-day sorcerers who have the power to make children say that black is white. Most lawyers don't go quite that far, but many do suggest that some therapists at least begin with the preconception that children have been abused. "I think therapists, especially on the licensed marriage-and-family counselor level, are looking for child molestation and wanting to find it," a California attorney says.

Such expressions of concern strike a responsive chord among those who would rather not believe the stories being told by children, but the problem is more complex than that. It arises in large part because the therapist's task is not to get at the truth in a legal sense. That's the job of the police and prosecutors, who need information that can be admitted into evidence at a trial. Whether the questions that elicit that information are suggestive or coercive is as important to the police as how they are answered, but the therapists are most concerned with the therapeutic truth. "We're not interested in putting people in prison where I work," one therapist says. "We're interested in helping children cope with things that have happened to them."

In seeking the therapeutic truth, however, the therapists raise the potential for suggestibility to new heights. The nexus of the problem they face is that many children who have been sexually abused are reluctant to talk about it. Perhaps they're afraid of getting in trouble themselves or of getting their abusers in trouble, or maybe they've been threatened with revenge. Maybe they're just too embarrassed to talk about what happened. Whatever the reason, when a child initially denies having been abused, a responsible therapist must consider the possibility that he is lying — or, to use the clinical term, is in denial.

"A child who has been frightened into not talking about being abused," one therapist says, "will behave with the therapist the way he's been behaving with his parents and everybody else until then, like everything is just fine. The child has been living a lie, maybe for weeks or months, maybe for years. He's learned long ago how to act like everything is normal. He's not going to give that up just because he's talking to a therapist. When you have children that are this frightened, who have been in secrecy and denial about something for years, who run in the corner and tell you they never went to that school, you know you've got a problem."

To break through what may be the barrier of denial, the therapist asks questions that a court would term unduly suggestive. "You can ask children generalized questions like 'What, if anything, unpleasant ever happened to you when you were at that school?' and they are not going to give you anything," one therapist says. "My experience is that they will not tell you a thing unless they either are asked very directly or have some sense that you already know something." The therapist also defends the technique, which defense lawyers are quick to label suggestive, of reassuring a child that other children have already told her about being abused. "I'm trying to let Billy know that it's all right to talk to me," the therapist says, "that all his friends have told me stuff and nothing happened to them, that they're fine, their parents are fine. It's a problem with the defense, of course."

The overriding dilemma, which is best illustrated by the Jordan and McMartin cases but is also now becoming a factor in most sexual abuse cases, is whether therapists should be used as part of a police and prosecution team. Many therapists are used in just this way, primarily because they are mostly women, while most police officers and prosecutors are men who feel less comfortable with children. Apart from the problems posed by legitimate therapeutic techniques, it is also the case that many who enter clinical social work or clinical psychology, the two professions from which most therapists are drawn, bring with them a bias in favor of victims. Not a few therapists have had troubled childhoods themselves, and for them their work is a means of exorcising their own experiences.

Even if they were not themselves abused as children, social workers in particular tend to be highly empathetic people. When they are confronted with what appears to be the mistreatment of children, their first response is often to begin building a case against the abuser rather than to sort through the objective facts in an evenhanded effort to establish what really happened to whom. When California attorney general John Van de Kamp examined the failed prosecution of the Bakersfield "Satanic" case, he reserved the largest measure of criticism for a social worker–cum–therapist, attached to the county's Child Protective Services agency, who "contributed greatly to the confusion and unprofessionalism surrounding the case by assuming the role of criminal rather than civil investigator."

Having discovered the multitude of difficulties in bringing a child sexual abuse case to court, prosecutors are beginning to back away from cases that are not open-and-shut. Most likely to come to trial are those cases in which the defendant is accused of abusing unrelated children and also has a previous conviction — in other words, a hard-core pedophile. Less likely to reach a courtroom are cases in which the complaining witness is under the age of five or over the age of twelve. Least likely of all are those in which the defendant is a woman, because of the difficulty of convincing jurors that women are capable of abusing children sexually. The degree of prosecutorial reluctance varies from state to state, even from county to county. "If you go to one place in the state," an Illinois therapist says, "there's an eager state's attorney who wants to 'get them all' and is realistic about his chances of that. You go to another place and he wants nothing to do with these cases, because he firmly believes that kids are just making it up and will back out at the last minute."

One prosecutor who wants to "get them all" is Don Weber, the state's attorney for Madison County, Illinois. "Every once in a while," Weber says, "some case will crop up in the newspapers — a nursery school, a schoolteacher. Then, three or four months later, the district attorney says, sort of sheepishly, 'Well, there's not enough evidence here, the girls were obviously put up to this,' and the case is dismissed. I think what's going on around the country, and it's very alarming, is that prosecutors are filing these charges and they expect it to be just like anything else, and then there's this uproar in the community. They decide they can't take the heat, and they figure the path of least resistance is not to prosecute. It's a very serious problem. You have to do this or you have to go get another job, because there's no place in this type of prosecution for weak-kneed yellowbellies."

No matter how determined a prosecutor may be, he is a prisoner of the system that prepares and presents him with such cases. In many places, that system is seriously flawed. In theory, whenever a child reports having been sexually abused, a number of agencies are alerted — the receiving hospital, one or more police departments, the state child protection bureau, the county family services agency, and perhaps a child counseling center. In a few cities, the management of sexual abuse cases is handled by integrated teams of highly trained specialists who have years of combined experience in interviewing and treating child victims. But the recognition of child sexual abuse as a major crime is so new that most agencies lack such training, experience, and coordination, and even the best of them is likely to be understaffed.

In Seattle, which has led the rest of the nation for years in acknowledging the scope and seriousness of child sexual abuse, there are still only eight prosecutors assigned to review 650 cases a year. Indianapolis, which files about eight hundred felony sexual abuse charges annually, has only seven, and in Denver there are only two prosecuting attorneys assigned exclusively to try such cases. Las Vegas has none, and though they often have more than their share of sexual abuse cases, neither do most smaller and middle-sized district attorney's offices. Police departments are equally shorthanded. In 1983, San Diego had nine officers assigned to investigate allegations of child sexual abuse, about the right number for a department that was opening thirty new cases a month. Over the next two years, the number of new cases rose to more than a hundred a month, but the number of officers assigned to handle them remained the same.

The problems faced by prosecutors and police are minimal compared to those encountered by the social workers — or, as they now prefer to be called, child protection workers. For an average starting salary of twelve thousand dollars a year, less than most dogcatchers or bus drivers earn, child protection workers subject themselves to a daily stream of battered, starving, and sexually abused children and do battle with a formidable bureaucracy at the same time. CP workers in some states must complete a dozen different forms after visiting a family with three children, and the average worker has a minimum of thirty such families on her case list.

In many cities the CP worker carries twice that number of cases. If she sees each family twice a month, that means she must fill out more than fourteen thousand pieces of paper every year. If she takes any serious action, such as removing a child from his family, the number of forms rises exponentially. With the long hours, low pay, red tape, and personal anguish that such work involves, it is not surprising that nearly every child protection agency is dangerously understaffed. "I'm not allowed to do real social work anymore," one Los Angeles worker says. "You can't go out and see ten children and just say hello and goodbye." Says another, "You just hold your breath and hope nothing will recur."

When the police officers, prosecutors, and caseworkers who face such pressures are handed yet another sexual abuse case to investigate, the chances are improving that the interviewing and other preparation will be less than complete. On top of that, even the best prosecutors and caseworkers burn out after a few years, and their replacements must begin the initiation process all over again. As appears to have happened in the case of Brian Taugher, it is because so many of those assigned to investigate sexual abuse cases are so harried or have such limited experience that so many recent prosecutions appear to have gone wrong.

Taugher, a senior staff lawyer in the California state attorney general's office, was separated from his wife, and the couple's two daughters were spending the day with their father. The sixteen-year-old was content to stay by the backyard pool, so Taugher and his nine-year-old daughter, Kathy, climbed into the car and headed for the beaches south of San Francisco. When they started home the sun had set, and by the time they arrived, Kathy had fallen asleep in the backseat. Thinking that it would be easier to carry the girl to her bed without having to fumble for his keys, Taugher left her in the car while he went to open the front door. As he unlocked the door, the telephone rang, unusual at that hour. The caller was the mother of one of Kathy's friends. "I'm very upset," the woman began, her voice rising with every word, "and I need to talk to you about something. You have molested my daughter. I want to know why you did this to my child."

As it turned out, the call had been placed at the suggestion of the Sacramento County sheriff's department, which was recording the conversation from the woman's house and which had already dispatched a car full of deputies to the Taugher residence. By the time Brian Taugher had hung up and headed back to the car to retrieve his daughter, the deputies were waiting outside with a warrant for his arrest and a pair of handcuffs. Locked in the backseat of a patrol car, Brian Taugher was taken to the sheriff's department for booking and fingerprinting; Kathy and her sister spent the night at the county children's home. Before the girls were allowed to go to sleep, they were examined by a doctor and questioned about whether their father had ever "touched" them. Both said he had not.

The arrest of an assistant attorney general on child molesting charges is not an everyday event, and by sunup camera crews from the local television stations had staked out Taugher's front yard. When those who knew Brian Taugher turned on their television sets that morning, they were astonished at what they saw and heard. Taugher had seemed a model of the bright, young professional on the way up, a first-rate lawyer with an important job in state government and a second career teaching law school at night. But there was something else that set Brian Taugher apart from the thousands of men and women charged with sexually abusing children during 1984. In his role as a top aide to attorney general John Van de Kamp, Taugher had drafted legislation to strengthen California's sexual abuse reporting laws.

Suspended from his sixty-two-thousand-dollar-a-year job, Taugher hired the best criminal lawyer he could find and prepared to stand trial against his ten-year-old accuser. According to the story the girl told police, the incident in question had taken place a couple of weeks before, following Kathy Taugher's ninth birthday party. The party hadn't been anything special, just a swim in the backyard pool and a treasure hunt, followed by hot dogs and a birthday cake and the unwrapping of presents. When the cake and hot dogs were gone, three of the girls went home, leaving the five others to spend the night in sleeping bags in Taugher's living room. Four of the five had spread their bags out on the floor. The fifth, several months older than the others and tall for her age, had rolled her sleeping bag out on the sofa. It was sometime during the night, the girl said, that a naked Brian Taugher had walked into the living room, unzipped her sleeping bag, pulled up her nightgown, and lain down on top of her. Their genitals had touched, but Taugher hadn't moved or spoken, nor had he tried to have intercourse with her. She was sure he hadn't had an orgasm.

The girl knew about intercourse and orgasm, she explained to the court, because she had recently received a fairly detailed lecture about sex from her mother that even included learning to learn to spell *penis* and *vagina*. After about five minutes, the girl said, Taugher got up and went away. When morning came, the group had breakfast and went for a last swim before being picked up by their parents, but the girl who had slept on the sofa said nothing to anyone about having been sexually abused. Nor would she for several days, until she told her mother while riding in the car that "Brian hurt me." The woman took her daughter to the family doctor, who thought he thought he saw some bruising near her vagina. As he was required to do under the California law that Brian Taugher himself had drafted, the doctor advised the Department of Social Services that one of his patients might have been sexually abused.

As Taugher's trial proceeded it became clear that, apart from the girl's testimony, the prosecution's case was hugely circumstantial. What had seemed to the doctor to be bruises on the girl's thighs proved upon further examination to be normal skin discoloration. Laboratory tests had found no trace of semen or pubic hair on the girl's nightgown or sleeping bag. None of the other girls who had been sleeping a few feet away could remember seeing or hearing anything. All that remained was the girl's testimony, and when she told the jury her story she did it in what some of those who attended the trial thought was a rather matter-of-fact way. When the girl was asked during cross-examination why she hadn't called for help, she was unable to answer, and something about the girl's description of the assault bothered Brian Taugher's lawyer enough that he decided to reconstruct the scene right there in the courtroom.

The lawyer, Michael Sands, had the sofa from Taugher's living room trundled into court, and on top of it he laid the girl's quilted blue sleeping bag. Then he invited the members of the jury to reenact the crime. Diane McKenzie, the jury foreman, played the part of the girl, with a juror named Darold Bott taking Taugher's role. Taugher stood six feet two inches tall, and Bott quickly discovered that, because the sofa's armrests were so high, there was no way someone as tall as that could lie down without bending his legs upward at the knees. In order to keep from falling over, a tall man in that position would have to support himself with one hand, which left only the other hand to unzip the sleeping bag. No matter how many times Bott tried to unzip the bag one-handed, he never could. "We tried it over and over again," he said later. "Her story just didn't stand up." Before the reenactment, at least two jurors had been dead-set for conviction, but now even they agreed the equation had been changed. There had been no way, they said later, that they could have found the defendant guilty beyond a reasonable doubt. Almost six months to the day after his arrest, Brian Taugher was acquitted.

Mike Sands didn't blame the girl as much as he blamed the prosecutors, the police, and the Department of Social Services for what he considered to have been a hasty and inadequate investigation.

The police, Sands said, had arrested his client not only without any corroborating evidence, but without even interviewing him about the girl's accusations. They had misinterpreted the initial medical evidence, and they hadn't taken particular pains to reconcile the discrepancies in the girl's statements. "She began to complain about Brian Taugher hurting her, and very possibly being pregnant," Sands recalled. "But from her description of what Brian Taugher did to her, she said she knew she couldn't be pregnant. Other statements she made were really inconsistent — she kept saying, 'Well, I think he did this, but I'm not sure.' She was very equivocal. We had all the girls who were in the same room testify. One of them woke up in the middle of the night and heard the alleged victim snoring. Those who had awakened in the middle of the night never saw Brian. They were asleep in the middle of the floor — he would have had to walk around them, or past them, to somehow get over to the couch."

There were other flaws in the official investigation, among them the fact that the sheriff's department had never checked the doctor's records to find out when the first complaint was made. But as it turned out, the biggest flaw of all had been the failure of the prosecutors and the police to reenact the abuse themselves before Mike Sands did it for them in court. "Once they knew they were dealing with somebody who was a high-ranking official of the Department of Justice, they rushed it faster than they should have," Sands said. "Then once they made the arrest, it hit every news media in town. If they had dismissed it, it would have been political suicide for the DA."

John Van de Kamp, the state attorney general and Brian Taugher's boss, said later that the Taugher case had been "a paradigm of how not to handle such cases." If the prosecution had done its job properly, he said, the case would never have come to trial. Twenty-seven thousand dollars in debt to his lawyer, Brian Taugher got his old job back and resigned himself to living with the indelible stain the experience had left on his reputation. "There are two crimes in America, treason and child molestation, that affect a person for the rest of his life," he said. "I will just have to deal with it."

Probably because of his background, Taugher was more sanguine than another in his situation might have been. Child abuse, he said, remained "one of the most heinous of all crimes. We didn't find child abuse when it was there, but now we are in danger of finding it when it is not there." A child abuse investigation that "boxes a child into pursuing a false accusation does as much harm to the child as to the person falsely accused," he said. "We owe it to ourselves to have the benefit of a full investigation before we start throwing charges around."

TEN
Justice

YOU'RE SEVEN YEARS OLD, and you're about to testify in court. The courtroom is the biggest room you've ever seen. Way up high, above everyone else, there's a man wearing a black robe. He has a hammer in his hand. If you make him mad, will he hit you with it? As you climb the steps to the witness stand, you're at the second highest place in the courtroom. When a policeman with a badge and a gun walks over, you wonder whether you've done something wrong. Is he going to arrest you and put you in jail? Instead, the policeman tells you to put your hand on a Bible while you repeat some words. When you sit down and look around, the person who abused you is right there in front of you, and he doesn't look very happy. Is he going to jump up and hurt you?

Unless you're an incest victim, your parents are sitting in the audience behind him, and behind them are dozens of people you don't know. Some of them look mad too; they must be friends of the person who abused you. A few of them seem to be paying close attention to what's going on, and they're writing in little notebooks. Depending on what state you're in, there may even be a television camera at the back of the courtroom. Off to one side sits a lady with a funny-looking typewriter and a thing stuck in her ear. Maybe that's the machine that tells whether or not you're lying. Two more policemen with guns are standing by the back door. Are they supposed to shoot you if you try to make a run for it? Which by now is exactly what you feel like doing.

"You'll have an eight- or nine-year-old who'll come into court," says Ken Freeman, a Los Angeles prosecutor who has tried more than a hundred sexual abuse cases, "and they'll be very, very nervous, rocking back and forth and fidgeting, and their mouth will be dry. I'll say, 'Susie, do you see your dad in the courtroom?' She'll say yes. I'll say, 'Point him out,' and she kind of looks the other way and timidly points to the man. Well, I say, 'Was there ever a time when you were alone with your dad and something happened?' She'll nod, and the judge will say, 'You have to say yes or no.' She'll start to get nervous, and she'll say yes. Then she'll start to cry. It's not just having to say something embarrassing — it's not just being in the courtroom, it's not just the public looking at them. They're terrified of the defendant. The kids have this feeling that here is this all-powerful individual, and they feel that somehow retribution is going to visit them if they testify."

The American judicial system traces its roots back to the thirteenth century and the Magna Carta, and in safeguarding the rights of adults accused of crimes, it has worked rather well. But neither the English noblemen who gathered in the meadow at Runnymede nor the framers of the Constitution envisioned a day when large numbers of children would be accusing adults of serious crimes.

When children commit crimes, their cases are usually heard by juvenile judges in courtrooms that are closed to the public. Until recently, however, no special considerations have been available to children who are the victims of crime. In response to a growing public pressure to "do something" about child sexual abuse, state legislatures have been searching for ways to make it easier for the victims of sexual abuse to testify against their abusers. During 1985 alone, more than 250 bills proposing some kind of judicial reform were introduced by legislators across the country. Though some of the reforms seem well advised, others have been conceived in anger and adopted in haste. Because many of them tend to confer an advantage on the prosecution, they involve potentially dangerous tinkering with the switches and dials of the Constitution.

As Oliver Wendell Holmes, Jr., once observed, "It is revolting to have no better reason for a rule of law than that it was laid down in the time of Henry IV. It is still more revolting if the grounds upon which it was laid down have vanished." Holmes might have been speaking of the need for a special hearing to assess the competence of young witnesses, a need that is called into question by new evidence that young children are often better able than adults to recall the details of recent events. When researchers at Atlanta's Emory University asked a group of adults and children to watch a videotaped basketball game, they instructed the audience to pay particular attention whenever the players passed the ball to one another. Midway through the game, a woman carrying an open umbrella strolled casually down the sideline. Afterward, none of the adults who had been watching the ball could remember either the woman or the umbrella. But a quarter of the nine-year-olds and three-quarters of the six-year-olds could.

Though fewer than half the states have taken such a step, in those where special competency requirements have been abolished, young children have given testimony that is more than adequate. "Three-year-olds are capable of giving you evidence which is useful," says Terry O'Brien, a Wyoming judge, "in spite of the fact that they may not know what an oath is and they may not know what telling the truth is. Most kids, unless they're very, very young, understand an obligation to be truthful. And even if they don't, that doesn't trouble me very much, because of the ability of the jury to assess that."

Another judge, Milwaukee's Charles Schudson, recalls a case in which he decided not to hold a competency hearing even though the principal witnesses were three, four, and six years old. "The three-year-old really was not responsive at all," Schudson said, "but I didn't declare that witness incompetent. I just let him go up there and do the best he could. With the four-year-old, the defense attorney took out a picture of a dog and said, 'What is this?' And the child said, 'That's a doggie.' He asked the child, 'What color are my shoes?' and this sort of thing. Those are the kinds of examinations that would have been used in a prerequisite competency state. They weren't being used in that way, but it was still proper. The four-year-old was able to say something, but not a whole lot.

"The six-year-old was crucial, the six-year-old was a key witness, and despite the fact that he gave some incorrect answers on the questions about colors and animals, and despite the fact that he said he didn't know the difference between what was true and what was false, I allowed him to testify. He did fine. Well, he did fine once I put him on his daddy's lap. He wouldn't say a thing when he was in the cold, hard chair and the father was in the courtroom just a few feet away. When he was clamming up, I just said, 'I'll bet you'd feel a lot better if you were on Daddy's lap.' The father wasn't involved in the case in any way. So he got on his dad's lap and described what he'd seen the baby-sitter do to his two little brothers. He did great."

Many of the attempts to facilitate the prosecution of child abusers have taken the form of new laws, but some have come in the form of appellate decisions that broaden the interpretation of existing statutes. On the theory that the prosecution's best weapon is a confident witness, most of the reforms are aimed at reducing the rigors of cross-examination for children. In some states, judges have been empowered to place limits on how long the cross-examination of children can go on. In others, they have been authorized to control the way in which questions are asked of children by the defense. Some states permit questions to be directed to the child through the judge, and other jurisdictions allow a parent or another trusted adult to take the witness stand along with the child. In a small but growing number of states, adults are even permitted to testify in behalf of a child who has told them about having been sexually abused.

Testimony about what one person tells another is called hearsay, and it is almost never admissible as evidence. Because hearsay statements aren't made in court and under oath, they are considered inherently unreliable. Perhaps the person who made the statement was mistaken, or wasn't telling the truth. Perhaps the person who heard the statement misunderstood it or has forgotten what was really said. Because it is next to impossible for a judge and jury to assess such pitfalls, only in two very special cases is hearsay testimony ordinarily admitted into evidence.

When one person tells another that he has committed a crime, the second person will usually be allowed to testify about the conversation. It's not likely that a person would lie about committing a crime or confess to one by mistake, and such concerns are overwhelmed by the potential significance of the statement. The other hearsay exception, known as an excited utterance, includes statements made by the victim of a crime that has just been committed. Declarations like "I've been robbed!" are considered likely to be true, because a person who is speaking during or immediately after a traumatic event is presumed not to have had the time or presence of mind to make something up. Those who overhear excited utterances and testify about them later are known as outcry witnesses.

The first hearsay exception doesn't play much part in sexual abuse cases, since most abusers don't often admit to others that they have sex with children. The second exception is more germane. If a child runs from a public restroom crying, "Mama, that man just touched me," the child's mother can testify, under the excited utterance exception, to having heard the statement. Time, however, is of the essence. The mother whose child arrives home from school and tells of having been abused by a teacher earlier in the day does not qualify as an outcry witness. It may be the first statement the child has made to anyone about the abuse, but it's already several hours old. Since an excited utterance by definition is one that happens at the moment, outcry witnesses are rarely available in sexual abuse cases. But in an attempt to plug what many prosecutors and judges now see as a crucial loophole, at least nine states have broadened the definition of an excited utterance to include statements made later by the victim. Similar proposals are awaiting action in several other states, and in a few, including Wisconsin, the hearsay exclusion has been broadened by judicial decisions.

The state with one of the broadest hearsay exceptions is Washington, which allows the admission of any testimony about a child's statements as long as the child is under ten and the circumstances under which the statement was made suggest that it is true. Robert Lasnik, a Seattle prosecutor who helped draft the Washington law, recalls a case in which a child told her mother and father while they were cooking dinner about having been abused some days before. "The little girl, who's three, says, 'Mommy, does milk come out of Daddy's penis?' " Lasnik said. "And the mother says, 'Well, no, why do you ask?' And the girl says, 'Well, it comes out of Uncle Joe's penis, and it tastes yucky.' " Because it had been a week since Uncle Joe last visited the family, the child's statement was not technically an excited utterance, but the Washington statute permitted the child's parents to testify anyway about what their daughter had said.

In most states where they are allowed at all, such "extended outcry" witnesses can be used only to buttress the courtroom testimony of the alleged victim. But in Washington, Texas, and a few other states, they can be used in place of the victim under certain circumstances. In the El Paso day-care case mentioned in chapter 6, the only prosecution witnesses to testify against the two defendants were the parents of the children who had been abused, the doctor who examined them, and the social worker who interviewed them. Because such broad hearsay exceptions make it possible to convict someone of child abuse entirely on the basis of secondhand evidence and testimony, they raise serious constitutional questions about whether a criminal defendant's Sixth Amendment right "to be confronted with the witnesses against him" and to question them through an attorney is being abridged.

Most of the attempts at judicial reform are intended to ease the sexual abuse victim's burden of testifying in court. But for many victims, the journey through the criminal justice system can be an ordeal that matches, and sometimes even surpasses, the abuse itself. The ordeal begins the moment the child tells someone about having been abused, and even under the best of circumstances the victim may be required to tell her story not once but several times — first to her parents, then to the doctor, then to the police, the child protection worker, the prosecutor, and finally a therapist. If there are delays, misunderstandings, and all the other confusions that result from overwork and a lack of coordination, she may have to repeat the process again and again. When discrepancies are noticed between the story the child gave the police and the version she told the prosecutors, both ask her to tell it over. When the prosecutors see that she's told her therapist something she forgot to tell them, back she goes to the courthouse for another interview.

It is not unusual for sexual abuse victims to be interviewed dozens of times before the date for the first courtroom appearance finally arrives. Even then, few children testify only once. Two child witnesses in one California sexual abuse case testified on fifty-five separate occasions, not including investigative interviews, motion hearings, and juvenile proceedings. "These children," the prosecutor said later, "have been victimized twice, first by their parents, who now are in prison, and secondly by a system that forces them to undergo — hour after hour, day after day — grueling cross-examination concerning their molestation. They become passive and zombielike whenever they are asked to recall the acts of abuse they have suffered. The bottom line is, we just can't put these kids on the stand again."

Only a year or so ago, the use of videotape was being heralded as the solution to the problem of multiple interviews and repetitive testimony for such witnesses. Children who could not testify effectively in open court, it was thought, might be able to do so in front of a television camera; the resulting tapes would not only be available for reference by other members of the investigative team, they could also be shown to the grand jury, at a preliminary hearing, and again to the judge and jury at trial. It seemed a promising idea. The child's story would be permanently recorded, so there should be no subsequent misunderstanding of what had been said. The story would be told in the child's own words, not by an extended outcry witness to whom the child had reported being abused. And the child would be spared the rigors of cross-examination in the defendant's presence.

The use of videotape is currently authorized in fourteen states, but the statutes that permit it vary widely. In an effort to comply with the demands of the Sixth Amendment, some states require that the defendant be present when the tape is made, though "out of sight and sound" of the child witness. Others leave it up to the defendant to decide whether to be present or not. A few go so far as to preclude a face-to-face confrontation when the defendant's alleged treatment of the child has involved torture or extreme brutality. In some states a

videotaped deposition can be used instead of live testimony only at a
pretrial hearing. In others it can also be used at the trial itself, if the
judge decides that appearing in person would cause the victim
substantial psychological harm. In Texas, where one of the first
authorizing statutes was passed, videotape is admissible only if the
child witness in question is otherwise competent and is available to
testify should he or she be called by the defense.

Videotape may make things easier on children, but it does not
guarantee a conviction, as a Connecticut prosecutor discovered during
the 1985 trial of a thirty-three-year-old woman charged with abusing a
four-year-old neighborhood girl. Instead of seeing and hearing the girl
herself, the jurors in the case watched a tape of the child answering
questions, through a mouthful of cracker crumbs, from the defendant's
lawyer. The tape had been made a week earlier, after the judge had
concluded that testifying in person would impose an undue psychological burden on the child. The judge was present at the taping, as
were his clerk and the prosecutor — but not the defendant, who was
watching the proceedings on a television monitor in another room
while communicating with her lawyer over the telephone. "Are we
watching a movie?" the woman's lawyer asked while the tape was being
played in court. "Or are we here for justice? This child knows she's in
the movies. It's just like 'Sesame Street.' " His objection that the
defendant's Sixth Amendment rights had been violated was overruled
by the judge, but the woman was acquitted anyway.

Because so many important legal questions remain unresolved,
even in those states where videotaped testimony is authorized, it is not
used nearly as often as it might be. Some prosecutors are afraid that
whatever convictions they obtain will be overturned on appeal, while
others believe that a televised picture of a child lacks the emotional
impact on jurors of seeing and hearing the child himself. Some also
point out that, because such tapes are often made fairly early in the
case, at a time when many children are not yet fully forthcoming about
having been abused, the portrait they present to the jury can be a less
than convincing one. Still others, watching the McMartin case
unfold, have grown concerned that tapes made by child therapists may
lend support to charges of brainwashing leveled by the defense.

In hopes of satisfying the Constitution's requirements while
minimizing the trauma to the child witness and also circumventing the
brainwashing problem, a few states have approved an arrangement,
like the one used in the Bronx day-care case and also briefly at the end
of the McMartin hearing, in which children of a certain age are able

to testify over live, closed-circuit television. The technique was tried for the first time in mid-1984, in the case of Campbell Hugh Greenup, the principal of an exclusive private elementary school in a Los Angeles suburb, who was charged with sexually abusing eight of his students, all girls, the youngest of them age five. The children and their parents sat not in the courtroom where Greenup's preliminary hearing was taking place, but in an empty jury room next door. In the jury room were two television monitors, one showing the general courtroom scene and another that displayed either Ken Freeman, the prosecutor, or Greenup's lawyer, depending on which one was asking the questions. A monitor perched on the witness stand in the courtroom showed the face of the child who was testifying.

"It's never easy to testify," Freeman said after Greenup had been ordered to stand trial. "But we had kids who would never have been able to make it in a normal courtroom situation. I talked to one child later and said, 'Well, what did you think?' and she said, 'I was so happy I didn't have to go and sit in that chair.' It was so scary to her, and she was a seven-year-old."

Like videotape, however, closed-circuit television is no guarantee of success — a mistrial was declared in the Greenup case when the jury could not agree on a verdict. When Greenup was retried the following year Freeman abandoned the closed-circuit television setup, in hopes that the children who had survived the first trial had probably gained enough confidence to testify effectively in person at the second one. He was right — after hearing five months of testimony from more than 140 witnesses, the second jury took only two hours to convict Campbell Hugh Greenup of sexually abusing six of his former students. Greenup was sentenced to thirty-six years in prison, the maximum possible, by a judge who condemned the man for having violated his "sacred trust" as a teacher. "You put parents in the situation of not believing their children," the judge said.

Campbell Greenup waived his right to confront his accusers face-to-face, but not all defendants are willing to make it easier for children to testify against them. Most defense lawyers, in fact, have continued to argue that anything that diminishes their ability to fully and fairly cross-examine a live witness before a judge or jury, whether it is a piece of videotape, a television monitor, a hearsay witness, or a child sitting on his mother's lap, abridges the defendant's constitutional rights. The ultimate arbiter of efforts to reform the judicial process is the United States Supreme Court, and none of these innovations has yet passed the Court's final test. The Supreme Court, in fact, hasn't had much to say about the Sixth Amendment in quite some time. Most of its landmark decisions in the realm of criminal procedure have concerned such things as a defendant's right to legal counsel and the circumstances under which a suspect's home and automobile may be searched.

No one suggests that the right to cross-examination includes the right to intimidate or frighten any witness. But is the constitutional requirement satisfied when a defendant watches his lawyer question a child on television? Is it satisfied by questioning the person to whom the child reported having been abused? Or is a defendant entitled to a verdict from a jury that has had the opportunity to gauge the nuances of his accuser's testimony firsthand? Sooner or later, the Court will have to decide precisely what confrontation and cross-examination must entail when the accuser is a frightened child, and it is hard to imagine even the current Court agreeing to anything that involves more than a token surrender of Sixth Amendment rights by one accused of a crime.[1] If that proves to be the case, then the movement toward procedural reforms in child sexual abuse cases will have been dealt a fatal blow.

Criminal defense lawyers understandably oppose the reform of hearsay laws and other new statutes that give judges greater authority to ease the burden of young witnesses. The American Bar Association, which has never been entirely representative of its rank and file, not only endorses such reforms but has proposed some of its own. One of the ABA's proposals involves an extension of the statute of limitations in crimes involving the abuse of children. At the moment, the limitations on reporting sexual abuse vary from place to place. Victims in Illinois must speak out within three years, but California gives them six years, and in most other states they have five. The problem, according to an ABA resolution adopted in 1985, is that "children who suffer sexual abuse are often quite reluctant to report their victimization. They are frequently likely to repress these incidents for years. The statute of limitations in criminal cases usually begins running on the day the crime was committed. In many cases, the statute may have expired by the time the abuse has come to light, and it is thus impossible to bring the accused offender to justice."

The best argument for extending the statute of limitations is a case in the small Northern California town of Quincy, where the district attorney was unable to act after several children accused the county sheriff of having abused them seven years before. "The crimes were serious," the prosecutor said later. "The evidence is strong enough that if it weren't for the statute of limitations I would prosecute, and the likelihood of felony convictions would be quite high." Another rationale is that abusers whose victims wait too long to speak up will be free to abuse again. But there is a danger that a child who makes an accusation years after the fact may not remember important details about who did what to whom. There is also the more fundamental question of why someone who abuses a child should be held answerable for ten or even twenty years after the fact, when the longest period of accountability for most other serious crimes is five years.

The statute of limitations is intended to moderate the already enormous prosecutorial power of the state by denying the prosecutors the ability to reach very far backward into history. Such important safeguards should not be easily tossed away, and the current effort to make those who sexually abuse children into a special class of criminal also overlooks the fact that many judges have difficulty in knowing what to do with such offenders even after they are convicted.

When Theodore Francis Frank was committed to California's Atascadero State Hospital, his sentence appeared to be an enlightened one. Rather than running for a certain number of years, it would expire when a panel of psychiatrists decided that Frank had been "rehabilitated." With his gray beard and bushy gray hair, Frank could have passed for a university professor, and to the staff at Atascadero he seemed to be a model patient. Unlike most of the child abusers there, he didn't try to deny his guilt or to blame his victims for having led him on. He readily described himself as a "good, clean child molester," and he acknowledged having abused more than 150 children. The admission went a long way toward convincing hospital officials that Frank had come to terms with his problem, and finally that he had conquered it altogether.

When Theodore Frank was released with a clean bill of mental health, his case was cited as an example of the legislative wisdom behind California's Mentally Disordered Sex Offender statute, the law that made such indeterminate sentences possible. Six weeks after he walked through Atascadero's front gate, Frank kidnapped a two-year-old girl named Amy Sue Seitz, tied her up, forced her to drink beer, raped her, tore off her nipples with a pair of pliers, then slowly strangled her to death. While the police were searching for Amy Sue's killer, Frank kidnapped, raped, and tortured two other young girls. When he was arrested, police found a diary in his Southern California apartment that was filled with fantasies of torture, rape, and murder — fresh fantasies composed since his release from Atascadero. "Children, made to order outlet for my anger and sex," Frank had written. "Innocent, trusting, scared, vulnerable, and submissive. I want to give pain to these little children. I want to molest them. I want to be sadistic. I want to harm them."

Stephen Lawrence Boatwright never killed or tortured any of the children he abused. "I loved every one of them," he told the judge, and most of the parents who dropped their children off at the Reno day-care center where he worked agreed that Boatwright had been an outstanding teacher. Though he was thirty-five and had served a hitch in the Air Force, Boatwright admitted to the doctors who examined him that he had never felt comfortable around adults. He hadn't been successful at much of anything, in fact, until his mother, who owned the center, gave him a job. For the first time he could remember, Boatwright felt like a capable, competent human being.

When Boatwright said he had never meant to harm the children, the doctors believed him, and the children agreed that he had always asked their permission before he touched them. Even the prosecutor in his case acknowledged that "sick as he may have been, he actually loved the children in his own way. He never threatened the kids, never told them not to tell anybody. He was very loving toward them, as opposed to people that show acts of violence to kids and say, 'This is going to happen to you or your parents if you don't cooperate.' " After his conviction, Boatwright plunged into an acute depression. He understood that he could not be allowed to remain free, but he asked the court to send him someplace where he could get help, and the three doctors who examined Boatwright endorsed his appeal. "He had some things going for him that many pedophiles don't have: a strong sense of conscience and a young, malleable personality that was essentially still unsocialized," one said. Boatwright got four life terms in prison, but he didn't get any help. As his lawyer put it later, the psychotherapy available at the Nevada state pen is "somewhere between slim and none."

Whether Stephen Boatwright's sentence seems overly harsh or not harsh enough, he is clearly an exception, because the sentences handed out to child abusers have traditionally been quite lenient. In many states, those convicted of sexually abusing children, particularly their own children, have received lighter sentences than those who rape other adults. A typical case is that of a young Colorado couple who pleaded guilty to sexually abusing an eight-year-old neighborhood girl. The husband assumed the role of abuser, while his wife prepared the girl by giving her liquor and dressing her in one of her own frilly blouses, then cleaned her up after her husband had finished.

As the moment arrived for the court to pass sentence, a Baptist minister appeared to testify that the husband had begun attending Bible study sessions since his arrest. He was "truly penitent," the minister said, "very sorry about it happening, not just sorry he was caught." A clinical psychologist who had seen the couple a dozen times testified that stress due to marital difficulties and financial problems was what had really triggered the abuse. But the couple's relationship had been improving, and he predicted that the husband was "not at all likely" to repeat his behavior. "He is deeply remorseful about his conduct and the harm he has done to the children he molested," the psychologist intoned. "I do not believe incarceration would benefit society or the victims of this offense."

The expert testimony was not lost on the judge, who sentenced the couple to twenty days in the county jail, to be followed by two years' probation. Shortly after their release, the couple left town and transferred their probation to their new home in Texas. "Most people say, 'Well, once they get on probation then they're going to be helped, and all the wrongs are going to be made right,' " said the angry prosecutor in the case. "And that just ain't so. Probation can only do certain things. About the best you can hope for is some type of minimal supervision, and that's only for a limited time. I don't know what the probation departments in Texas are like, but I imagine they're the same as they are here, which means overworked and understaffed."

As the issue of child abuse has garnered more public attention, judges whose instinct is to go easy on child molesters are discovering that they run an increasing risk of provoking the public ire. In St. Louis, fifty people held a candlelight vigil outside the home of the judge who imposed a sentence of two years' probation for the rape of an eight-year-old girl. There was an even angrier protest in Cincinnati, after a judge sentenced two men who admitted raping another eight-year-old to ninety days in jail and then justified the sentence on the grounds that the child had been a "willing participant" in the abuse.

Much of the pressure for harsher sentences comes from Society's League Against Molestation, a national organization known as SLAM that was founded by a California woman named Patti Linebaugh, the grandmother of Amy Sue Seitz. "Whether molestation is or is not an illness," Linebaugh says, "it is a crime. And no matter what the root causes, one way to stop it is to lock the molesters up." It is largely because of such outcries that some sentences for child abusers have lately become much less forgiving: like Stephen Boatwright, a number of child abusers have recently been sentenced to consecutive life terms.

In many cases, however, harsher sentences are more a response to public opinion than the result of a careful determination of the facts in the case and a consideration of the likelihood that the defendant will abuse again.

"First of all," says Andrew von Hirsh of the Rutgers law school, "most states don't have guidelines on this subject. Guidelines on sentencing are a fairly new development. Then, because a lot of sex abusers are middle-class, you get all these rehabilitative and other urges, either to treat people lightly or very severely. It's also a fashionable issue, and a fashionable issue will mean that judges will oscillate between throwing away the key to make an example of the fellow and 'Poor Schmidtlapp, he's a family man . . .' "

Because of child molesters, like Theodore Frank, who have been pronounced cured and set free only to abuse again, the indeterminate sentence is rapidly falling out of legislative vogue. In the aftermath of the Frank case, the California legislature rescinded the Mentally Disordered Sex Offender law, and several other states have followed suit. In their search for an alternative means of sentencing child sexual abusers, state legislators might consider Minnesota's guidelines, which are held up as a model by von Hirsh and other experts in the law. "We have guidelines for all our offenses," says Kay Knapp, the director of that state's sentencing guidelines commission, "and that includes the sexual abuse of children. Every offense is ranked under the guidelines, and the sentence is based on the severity of the offense and the criminal history score of the offender."

In Minnesota there are actually two parallel sets of statutes, the first a criminal sexual conduct law that covers offenses ranging from the first to the fourth degree. In cases of sexual abuse, a first-degree offense includes either penetration, or the less serious abuse of a very young victim, or the use of force that results in some kind of injury to the child. A second-degree offense involves any sexual contact with a very young victim. A third-degree violation includes penetration accomplished without the use of physical force, though with some other kind of coercion. A fourth-degree offense involves neither force nor coercion. For those convicted of a first-degree violation, the sentence is forty-three months in prison, no more and no less; a judge can depart from that sentence only if he can show that there are "substantial and compelling circumstances" that warrant such a departure.

The second set of Minnesota statutes covers sexual abuse within the family, and it carries the same presumptive sentences as the statutes on criminal abuse. Under the Minnesota "incest laws," however, a judge can stay whatever sentence is mandated by the guidelines if he finds doing so to be "in the best interests of the family." The Minnesota guidelines are less than six years old and so far have worked rather well, but not many states have yet followed their example. Perhaps surprisingly, the principal opposition to mandated sentences for child abusers comes not from defense lawyers but from psychotherapists. "The treatment community is very much in favor of considerable discretion," Knapp says. "They like to have all kinds of flexibility, and they like huge clubs hanging over offenders' heads so they have a lot of power over the offender when they're in a treatment program. They almost always want a twenty-year sentence hanging over the guy, and then if they don't do well in treatment they want them to get all twenty years."

Whether they involve the rule of cross-examination or sentencing guidelines, calls for the reform of judicial procedure in sexual abuse cases arise from an overriding determination that those who sexually abuse children must not go unpunished. But as states move further away from a strict interpretation of constitutional protections for criminal defendants, they threaten to infringe upon the philosophies of equal justice and individual rights that are central to the nature of American society.

Few would agree with Ralph Underwager, a Minneapolis psychologist who testified on behalf of several defendants in the Jordan case, and who declared it "more desirable that a thousand children in abuse situations are not discovered than for one innocent person to be convicted wrongly."[2] In the wake of Jordan and McMartin, however, some of those who have devoted their careers to the protection of children are beginning to wonder whether such prosecutions are worth the cost, either to society or to the victims of abuse.

Eli Newberger, a pediatrician on the staff of Boston's Children's Hospital and a principal authority on the sexual abuse of children, surprised many of his colleagues recently when he declared that prosecuting child abusers had become "an increasingly prevalent form of child abuse." Child molestation trials, Newberger said, were really morality plays that also happened to provide work for lawyers and publicity for prosecutors. The children who had been abused were being treated primarily as bearers of evidence, with little concern shown for their well-being. Such prosecutions also permitted society to "shoot the messenger," the social workers and therapists who spoke for the victims of child abuse, and made it easy to justify abandoning the social welfare approach to sexual abuse in favor of the criminal justice approach. Worst of all, Newberger said, the prosecutions led to the mistaken impression that a solution to a complex and disturbing problem had been found.

ELEVEN
Therapy

U NLIKE BANK ROBBERY or even murder, the sexual abuse of children is the pure product of an emotional disorder. As such, the concerns it poses for society are unique. Nobody talks about "curing" bank robbers, but the question of whether some child abusers can be cured — and, if so, which ones — is still open. Many judges do think that some kinds of child abusers can be successfully treated, and that not all of them need to be locked up while the treatment is taking place. "The first thing you have to consider is that there are child sex abusers and there are child sex abusers," says Mike Fondi, a Nevada judge who sees many such cases. "There's the first-time offender who did this thing not realizing why he was doing it, felt guilt, reported to a clergyman or a counselor, or turned himself in to the cops. This guy is crying out for help. This kind I would deem the person who is most able to be worked with. If he pleaded guilty, I'd put him on probation with a prison sentence hanging over his head and require him to get counseling."

The notion that incest results as much from the abusive parent's troubled relationship with his family — and his family members' faulty relationships with one another — as from a sexual attraction to children has led many judges to conclude that incest offenders have the best chance of controlling their behavior through psychotherapy. "The thing that has always struck me is that incest is a family problem," says Terry O'Brien, a Wyoming judge. "It's not one, in my view, that's owned exclusively by the male. If you look at the circumstances, usually you find a failed family in any number of respects. The family is typically introverted. Normally they don't belong to clubs, they don't go out and socialize. A lot of times they have very strong religious convictions, very puritanical sorts of things.

I think you have to try to do some things with the family. I think it's imperative that the child receive counseling, and that the father admit to the child that it was his doing, not the child's doing, to relieve the child of the guilt and anxiety that go along with these things. I put an awful lot of these guys on probation. I usually give them some time in the county jail, like thirty days, but that's an attention-getting thing more than anything else. I want these people to know this is damn serious. Also, I think it's a pretty visible symbol for the girl that Dad did something wrong, because Dad's in jail. Kids know that people go to jail because they've been naughty."

Mainly because of such opinions, several states have begun "pretrial diversion" programs in which incest offenders who acknowledge their guilt are sentenced to undergo psychotherapy rather than go to prison. But such programs are not open to everyone. "We have very strict guidelines here," says Dennis Moore, the district attorney for Johnson County, Kansas, whose program has become something of a national model. "For a father who's sexually molesting a daughter and who is otherwise apparently amenable to treatment — and I rely on treatment personnel to give me that recommendation — if they have no prior convictions, if there was no force or threat of force used, they may be admitted into a diversion program. They're required, if that happens, to move out of the home, to have no contact with the child or any other children at risk until we give them the OK to do that, and you're talking probably four to six months. The father is required to involve himself in weekly individual treatment and weekly group treatment."

Diversion programs are becoming popular because they save the state the time and money involved in prosecuting an abuser and imprisoning him if he is convicted, but there are other arguments in their favor. One, as the case of Stephen Boatwright shows, is that very little therapy worthy of the name is available behind bars; another is that sending an incestuous parent to prison is likely to heighten the guilt his victim probably feels for having reported the abuse. Some judges also believe that only through the sort of family therapy many diversion programs entail are some incest victims' mothers likely to come to terms with their failure to recognize what was taking place.

"One of the things you usually see in these cases is a very passive, dependent woman," Judge O'Brien says. "Usually you see some role reversal with the mother and the daughter. In probably ninety percent of the cases, the mother herself was sexually abused as a child. You have to convince the mother that it happened, because most of these women have incredible systems of rationalization. I had one case where this guy came into court and admitted to cunnilingus and intercourse with his stepdaughter over a period of years. He went into detail about where they were, what he did, what she did. And he walked out of the courtroom and told the mother that he really hadn't done any of those things, that he just said that to satiate me. And she believed him, because she wanted so badly to believe him."

Because of the observation that incest is symptomatic of a multitude of other problems — the abuser's inability to handle stress and to emphathize, his troubled relations with his wife or his employer, even his alcohol or drug abuse — the fashion of the moment is to take a "holistic" approach to treatment that may combine "empathy training" with instruction in "interpersonal relations," participation in Alcoholics Anonymous, and even marital counseling. A widely used approach is the one developed fifteen years ago by Henry Giaretto, a California psychologist who founded the Child Sexual Abuse Treatment Program for Santa Clara County, south of San Francisco, and who by now has seen something like twenty thousand incestuous parents.

The Giaretto approach is loosely based on the psychodynamic theory of personality disorders, an idea set forth by Sandor Rado, a Hungarian-born psychoanalyst who established the first American graduate school of psychoanalysis, at New York City's Columbia University. Reduced to its essentials, psychodynamic theory suggests that while inherited predispositions cannot be overlooked entirely, much of what is wrong with people is a product of flawed relationships between themselves and their parents, their spouses, and their children. Though Giaretto's theories do not speak directly to the issue of narcissism, his solution is to repair the troubled "dynamics" within the family by raising the self-esteem of father, mother, and victim alike. A court order mandating diversion to Giaretto's program usually requires the incestuous parent to leave the home. Often, the victim will also be moved temporarily to the home of a close relative or a foster parent.

What occurs next is essentially a slow reunification of the family. All of those involved receive individual counseling, as well as separate sessions for mother and daughter together, father and daughter together, and father and mother together. The chief goal of such therapy for the child is to convince her that the responsibility for what happened lies with her abuser — and also with the other parent, who failed to protect her from the abuse. Among Giaretto's other concerns is establishing a sound relationship between the victim and a mother who may feel resentment, jealousy, and anger toward her child, either for having reported the abuse or for having allowed it to happen in the first place. The principal therapeutic aim for the abuser is his acknowledgment that he, and not his child, is responsible for what has happened. Only when the abuser assumes that responsibility do he and his child finally meet in counseling.

Eventually the whole family undergoes counseling together, but they are reunited under the same roof only when everyone agrees that the abuse will not recur. The victims who enter Giaretto's program spend an average of only ninety days in temporary foster care, and 90 percent are ultimately reunited with their fathers and mothers. Giaretto says that very few later display self-destructive or promiscuous behavior, and that a majority of the parents say their marriages are actually improved by the court-ordered counseling.

Giaretto's statistics are impressive, but the idea that incest offenders are more easily treatable than other abusers depends mainly on whether their recidivism rate is lower. Giaretto reports that fewer than 1 percent of the incestuous fathers who have been through his program have been caught abusing children afterward; but where incest is concerned, the question of recidiyism is cloudy. Vernon Quinsey, a Canadian researcher, puts the recidivism rate for all incest abusers at around 5 percent, whether they have undergone therapy or not. Other studies have produced much higher figures, including one that puts the number at 19 percent, compared to 29 percent for those who abuse unrelated children. [1]

As with any crime, the recidivism statistics for incest don't count every offender who abuses children again, only those who get caught, and because most pretrial diversion programs are so new, they have not yet produced very good statistics on what happens to the participants over the longer term. Whether as a practical matter or a moral one, however, it is unlikely that an incestuous parent will abuse again within the first few months of being caught, or in some cases even within the first few years. Because most incest relationships end as the victim enters adolescence, it is possible that by then there may be no other child home to replace her.

Even if psychodynamic therapy does play a role in lowering the short-term recidivism rate for incest, it is likely to leave the abuser's fundamental narcissism relatively untouched. The resolution of serious narcissistic personality disorders cannot be achieved without intensive psychotherapy, and even then such disorders are among the most resistant to treatment. Without long-term psychotherapy the narcissistic abuser may eventually turn again to sex with children, and if he is one of those who fit the description of the "crossover" abuser, they may be other people's children.

For these reasons, some judges and therapists think that incest abusers are among the worst candidates for treatment rather than the best. "You have a man who's thirty-seven years old, and you find out that for the past twelve years he's been involved in incestuous relations with his daughters," says a Boston judge. "And you're telling me he's a good candidate for treatment? You're telling me he's not a pedophile?" One therapist who thinks no incest abuser is a good risk is Mike Ryan, a psychologist on the staff of the Menard Institute, the psychiatric treatment facility of the Ilinois prison system. "I used to think there were some folks that were excellent candidates for therapy," Ryan says, "and we spent a lot of time trying to discriminate who was who. Time and time again we thought we'd built the safeguards in — we thought Dad was a good treatment candidate, we thought the family was viable — and all of a sudden something surfaces where the kid is becoming sexually involved with Dad again."

Because successful psychotherapy requires a large degree of willing participation by the patient, most therapists agree that anyone who is ordered to seek therapy by a court is a less than ideal candidate, no matter how willing he may seem to be. One lawyer who specializes in the defense of child abusers admits that, in an effort to obtain the lightest sentence possible for his clients, "I always advise them to emphasize their remorse, their concern for the victim's family, and their sincerity in starting an effective therapeutic plan." Among child abusers, therapists say, the only first-rate candidates are those who turn themselves in, and they are few and far between.

As with an incestuous father, the central question a judge must confront in deciding whether to send a hard-core pedophile to prison is whether the person is likely to abuse again. Here, too, judges depend mainly on psychiatric evaluations for guidance, but the therapists who are called on to render such opinions are in much disagreement about whether any pedophile constitutes a "good risk." "Let me tell you who's not treatable," says Roger Smith, a therapist at Oregon State Hospital. "First of all, the people who continue to deny the crime. With child molesters, denial is the major thing you have to overcome. 'I don't know about you, Doc,' they'll say, 'but there ain't nothing wrong with me. I didn't even do it — the girl's lying.' What often happens to people who are convicted is that they rationalize that they're doing the kid a favor, they're teaching him about sex. The other thing they do is they get religion in prison, which is very common for child molesters. They come in reporting born-again experiences, that all their guilt has been taken away, and that they're totally forgiven. We've got nothing to work with at that point. I think it's a major problem, because it's an easy way out. It seems to resolve all their guilt, and it doesn't touch their fantasy structure at all."

Therapists are the first to acknowledge that predicting who can be successfully treated and who cannot on the basis of a psychological assessment is risky business, and many are growing uncomfortable with the seer's role into which they have been cast by the courts. "Why are we locking people up on the testimony of psychiatrists, or giving them probation?" one psychiatrist asks. "One of the things we always struggle with is whether people in these situations are telling us the truth. Therapists are pretty good at telling when people are fooling themselves, but society looks to us to do this other thing, which is to tell when they're lying to us, and that I don't think we do well at all. We have grossly misled the public about our ability to predict things."

Whenever there is doubt about whether an abuser will abuse again — and with the confirmed pedophile it is usually not a matter of whether but when — the most prudent course is to lock the person up. Despite the fact that a few pedophiles say they find prison beneficial and talk about their psychological need to be punished, prison is not a therapeutic experience. No state has what professional therapists consider adequate psychotherapy available to its prison inmates, and many states have none at all. In most states there is a prison hospital to which child abusers can be remanded, but such institutions are usually more custodial than anything else.

For convicted abusers who are sent to regular prisons, there may be at most a weekly, and not a very productive, hour with the prison psychologist. A few of the more enlightened states have set up special treatment and evaluation programs for child sexual abusers. But funds are not readily forthcoming from legislators, who fear accusations that they are "coddling" child molesters, and those programs that do exist are quite limited in scope. The sex offender program at the Menard Institute has room for only forty inmates, and only fifty are accepted into a California program that permits child abusers to spend the last two years of their sentence undergoing treatment and observation at a hospital.

To compound the therapeutic problem, the relatively few therapists who are attempting to devise treatment programs for pedophiles are themselves divided by a debate over how such individuals can best be treated, and even whether they are treatable at all. One small school of researchers thinks the desire to have sex with children might be biological, and they point to evidence that some individuals who are sexually attracted to children exhibit a higher than usual incidence of a genetic phenomenon known as Klinefelter's syndrome. A few psychotherapists, on the other hand, claim to have successfully used the techniques of classical psychoanalysis to treat pedophilia, or at least the narcissism that surrounds and inspires it. But psychoanalysis is an emotionally consuming process that requires a great deal of commitment and effort by the patient, qualities most pedophiles do not bring to therapy.

At the moment, the main approach to the treatment of pedophilia is one derived from the theory of behavior modification proposed by J. B. Watson fifty years ago and since refined by B. F. Skinner, the Harvard psychologist. Rather than locating and attacking its root psychological causes, behavior therapy strives to eradicate unwanted behavior by replacing it with other behavior. Behaviorists believe that all behavior, including the desire to have sex with children, is learned, and that it can also be unlearned. Behaviorists aren't interested in the infantile origins of the pedophile's narcissism, or in the childhood experiences that helped to form his compulsive-addictive personality, or in how his faulty relationships with adult women have contributed to his sexual attraction to children. "Men molest children because they're attracted to children," declares Emory University's Gene Able, a prominent behaviorist. "It's that simple. Analytical treatment is a waste of time. We see lots of people who have spent years learning they didn't get a little red wagon when they were six. We don't care about little red wagons. We're interested in changing behavior, because once it gets started, the behavior takes on a life of its own."

Whether its subjects are pedophiles or laboratory rats being taught to run a maze, behavior therapy is fundamentally a reeducation process. With some pedophiles, as with some rats, it appears to work. In one kind of program, an icon of the unwanted behavior, such as a picture of a naked child, is associated with something unpleasant — a painful electric shock, a drug that induces vomiting, or a chemical with a putrid smell. A less drastic form of behavioral therapy involves shifting the pedophile's fantasy structure away from children through the use of denial and reward. Because much of the pedophile's attraction to children is reinforced through fantasy, the therapeutic aim is to change not only what the pedophile does but what he thinks about doing — in clinical terms, to alter his nondeviant arousal patterns.

The therapist may begin by showing the pedophile erotic pictures of young girls and allowing him to become sexually aroused. Eventually the pictures are paired with, and then replaced by, pictures of older girls, and then of young women. Finally, only pictures of grown women are presented. In several cases where this technique has been used, the subject's erotic interest in young girls appears to have declined, particularly when the correct responses to the pictures are accompanied by rewards like allowing the subject to masturbate to orgasm. But the question of recidivism where pedophiles are concerned is just as murky as for incest abusers, and behavior alteration programs have other shortcomings. Because they can take years to complete, such programs are very expensive, and many therapists are opposed to any form of treatment that involves discomfort or pain. Not all pedophiles, moreover, are susceptible to such therapy.

Though Stephen Boatwright's doctors thought he might have made a good candidate for a behaviorist approach, it is doubtful that any amount of therapy would have been successful for Theodore Frank. To the extent that such an approach succeeds at all, it will be with the relatively small number of pedophiles who genuinely wish to rid themselves of their attraction for children. Looked at in this light, the almost total lack of prison therapy for child abusers doesn't really matter, because it is those who commit the most serious abuses, who have had the most victims, and who display the least remorse over what they've done who tend to draw the longest prison terms. Although there are fine shadings of disagreement, many therapists believe that such confirmed abusers are unlikely to benefit from any kind of treatment.

"When you have a man who has been involved in this kind of deviance, you find that if he's not been involved in molesting kids most of his life, he's thought about it," says Rob Freeman-Longo, who works with Roger Smith at Oregon State Hospital. "His sexual orientation to children has always been there. When you're working with a person like that, it's like me telling you that as of tomorrow you will not have sex with adult women or men, you can only have sex with a kid. You're saying to a pedophile, 'OK, you've been interested in kids for thirty years now, but we're going to say you can't have sex with anybody but adults.' Some people will say that guy's not treatable, but I hate to use that term. I don't think it's the person who's not treatable — we just don't have the technology to treat that person yet, or the knowledge."

Therapy or no therapy, prison does accomplish one important

thing. It keeps child molesters away from children. The problem is that there aren't enough prisons to hold all the pedophiles. The half-million inmates in this country are already jammed into facilities built to hold half that number, and the inmate population goes up every year by enough to fill California's Folsom Prison four times over. But even if there were room enough, warehousing child abusers is not a permanent solution to the problem of child abuse, because even with the current trend toward harsher sentences, most of them eventually get out.

In most states, an inmate must serve only a third of his minimum term before he is eligible for parole, which means that a child molester who receives a fairly stiff sentence of twenty-five to forty years will come up for release in a little over eight years. Unless he is a genuinely regressed abuser, the child molester who cannot be successfully treated or otherwise dissuaded from having sex with children has probably been abusing them for years. The longer the compulsion to have sex with children goes on, the stronger it becomes, and by the time a pedophile has had four or five victims, it's usually too late. When such men are released from prison, the chances are excellent that they will abuse again. Muggers, armed robbers, and other violent criminals tend to outgrow their criminal behavior, or at least the violent aspects of it, as they approach middle age, but unless it is successfully treated, the sexual attraction to children lasts a lifetime. As one therapist puts it, "Just when I set an upper age limit, I find a man who commits his first offense at the age of seventy-seven."

Efforts to find some solution more permanent than incarceration have not met with much success. One option is castration, the surgical removal of the testicles. Though a number of European countries offer convicted sex offenders castration as an alternative to lengthy prison sentences, it has been used rarely in this country because of public squeamishness and the reluctance of American surgeons to perform the operation. A few years ago, when a San Diego judge gave two convicted child abusers the option of going to prison or being castrated, both men chose castration. But then, the judge recalled, "the local ACLU chapter decided to take a stand. The main obstacle was a vocal group within the local medical society, which said it harked back to Hitler's medical experiments, and that no ethical doctor could participate. So it became impossible to get either a doctor or a hospital to perform the surgery. In spite of their stated desire, they went to prison. I gave up after that."

Even though castration diminishes the supply of testosterone, the male sex hormone, and with it the sex drive, it is not an infallible remedy. Some European studies have found that a third of the men who are castrated are able to continue having sex, and the effects of castration are also reversible. A California man who agreed back in 1946 to be castrated in lieu of going to prison was in court again forty years later, to plead guilty to having abused three young girls he met by answering a newspaper advertisement for a baby-sitter. When the judge asked the obvious question, the man explained that he had been injecting himself with male hormones to offset the effects of the castration.

Less offensive to many is the use of a female hormone, marketed as a birth-control aid called Depo-Provera, that also diminishes the male sex drive. The drug made headlines in 1984 when Roger Gauntlett, a forty-three-year-old Michigan man convicted of abusing his teenage stepdaughter, was sentenced to be treated with Depo-Provera; Gauntlett happened to be the great-grandson of W. E. Upjohn, the founder of the pharmaceutical company that produces the substance. When Gauntlett appealed his sentence as unconstitutional, the Michigan Court of Appeals agreed and resentenced him to five to fifteen years in state prison.

Despite the questions of constitutionality that the use of Depo-Provera entails, its proponents insist that the drug holds great promise for the treatment of pedophilia, and experiments at Oregon State Hospital, Johns Hopkins University, and elsewhere suggest that some child abusers who genuinely wish to lose their attraction for children may be helped by the drug. Most others, however, are not helped, because Depo-Provera does nothing to diminish nonsexual, narcissistic drives like the need for control and affection. The drug's future is also called into question by studies showing that as many as a third of the men who are injected with Depo-Provera can still become sexually aroused, and it is useless where female abusers are concerned.

While the search for ways to find and stop those who are sexually abusing children continues, most of the research currently under way involves developing better methods of treating adult men and women who have been having sex with children, many of them for years. What such an approach overlooks is the fact that most confirmed pedophiles don't begin molesting children on the day they turn twenty-one. When pedophiles are asked how old they were when they began having sex with children, many place the onset of their behavior in their teenage years or even earlier; more than three-quarters of one group studied said they began abusing younger children before they were twelve. Not surprisingly, most children who abuse other children have also been sexually abused. "I don't know what you find in a seven-year-old that makes them do sexual violence to a two-year-old if they haven't had that in their own backgrounds," a child therapist says. "I really worry about these kids being out in the community, and some of them are seven and eight."

It is sexually abusive children who ultimately do the most damage, since the abuser who begins abusing while still a child is likely to commit hundreds of sex crimes during his lifetime.[2] If such children could be placed in treatment the moment they began to make the transition from victim to victimizer, it might be possible to interrupt the abusive cycle at the outset. But the treatment of adolescent abusers depends on the identification of abusive children, and most sexual abuse committed by children is not recognized for what it is. Children who abuse other children tend to be what therapists call "pseudo-mature." They look and act like other children their age, but because they're emotionally underdeveloped, they prefer to spend time with those who are younger than themselves.

When abuser and victim are both very young, the beginnings of a lifelong compulsion to have sex with children may be easily passed off as "playing doctor." In somewhat older children, what may be the emergence of a grown-up pedophile is likely to be dismissed as preadolescent sex play. A teenage boy who sexually assaults a girl his own age is often seen as "overamorous," or the victim of a teenage tease. Even when sexually abusive children do come to the attention of authorities, most states have no effective way of ensuring that they receive the intensive treatment necessary to short-circuit their attraction to sex with other children. For fear of branding children with a lifelong stigma, most juvenile courts and child protection agencies are still reluctant to label juvenile sex offenders as what they are.

The question of whether those who sexually abuse children can be successfully treated, and if so, how, is in urgent need of an answer. But the urgency should not eclipse another question of equal importance: What are the effects of sexual abuse on those who do not grow up to become child abusers, and how can such victims best be treated? The psychological consequences of sexual abuse are far too little understood. What is known is that, one way or another, not many children emerge from such an experience unscathed. Many younger victims revert to infantile behavior like sucking their thumbs and wetting their beds. Some set fire to their houses or mutilate their pets, and a few even attempt suicide by stabbing themselves with knives, running in front of moving cars, or jumping from high places.

Although most reactions are less extreme, they are not necessarily less serious. When the University of Chicago's Jon Conte compared 369 sexual abuse victims with children who had not been abused, he found that the victims had more nightmares, were more depressed, had more problems in school, daydreamed more, and had more trouble remembering things. They were more "aggressive and fearful," less "rational and confident," and more likely to withdraw from the normal activities of life. Their self-images were poorer, and they were more anxious to please adults.

Because the probable magnitude of child sexual abuse has not been recognized until so recently, much less is known about what happens to such children as they grow up. So many adult victims have never told anyone about their childhood abuse that it's difficult to make generalized statements about the long-term psychological and social results. Still, there are some clues. Sixty percent of two hundred prostitutes interviewed in San Francisco had histories of childhood sexual abuse. So did 75 percent of those in New York City, 65 percent in Seattle, and 90 percent in San Diego. When five hundred older teenagers in a California drug abuse rehabilitation program were asked about their childhood sexual experiences, 70 percent said they had been abused.

A survey of seventy-five women in a Minneapolis alcohol dependency program found that more than half had been abused as children, mostly by their fathers. When 118 adult female drug addicts in New York City were asked the same question, nearly half said they were victims of incest. When women who admitted severely beating their children were questioned in a California survey, 82 percent said they had been sexually abused by their fathers. In another study, nearly half of a group of women who compulsively cut their arms and legs with knives, burned their bodies with cigarettes and acid, swallowed toxic substances, or poked themselves with pins and needles had suffered sexual abuse as children. Most of the other women in the group had suffered serious physical abuse.

There is also some evidence that the percentage of rape victims who were sexually abused as children may be higher than for the female population as a whole. When Henry Giaretto asked female victims of child sexual abuse whether they had been raped as adults, 60 percent said they had. When Columbia-Presbyterian's Judith Becker approached the question from the opposite direction by asking women who had been raped if they had been sexually abused as children, a third said they had.

Becker ascribes her findings to a characteristic she calls "learned helplessness," a personality trait acquired by a child who is being abused and who realizes that he or she is powerless to fight back. "It's a myth that rapists are looking for attractive women, women in high heels and shorts," Becker says. "That's not it. It's the woman who looks very vulnerable, who looks like she's not going to fight. And if you've developed this phenomenon of learned helplessness, then you're really at risk for being violated by one of these rapists." Many of the rape victims surveyed by Giaretto went further, admitting that they had consciously put themselves in unnecessarily hazardous situations by walking down dark and dangerous streets or striking up suggestive conversations with strange men.

Not all sexually abused children become prostitutes, drug addicts, child beaters, or rape victims. Most, in fact, do not, but the majority of these do not go on to lead happy lives. The victims surveyed by the *Los Angeles Times* seemed much more distressed and unsettled than the nonvictims, and many others complain of depression and anxiety, of relationships that are superficial and empty, and of feeling that everyday events are beyond their control. The uncertainty that surrounds the question of how victims respond to the trauma of sexual abuse is compounded by some fresh evidence, not yet fully evaluated or understood, that a minority appear to suffer no lasting emotional harm.

According to UCLA's Gail Wyatt, some of the victims in her study reported that their abuse "was done in such a loving and warm way that the child never knew this was something inappropriate, until years later when someone labeled it for them. It was a pleasurable experience, not traumatic, there was no physical coercion involved. But you can look at someone else who had that very same experience, being fondled by an uncle every time the uncle came over for a holiday, and that woman might say it was one of the most horrendous experiences of her life, shaped her attitude toward men, created difficulty in her sexual relationships, and on and on and on. I don't think we know enough about the personalities of individuals, their coping mechanisms, to really say which incidents have an impact and which ones don't."

One possibility is that younger victims may suffer less anguish than older ones, simply because they're too young to understand the significance of what's happening to them. Personality differences are also likely to be a factor, since some children are simply more rugged than others and better able to survive any trauma. Other determinants may be the nature and severity of the abuse, the length of time that it goes on, and the child's relationship to the abuser. Although far more research is needed into the importance of these factors and probably others not yet identified, the impression that some victims are left untouched by sexual abuse can be deceiving, and it is a mistake to minimize the potential impact of even the least serious occurrences of sexual abuse.

Whatever the nature of their experience, it is much harder than might be imagined for the victims of sexual abuse to find effective psychotherapy. Psychoanalysts and psychiatrists who spend years studying such disorders as schizophrenia and manic-depressive psychosis are often reluctant to become involved in what they view as counseling, and some still hold the view that women who claim to have been sexually abused as children are merely fantasizing.

One well-known psychiatrist suggests that, despite their medical degrees and other impressive credentials, some of his colleagues have no business treating anybody for anything. "Some of the least well-adjusted people I've ever met are in this profession," he says. "Thirty percent of them I wouldn't trust with my dog." When the *American Journal of Psychiatry* surveyed 1,442 of its psychiatrist subscribers, 7 percent of the men and 3 percent of the women acknowledged that they had had sex with their patients during therapy. A Minneapolis psychologist who reviewed some four hundred complaints of sexual misconduct by psychotherapists concluded that many of the therapists were themselves suffering from narcissistic personality disorders, and that a smaller number were actually schizophrenic or psychotic.

Further down the treatment ladder are the counselors. The Los Angeles telephone directory contains listings for twenty-one different kinds, including crisis counselors, divorce counselors, drug abuse counselors, parental guidance counselors, and spiritual counselors, who offer a host of therapies identified as primal, humanistic, encounter, stress, growth, gestalt, Reichian, "feeling," rational, core, orgonomy, Jungian, group, bioenergetics, existential, holistic, behavior, and Rolfing. Some of these therapists are skilled clinicians with graduate degrees in psychology, but because there's no academic specialty in sexual abuse therapy, no special credentials or experience are required to treat its victims. Even in the relatively few states that regulate the field strictly, those with training in anthropology, literature, and religion can qualify as licensed marriage, family, and child counselors. In some states, anybody with the money to rent a suite of offices and some Scandinavian furniture can call himself a psychotherapist and charge patients for counseling.

If the adult victim of sexual abuse has the funds to suffer trial and error, sooner or later she may come across a therapist who comprehends the source of her distress and knows how to resolve it. "Probably the most important thing I got from therapy," one such victim says, "is the realization that the things I'm frightened of are much smaller than the fears they generate. Having confronted my biggest, darkest secret and lived to tell about it has given me more confidence about dealing with all the other dark parts of my life. It's one thing to have a person on the outside tell you to 'get over being molested.' It's quite another to talk about what such an incident does to your life and how you can learn to live with it, with someone else to whom it has happened. I don't know that any of us ever overcome it or truly forget it. I have been able to recognize, consciously at least, that what happened was not my fault. I'm beginning to realize that unconsciously as well, to let my guilt go, but it's taking longer. I realized that I would never think that what happened to everyone else in the group could possibly have been their fault, and this helped me to see that no rational person would believe that what happened to me was my fault either. One of the biggest benefits was realizing that it was perfectly normal to still be bothered about it all these years later."

As the woman's experience illustrates, successful treatment can sometimes be a relatively straightforward matter of convincing the adult victims of child abuse that they are not responsible for having been abused. But those adults who have been abused in more serious ways or over a longer period of time are more difficult to treat, and those without the money to finance the search for effective therapy are likely to be less than successful in finding it. Most large cities have community mental health programs that offer counseling for free or at reduced rates, but such programs have never had adequate funding, and recent cutbacks in federal and state aid to social services have further diminished their capacity to render help.

For the parents of a son or daughter who has been sexually abused, pursuing adequate child therapy can be a supremely frustrating experience. Because not much is known about how children's minds really work, there's no real consensus on how to treat abused children. Even though most adult disorders have their roots in childhood, modern psychiatry has chosen to concern itself almost entirely with the finished product. The few psychiatrists who acknowledge what seems a principal shortcoming of their profession admit that most of their colleagues do not find children very interesting patients, and also that child psychiatry does not pay very well.

To the extent that it can be called a field at all, the field of sexual-abuse treatment for children is less than ten years old, which means that hardly anyone in it has more than a decade's worth of experience. The number of qualified sexual-abuse therapists with even half that much training would not fill a large hotel ballroom, and most of those are self-trained practitioners who have picked up their knowledge on the job. "Little kids are hard to figure out," one child therapist says. "It's like learning a foreign language, and every child speaks his or her own dialect. Just as a person coming from another country needs an interpreter, so do children. Children are not miniature adults. Even those of the same age are quite different. I keep feeling like every month I learn more about what I don't know. If I'm an expert at anything, it's in what not to do."

The understanding of why some victims are more traumatized than others by sexual abuse, and how best to treat those who fall into each category, awaits a good deal more research. The answer is likely to be found only through monitoring young victims closely as they grow into adolescence and adulthood, but nearly all the information now available on victims consists of individual profiles gleaned over a brief period of time. If child sexual abuse victims are lucky enough to be among the relatively small number who receive any therapy at all, they may be evaluated over a few weeks or months or at most a couple of years. Since the data comes from hospitals and clinics scattered across the country, it lumps together victims who have been abused in many different ways by many different kinds of people.

Such information has its uses, but many researchers believe that if the abusive cycle is ever to be understood, it will be necessary to study the same victims for the rest of their lives. Because these so-called longitudinal studies require keeping close tabs on children as they grow up, marry, have children of their own, and move from place to place, they are extraordinarily expensive. Researchers at UCLA were recently awarded $450,000 by the National Center on Child Abuse and Neglect (NCCAN) to pay for just the first three years of a proposed longitudinal study of some of the McMartin preschool students. The project may ultimately prove invaluable, since the advantage of conducting such a study in a macro day-care case is that it permits the long-term observation of children from similar social and economic backgrounds.

Because longitudinal studies take decades to complete, the answers they offer will not be quick in coming, and because research into child behavior is not accorded the same status as research on adults, there are not many such studies under way. In fact, the paucity of solid research on all aspects of sexual abuse is remarkable. The Child Abuse Prevention and Treatment Act of 1974 established NCCAN to coordinate federal funding for treatment and research. But NCCAN has never had enough money, and nowadays it has even less. When Jimmy Carter was in the White House, the agency's four-year budget totaled $79 million; during the four years of the first Reagan Administration, it fell to $71 million total.

In 1986, after two years of intensive publicity on the subject of child abuse, NCCAN's annual budget was increased to $26 million — less than half the amount of foreign aid given during the same period to the government of Haitian dictator Jean-Claude Duvalier. The low priority accorded child abuse research reflects the degree to which the scope and seriousness of child abuse in America are still not recognized for what they are. But it is also a measure of the failure, by government and by large segments of the academic community as well, to acknowledge the necessity and legitimacy of such research.

TWELVE
Prevention

A MERICA SOMETIMES seems to be the most prevention-minded nation on earth. It's practically impossible to turn on a television or radio without being overwhelmed by appeals for help in preventing everything from heart attacks to forest fires to accidents in the home. As reports of child sexual abuse continue to rise faster than those of any other crime, many who are concerned for the welfare of children have begun a campaign to prevent child sexual abuse. At the moment, the most popular approach is teaching children how to protect themselves from child abusers. If children can only be taught to say no to adults who want sex, or so the thinking goes, the problem will be solved of its own accord. But most sexual-abuse prevention programs have serious shortcomings, not the least of which is their squeamishness about the subject at hand, and there are questions about how well even the best of them work.

There are hundreds of prevention materials available, most produced by child therapists, rape crisis centers, teachers, hospitals, and writers of children's books. New programs arrive on the market each week in such numbers that newsletters are now being published to help keep track of them all. In attempting to convey their message, they use every device imaginable — storybooks, movies, videotapes, television programs, filmstrips, comic and coloring books, puppets, even live theater. A few have enlisted Hollywood stars such as John Houseman and Henry Winkler to instruct children on how to protect themselves. Most of the programs are produced by nonprofit organizations, but some writers and publishers have discovered that they can cash in on parents' fears, and the competition is so intense that a few authors have resorted to hucksterism and outright scare tactics.

Though prevention programs differ widely in approach, nearly all attempt to establish three fundamental ideas: that a child's body is the child's "property," that a child can "say no" to an abusive adult, and that a child who is molested must immediately "tell someone" who will take action. Such messages are hard to argue with on their face, but they are conveyed in a variety of ways. Some are silly, like Trooper B. Safe, a fifteen-thousand-dollar robot with a flashing red light and siren that is used by police in several states to teach children to avoid child molesters. Dressed in a state trooper's uniform and speaking through a voice synthesizer, the robot promises to protect "humanoids who live in the intergalactic space-sphere called Earth," paying special attention to the "small, younger human units." Most prevention programs adopt a more serious tone, but many are flawed in other ways, and some are downright dangerous.

One of the best-selling books on the subject is *Never Talk to Strangers*, first published by Golden Books in 1967 and reissued last year. The book uses what its publisher describes as fantasy and humor to convey its message "in a nonthreatening way." The illustrations it contains show children in familiar settings — at home, at the store, at the bus stop, at the playground — when an unfamiliar and presumably threatening character appears on the scene. None of these strangers, however, is human. "If you are hanging from a trapeze," the book begins, "and up sneaks a camel with bony knees, remember this rule, if you please — Never talk to strangers!" It goes on to warn children about grouchy grizzly bears, parachuting hawks, a rhinoceros waiting for a bus, coyotes who ask the time, cars with a whale at the wheel, and bees carrying bass bassoons.

The use of animals to represent potential abusers is no doubt inspired by the idea that children will be less frightened by a picture of a rhinoceros wearing a tutu than by one of a malevolent stranger in a raincoat, and other prevention programs use chipmunks, mice, or bears to make their point. The problem with such anthropomorphic presentations is illustrated by a filmstrip featuring Penelope Mouse, who has an otherwise unidentified "strange experience" at her Uncle Sid's house. When a group of schoolchildren who had been shown the filmstrip were asked later what its message was, they agreed that sexual abuse must be a serious problem among mice.

Another best-selling book is *It's O.K. to Say No!*,[1] endorsed by the Catholic Youth & Community Service and the Children's Justice Foundation. The book mostly contains warnings about "child molesters" who frequent public restrooms and video arcades, with a few cautionary words about neighbors, teachers, and baby-sitters thrown in. But *It's O.K. to Say No!* never says what it's OK to say no to. In one story, a girl named Tina spends the night at the home of Lucy, her friend. After Tina's in bed, Lucy's big brother comes into her room and starts saying "strange things" that make Tina feel "uncomfortable." But what things? Why does Tina feel uncomfortable? The reader never finds out. Because *It's O.K. to Say No!* and similar storybooks are designed for parents to share with their children, their squeamishness may be an acknowledgment that many parents feel uneasy talking with their children about any aspect of sex. But those programs designed for presentation in the classroom or to youth groups by trained instructors are scarcely more forthcoming.

One of the most popular is *Red Flag, Green Flag,* a multimedia program developed by the Rape and Abuse Crisis Center of Fargo-Moorhead, North Dakota, the centerpiece of which is a coloring book that helps children learn the difference between a "green flag touch" and a "red flag touch." The program is typical of those that, in seeking ways to avoid actually talking about sex, distinguish between "good" touches, such as a hug or a pat on the head, and "bad" touches. Such jargon involves a number of potential contradictions, such as the possibility that a child whose genitals are being fondled might find the sensation pleasant. A few programs have tried to resolve such contradictions by introducing a third category called "confusing" touch, which they define as a touch that might feel good but is bad nonetheless. But the idea of confusing touches is just that, because it doesn't address what often happens in the real world.

Nor do such programs recognize that children often take things literally. Is an abuser who asks a child to perform fellatio touching the child, or is the child touching the abuser? Programs that warn children about adults who might "bother" or "hurt" them are equally misleading, since a child who's being sexually abused is probably not being physically hurt. "We're giving children an outrageous double message," says Cordelia Anderson of the Illusion Theater in Minneapolis, which produced the first live-theater prevention program back in 1979. "We're saying that we want to talk to you about *it,* that if you have any questions about *it* I want you to ask me about *it,* that it's not OK if someone does *it* to you, and that if *it* happens it's not your fault. But what *it* means is so bad that I can't even say the words."

With the same misguided decorum they reserve for talking about "touching," most prevention programs refuse to call penises and vaginas by their proper names, referring instead to mysterious "private

zones" or "places where your bathing suit covers." The *Red Flag,
Green Flag* coloring book contains a drawing of an androgynous child
whose arms, legs, chest, and other body parts are identified for what
they are, while the region beween the child's legs is merely labeled
"genitals (private parts)." Upon closer inspection, it becomes apparent
that the child in the drawing has no genitals or private parts.

Another serious shortcoming is the exclusive focus of many prevention programs on the danger posed by strange adults. One film,
produced by the Boulder, Colorado, police department, shows a shady-
looking character luring a little girl into some bushes, where she is heard
to scream — the same sort of "stranger danger" movie that American
schoolchildren have been watching for decades with no noticeable effect
on the incidence of sexual abuse. There's nothing really wrong with
warning children never to accept candy or a ride from adults they don't
know or never to open the door for a stranger, since some pedophiles do
abuse strange children. It's just that most of them do not. Of the adult
victims surveyed by the *Los Angeles Times*, only a quarter recalled
having been abused by someone they didn't know.

Programs that teach children to memorize their home telephone
number or that of the local police department might be helpful for a
child who becomes lost, but they have very little to do with preventing
sexual abuse. Some programs feature "assertiveness training" for
children, teaching them to defend themselves physically by stomping
on an abuser's foot or bending his pinky. But the idea that a child can
repulse an attack by an adult is both ludicrous and dangerous to the
child. Those who promote such programs maintain that, while
warning children about strangers may not cover the spectrum of child
abuse, such advice cannot hurt. Apart from the possibility that such
messages may frighten some children unduly, the distinctions they
draw about which adults should be trusted and which should not are
often vague.

Never Talk to Strangers suggests that it's fine for a child to talk to
any adult who is introduced by someone the child knows. "If your
father introduces you to a roly-poly kangaroo," the book advises, "say
politely, 'How do you do?' That's not talking to strangers because your
family knows her." Or: "If your teacher says she'd like you to meet a
lilac llama who's very sweet, invite her over and serve a treat. That's
not talking to strangers because your teacher knows her." Worst of all:
"If a pal of yours you've always known brings around a prancing roan,
welcome him in a friendly tone. That's not talking to strangers because
your pal knows him."

A brochure distributed to parents by the Fairfax, Virginia, police department goes further still, saying, "It should be emphasized to children that only doctors or a parent or guardian are permitted to touch them in a personal manner." Considering the number of doctors who have been convicted of abusing children sexually, they hardly deserve a special exemption. But the real problem with sexual-abuse prevention programs is that they ignore the vastly greater danger to children from adults they know, particularly their own parents. Very few programs warn children about the possibility of sexual abuse by relatives, and there are almost none that discuss parent-child incest. Those who design such materials defend their skittishness by pointing to the parent-teacher protests that have sprung up even when the most innocuous programs have been introduced into local schools.

"I'd walk into gymnasiums with two hundred and fifty parents, and they'd be saying things like 'Rape crisis for my kindergartner, no way,'" one Utah child abuse counselor recalls. "I was in a parent meeting once where a woman got up and said, 'I'm running for PTA president next year so we won't have programs in the schools like this one.' I remember doing training in one school system where the principal just got outraged. He said, 'You make this sound like it's happening everywhere. I've been an administrator here five years, and we haven't had this problem.' And one of the assistant principals stood up and said, 'Well, there's six kids right now in the school, and furthermore I was a victim.'"

Some parents oppose prevention programs on the ground that they "put ideas about sex in children's heads." Others are concerned that sexual-abuse prevention might somehow be akin to sex education. Because many parents find it hardest to acknowledge the possibility that their children may be at risk from family members, sexual abuse counselors argue that in most cities an "incest prevention program" would have no chance of gaining acceptance. "To be perfectly honest with you, we're not all that upfront about it," says a sexual-abuse prevention worker in Greenville, South Carolina, the ultraconservative home of fundamentalist Bob Jones University. "That would make a lot of people real nervous."

Perhaps surprisingly, the bulk of the opposition to such programs appears not to come from parents who are abusing their children sexually. "Most abusive parents don't consider what they're doing to be abuse," says a counselor who administers prevention programs for both children and adults. "It's wild. I've had people come up to me after I've given my talk and explain in great detail what they're doing with their kids. I had a gynecologist come up, and from what he said I had real concern about what he was doing with his own daughter. They don't see any relationship between what I've been talking about for the last hour and what's going on in their homes."

Parents are not the only ones who object to such programs. As one California social worker points out, teachers who are called on to administer such programs "feel like this burden has been dumped on them, and their response is that this is something that should be taught at home. This is an area that they just don't see as their business. Teachers are loaded with a million different things to do that don't have anything to do with teaching kids, and they think that anything that doesn't have to do with teaching kids just shouldn't be part of their job. They're tired of the community looking to them for the solution to all its problems."

When teachers object to presenting such programs to their students, the only recourse open to school administrators is to bring outside presenters into the classroom. Whether they are local police officers or social workers or simply well-intentioned parents, such presenters are not likely to be very well versed in the subject at hand, which renders the presentation even less effective. A few have no business being near children at all, like the Maine man who, as "Sparky the Clown," put on plays about the dangers of sexual abuse until he himself was charged with the sexual abuse of twenty-eight children.

Prevention programs may give those who prepare and produce them a sense that they're doing something about child abuse, but there are serious questions about whether even the best programs are worth the effort. When children who have been exposed to prevention programs are asked later about what they remember, the answer is usually "Not very much," and the level of recall doesn't seem to depend on the quality of the program. One study found that children who were exposed to one of the better programs had forgotten much of the information it contained after only two months, and nearly all of it after less than a year.

Even when children do remember a particular concept, they're less than likely to be able to apply it to a real-life situation. Another study found that, while nearly all the children exposed to an assertiveness program could later repeat the definition of "assertiveness," fewer than half could give an example of an assertive reply to be used in an abusive situation. Younger children especially tend to parrot the answers they've been taught. When they're asked whom

they'd tell about being abused, they may say their mother or their
father, but when the time comes, there may be a gap between saying
and doing.

It is a basic principle of education that people, especially young
people, learn much more efficiently if they have some personal
experience that bears on what they're learning. Trying to explain the
dangers of sexual abuse to a child who hasn't been abused is difficult,
particularly when the presentation is not straightforward. A child who
has been abused, on the other hand, is likely to understand immediately what is being said. If prevention programs have any real value, it
may be that they prompt some victims to come forward. "We know
that these programs are good for one thing," says a pediatrician who
has studied the question. "They're good for identifying kids who have
already been sexually abused. When you do one of these shows,
inevitably one or two kids out of a group will come forward and say,
'Well, that happened to me.' "

Even in such cases, however, sexual-abuse prevention programs
are likely to be effective primarily with younger children who are being
abused by someone outside their families. Far less clear is the value of
such programs in preventing the most prevalent kinds of abuse, mainly
incest and voluntary relationships between older children and pedophiles. The fact that such programs do encourage some victims to
report may be reason enough to continue with them. But the content
of most programs needs to be vastly improved to reflect what happens
in the real world. In view of some of the testimony in recent child
abuse cases, for example, one thing children should be taught is how
to overcome the fear created by watching small animals killed before
their eyes.[2] But no matter what information the prevention programs
contain, teaching children to "say no" to sexual abuse is a simplistic
answer to an extraordinarily complicated problem.

On a snowy Sunday afternoon in January 1985, Judith Becker,
Kee MacFarlane, David Finkelhor, and a dozen other child abuse
researchers from the United States and Canada gathered at "Wingspread," the largest and last of Frank Lloyd Wright's prairie houses,
just outside Racine, Wisconsin. It was an eclectic group — child
therapists, social workers, a sociologist, several psychologists, two
psychiatrists, even a writer. For three days and nights they talked, in
panel discussions and among themselves, but no matter how the
discussions began they inevitably returned to a single question: Could
the sexual abuse of children in America ever be eradicated?

Some of those in attendance were less pessimistic than others, but all of them agreed that it was unfair to put the burden of preventing sexual abuse on children. The fact that most prevention programs were so flawed, the group thought, made it imperative that the prevention effort be directed elsewhere. Another thing they agreed on was the urgent need to find those victims who were going undiscovered. For every victim who spoke out, some thought, there were ten who remained silent. Others thought the real number was closer to a hundred for every one. Finding more victims might not solve the problem of sexual abuse, since victims by definition have already been abused. But not only will identifying such children take their abusers out of commission, treating them may also reduce the future population of abusers.

If many such children weren't coming forward, the Wingspread group thought, then it was incumbent upon doctors, teachers, and other professionals who have contact with children to learn to recognize the symptoms of sexual abuse. During the first half of this century, most states enacted some sort of law prohibiting the mistreatment of children, but not until the mid-1960s were laws passed requiring mistreatment to be reported to child protection authorities. The first mandatory reporting statutes were aimed only at doctors, but they have since been broadened to include many others who have temporary custody of, or responsibility for, children. Every state now has such a law, and most are directed at teachers, mental health professionals, police officers, and clergymen. Some even include dentists, paramedics, audiologists, podiatrists, optometrists, and barbers. In most cases, those covered by reporting laws must notify child protection authorities immediately if they suspect that a child has been sexually or physically abused, and most laws carry criminal penalties for failing to do so.

Despite the rise in the number of child abuse reports, from 150,000 in 1963 to more than 1.3 million in 1982, there is evidence that the reporting laws still do not work as well as they might.[3] Seven years ago a federal government study found that two-thirds of all cases of suspected child abuse were not being reported by those covered under the statutes, including 87 percent of those cases known to teachers and other school personnel. The explanations the teachers gave for keeping quiet included their ignorance of what the law required, their misconception that solid evidence of abuse was necessary before a report could be made, and their fear that they would be sued by the alleged abuser if their suspicions were incorrect.

Since then, most states have taken steps to ensure that those covered by such laws are aware of their responsibilities, and many have also passed amendments protecting such individuals from civil lawsuits for making an erroneous report in good faith. But a great deal of suspected child abuse is still going unreported. A 1985 study by New York City found that four out of ten teachers there had failed to report at least one case of suspected abuse, as had 18 percent of the city's hospital personnel and 8 percent of its police officers. Nearly all of those questioned said they were aware of what the law required, and most had received some sort of training in identifying the symptoms of abuse. But many said that nothing had been done when they had made such reports in the past, and they had come to doubt the ability or the willingness of the child protection authorities to act.

Not all of the blame for the failure to report can be attributed to the professionals. State child protection authorities must make it easier to make a child abuse report. The Illinois child abuse hotline, considered by many a model system for reporting, has often been a failure in practice. In one study reported by the *Chicago Tribune*, 28 percent of hotline callers either hung up after reaching a recording or had to wait for more than an hour and a half before a child protection worker called them back. "That's not a hotline, when you call people back," one state official said. "The idea of a hotline is to take a call and deal with it, and we're not doing that."

Sometimes the reluctance to report suspected child abuse is a matter of conscience, as with clergymen who fear that to make known what they are told in confidence will have a chilling effect on parishioners seeking forgiveness. Doctors have no such excuse, but the 1980 federal study found that almost half of the cases of abuse suspected by doctors were going unreported. Only 14 percent of the child abuse reports made in this country last year came from physicians, and according to the *Los Angeles Times*, fewer than half of the children in Los Angeles County found to have venereal disease are ever reported by doctors to that county's child protection agency.[4]

The tardiness of doctors in recognizing and reporting the sexual abuse of children follows their earlier reluctance to acknowledge that children were being physically abused. Barely twenty years ago, children who had been beaten and battered were often diagnosed as suffering from "spontaneous subdural hematoma," a brain hemorrhage that appears for no reason, or "osteogenesis imperfecta tarda," a congenital weakness of the bones. Such diagnoses have become less common as the physical abuse of children has gained recognition as a major problem, and the failure of many doctors to report cases of sexual abuse also seems to stem in part from their lack of knowledge about its prevalence and character.

It is a shortcoming the medical profession is moving slowly to correct. Not until 1983 did the American Medical Association hold its first national conference on the subject, and only in the past couple of years has the American Board of Pediatrics begun to require some sexual-abuse training in hospital residency programs. The symptomatology of sexual abuse is not yet a required subject for board certification examinations in pediatrics, psychiatry, or other related fields, and most medical students still receive a single two-hour lecture on the topic. Because so little is known about why adults have sex with children and how victims should be treated, the subject of sexual abuse, unlike that of pneumonia or liver disease, doesn't come with any conclusive theory attached.

Since there's no commonly accepted etiology, some professors of medicine who might otherwise be willing to teach the subject aren't sure of what to teach. Others object to it on the grounds that the available research is sketchy and the subject matter "more emotional than intellectual." As a result, whatever expertise a practicing physician does have is likely to have been acquired during an internship or residency at a receiving hospital. But even highly trained specialists are less than likely to spot the symptoms of sexual abuse. It may never occur to the urologist, for example, that a child with a urinary tract infection or who is a chronic bed wetter might be the victim of abuse.

Because they see children exclusively, pediatricians are becoming more quickly attuned to such subtleties than most other doctors. When a child who is suspected of having been abused is taken to a pediatrician, the chances are good that some of the most appropriate things will be done. Bruises, abrasions, and lacerations of the genitals and the surrounding area will probably be noted, and most pediatricians will order a vaginal culture for gonorrhea. But the child's throat and anus may not be cultured, and diseases like chlamydia and herpes may not be tested for at all. A new and simple test for the presence of sperm, important because it can also help to identify the child's abuser, is even less likely to be performed.

Unless the possibility of abuse has been raised in advance of a pediatric examination, however, it is unlikely that any of these procedures will be performed. Rather than suspecting gonorrhea, a doctor who encounters a vaginal discharge in a "well" child is likely to blame it on underwear that is too tight or to suggest that the child's mother change her bubble bath. The psychosomatic symptoms that often accompany abuse, such as abdominal pain, headaches, and overly passive or withdrawn behavior, are even less often seen for what they really are.

C. Henry Kempe, the late Denver pediatrician who coined the term "Battered Child Syndrome" back in 1962, once wrote that "the child who does not cry when he is stuck with a needle is either very sick with his basic illness, or he is very sick emotionally, because he has been trained at home not to cry when he is hurt." Kempe also warned his fellow physicians that the child "who is going around saying to one and all, 'I like you,' in an indiscriminate fashion, the child who does not object to being separated from his parents, [and] the child who lies perfectly still when being dressed and undressed . . . is telling you that he is doing those very things at home."[5]

Despite the persuasive evidence to the contrary, some doctors still refuse to believe that any children are sexually abused. One social worker recalled that "one of the most shocking, painful experiences I ever had was when I was working with a young woman who was drug-addicted, and she made an attempt to kill her mother. I don't think it was a serious attempt, but we chose to commit her to an adolescent unit at a teaching hospital. I called the head resident — this is a man who's in a teaching position. I said, 'Have you been able to talk to this child about sexual abuse? Because she was also molested by her mother's boyfriend.' And he said, 'Well, it really takes two to tango.' I couldn't continue my conversation with this person."

A doctor's reluctance to report the possibility of sexual abuse stems less often from disbelief than from other motives, not all of them conscious. Even when a doctor half suspects that abuse has occurred, it's easy for him to deny the possibility to himself when there are no overt symptoms at all. "You have to remember that doctors, like lawyers, look at the world in a very specific way," one pediatrician says. "They're very factually oriented. Doctors are used to dealing with very clear evidence of a known disease. There's still a feeling out there that unless there's a clinical symptom, you don't have to do anything, even though we all know there may be no clinical symptoms."

"We're human too, despite public opinion," another pediatrician says. "A lot of doctors have known their patients for a long time, and if a thought crosses their minds, particularly about sexual abuse, there's first the denial and then, 'Well, I'll see how I can handle it myself, gently and over a period of time, because I don't want to alienate this family.' "

When such suspicions do occur, some doctors may decide that it

is in their own best interest to do nothing. When 120 Denver
pediatricians were asked how they viewed sexual abuse cases, the most
common response was that they took too much time out of the doctor's
schedule. "When you've got an office full of children with tempera-
tures of a hundred and four and suddenly you're confronted during the
middle of a well-child exam with a vaginal discharge, you're an hour
behind," a pediatrician says. "These aren't quick cases. This isn't like
an ear check. If you're going to do an adequate history, these cases are
going to take a long time.

"Also, pediatricians are about the lowest-paid group. If you have
to have three kids an hour to make a living, you would be very
reluctant to shut down your practice for three hours to do the kind of
sexual-abuse evaluation that's needed. Where are the incentives? You
can't sit in an office with a parent who's raised the question of sexual
abuse and say, 'We'll do this lab test, call me in the morning.' That's
an emotionally charged situation. The minute you start talking about
the potential of a child being sexually abused, you better take some
time to talk to that mother." Even a doctor who takes the time runs the
risk of provoking the parent's anger. "I often get told that I'm going to
get sued," another pediatrician says. "Families say to me, 'I'm going to
sue your ass off, and I'm going to sue the hospital,' and things like that.
I get told that five times a week, even when I explain to them that it's
my legally mandated responsibility to report the situation."

The doctor who brushes all other considerations aside and reports
his suspicions can look forward in the weeks and months ahead to
devoting a good deal of time to the case he has spawned. As the
discoverer of the abuse, he will be interviewed by a steady stream of
police officers, child welfare workers, and prosecutors. Unless the
abuser pleads guilty, the doctor will have to testify at a preliminary
hearing and then at a trial, and since he is appearing for the
prosecution, he is not likely to be well treated by the defendant's
lawyer. "I used to have very little sympathy for physicians who didn't
want to cooperate and take time out of their busy schedules to go to
court," says a pediatrician who has testified in a number of sexual
abuse cases. "But having been abysmally treated at times by the legal
profession, I can see why physicians just don't want to expose
themselves to that sort of trauma. Unless you do it anonymously,
reporting puts you in the position of being further involved in what
happens. You find that quite often the lawyers and sometimes the
courts are not very considerate of your time and of what this costs you,
just not very considerate of you as a professional."

The Wingspread group acknowledged that while doctors might in theory be better equipped than other professionals to spot the symptoms of sexual abuse, they had less opportunity to do so. A child's pediatrician sees a child once or twice a year; his teacher sees the same child for five or six hours a day. Like doctors, however, teachers often don't recognize abuse for what it is. Some teachers in Jordan, Minnesota, recalled that several of the children there who later claimed to have been abused had behaved oddly for months before the first charges in the case were filed. One boy was described by his teacher as having had "a lot of nervous energy. He couldn't sit down in his chair. He would stand by his desk. He had a hard time concentrating on anything." Another boy drooled constantly. "He was very oral about things," his teacher said, "and he'd always cram things in his mouth, like shoelaces and crayons."

A third child, "a very cute little girl," developed a sudden craving for affection. "She would tell me things that were not true to get attention," her teacher said. "One time, she brought me a necklace for nothing. It was kind of sad." Another child, a second-grader, "was always tired. She would lay on her desk on one side. She was in the back of the room sleeping when twenty-two other kids were romping around the room. Her expression, her body language, both were the absolute absence of emotion. She had the longest face of any child I've ever had in my room — not even sad, just a lack of expression. All these kids had symptoms of something definitely bothering them, but I had no idea this was going on. I didn't know what to look for."

Apart from their inability to recognize many of its symptoms, teachers have the same disincentives as doctors for reporting suspected child abuse — fears of angry parents, of involvement in the criminal justice process, or of being wrong — and those who don't want the aggravation that goes with making such a report often find it easier to say nothing. To compound the dilemma they face, teachers who do try to act on their suspicions are likely to encounter resistance from their own superiors. A principal who fears publicity or angry parents may say he will "handle the problem" and then do nothing, and the teacher who takes it upon himself to call the police may be told that he's causing trouble and warned to stop, even threatened with losing his job.

The reluctance of school administrators to act when they suspect that a student is being abused pales beside their reaction when a teacher is accused of abuse. Anticipating reprisals from the teacher's union and suggestions by the school board that they have been derelict themselves, many principals instinctively try to find some way to sweep the matter under the rug. When an eleven-year-old girl accused a Chicago teacher of abusing her, the principal allowed the man to continue teaching — and left it to the girl's parents to inform police. When the police examined the teacher's personnel file, they found two letters from parents accusing the man of having fondled their daughters and a year-old letter from the principal warning the man not to be alone in his classroom with any of his students.

If there is a record for the longest-running sexual abuse cover-up, it must be held by the Los Angeles public school system. The cover-up began to unravel in December 1984, when three girls at a south-central elementary school told their parents that female students were being touched, rubbed, hugged, fondled, and otherwise molested during recess and lunchtime by forty-eight-year-old Terry Bartholome, a seventeen-year veteran of the Los Angeles schools. On paper, Bartholome was an outstanding educator whose official record was filled with commendations. But the record also showed that when he was first hired, school officials were aware that Bartholome had been charged with having exposed himself to a group of nurses in Tacoma, Washington, six years before.

Worse yet, there was evidence in the file that students at the two schools where Bartholome had taught had been accusing the man of sexually molesting them for more than three years. Confronted by his principal when the first accusations were made, Bartholome denied all. When another teacher heard the rumors about Bartholome and approached the principal, she was told to "leave it alone." When the reports persisted, Bartholome was transferred to another school and assigned to a class of third-graders in the belief that he would not molest the younger children. "What else could we do?" a school board official asked later. "He was a fully qualified teacher, and we couldn't prove a thing." To the teachers in the Los Angeles school system, the practice was known as "Pass the Trash."

The principal at Bartholome's new school was told the reason for the transfer and asked by her superiors to keep an eye on the man. In November 1983, she received the first of what would be several new complaints from parents that Bartholome was "bothering little girls in the classroom." Though the principal was required by law to report the complaints to police, she said she had been instructed to direct them instead to her immediate superior, a regional administrator named Stuart Bernstein. Bernstein's response had been to tell her to call Bartholome into her office and to order him to correct his classroom conduct. When the complaints about Bartholome continued, Bernstein told the woman to gather "more information" and to have the third-graders put their accusations in writing. Not until another two weeks had elapsed did Bernstein finally call the police, and only then after learning that Bartholome had already confessed his pedophilia to a teacher's aide.

"This is a very, very bad situation," a school board official said later. "Nobody is trying to downplay it. We had the facts. Why we didn't move faster, I don't know." Said another board member, "The administrators never rose above memo writing, paper shuffling, and telephone conversations between the school and the regional office." When the full story was pieced together, it emerged that not only had Bartholome fondled his students, he had lain down on a classroom table and masturbated in front of them. On days when Bartholome wore a special pair of trousers from which the pockets had been removed, he encouraged his girl students to reach inside and "take out the change." One girl quoted the teacher as having said, "My wife won't give me none, y'all are going to give me some." After his arrest, Bartholome blamed the children. The girls, he told police, had been "very mature" for their ages, and had "giggled and dared each other to do sexual things to me."

When Bartholome took the witness stand at his trial, he admitted having twice masturbated in front of his students but denied having molested or raped them. Convicted of the sexual abuse of seventeen children, Terry Bartholome was sentenced to forty-four years in prison. Regional administrator Bernstein, charged with five counts of failing to report suspected child abuse, said at his own trial that he had delayed calling the police because he had no facts to support a "reasonable suspicion" that the allegations were true. When Bernstein checked Bartholome's file and found a record of the allegations made against him at his first school, he testified that he discounted them, because "we receive anonymous letters all the time regarding employees." He was convicted in a second trial of failing to report a reasonable suspicion of child abuse. "I don't think there's any question that what happened could have been prevented," the prosecutor in the case said later. "There were enough red alerts and enough signals given to people whose concern for children should have caused them to act immediately and definitively."

Bernstein appealed the conviction, maintaining that the report he made to the police department operated by the Los Angeles Unified School District satisfied the statutory requirement to report suspected child abuse to the appropriate child protection authority (the prosecutors in the case had argued that Bernstein was obligated by law to have called the Los Angeles city police).[6]

The Bartholome case broke during the summer of 1985, and when school resumed that fall, the city made its teachers and principals sign a statement attesting to their understanding of the mandatory reporting law. Particularly stressed was the requirement that the teachers and principals were obligated to call the police themselves when they suspected that a child was being abused, rather than pass the responsibility to their superiors. The teachers were given explicit instructions on how to make such reports, and were even provided with a list of telephone numbers to call. They were also required to watch an hour-long television program that explained the reporting laws in still greater detail. The message apparently got through. During the first four weeks of classes, the school district's child abuse office received 602 reports of suspected abuse, compared to an average of 150 reports a month the year before.

Terry Bartholome's colleagues, at least, didn't try to defend him. When he approached the teacher's union for assistance in hiring a lawyer, he was told, in the words of the union's president, to "get lost." But when a sexual abuse case involving a teacher reaches the criminal justice system, it is not unusual for the other teachers to close ranks behind the one who has been accused. Richard Vanhook, a junior high school teacher from downstate Illinois, used a classic line with his victims. "Do you want me to treat you like my student," he would ask them, "or do you want me to treat you like my girlfriend?" The Vanhook case surfaced in much the same way the Bartholome case had, after five fifth-grade girls reported that Vanhook had been fondling and kissing them in the library and the girls' bathroom. But when the local grand jury weighed Vanhook's reputation against the girls' stories, it refused to return an indictment. "This guy was a teacher, he was a swimming coach, nobody in the community could believe that he would do this," said Don Weber, the prosecutor in neighboring Madison County.

According to Weber, what followed the grand jury's decision not to indict was "the most sickening two weeks of media coverage I've ever seen in my life. The man was hailed as a hero, there were stories about the trauma to him and his family. The police came over to my county — the school district is in both jurisdictions — and they said, 'Can you do anything about it?' I really didn't want the case, but I took this oath to uphold the law, so I said OK. The police by then had uncovered more victims, some going back as far as ten years. The investigation involved sexual molestation of young girls at Edwardsville Junior High School, at Collinsville Junior High School, at the new Collinsville High School and the old Collinsville High School. Of the two hundred girls they interviewed, at least half had been molested in some fashion by Mr. Vanhook."

The day before the new grand jury began its investigation, Weber said, "the president of the teacher's union came to see me. He told me they were not happy with me, and that if things didn't come out well at the grand jury the next day, I wasn't going to be reelected. A teacher sat outside the grand jury room and took down the names of every single student that testified, then printed them up and distributed them to all the teachers in the school district with the warning, 'You have to watch out for these people, because they're liars.' We finally got a conviction, but two days before Vanhook was scheduled to be sentenced, he committed suicide. He had the biggest funeral in the history of Collinsville, Illinois."

The Wingspread group agreed that there was little question that doctors, teachers, and others who have temporary responsibility for children can do much more than they presently are doing to find and get help for those who are being sexually abused, but the panelists acknowledged that doctors and teachers could only do so much. The ultimate responsibility for protecting children, the group thought, lay with parents and primary guardians, but the biggest problem facing child protection workers and others concerned with the safety of children is that there are so many parents who should never have become parents to begin with. Either such men and women never intended to have children in the first place, or they are so out of touch with themselves and the real world that they had no notion of the sacrifice and struggle that child-rearing entails, or they are impaired by drug or alcohol abuse, or they themselves were so badly treated as children that they have no model of decent parental behavior on which to draw. Whatever the reason, they simply aren't cut out to be parents. But who's going to tell them so? In this society, as in virtually all others, bearing children is looked upon as a fundamental human right. State and local governments may invoke their power to take children from their homes after abuse is suspected or discovered, but no government is ever going to assert the power to license potential parents in advance, to decide which of its citizens may bear children and which may not. And in a way that's too bad, because there are an awful lot of miserable parents in the world — a recent public-opinion poll found that 70 percent of American mothers questioned would not have children if they had it to do over again. Whether or not they are abusive themselves, unhappy parents are unlikely to do nearly enough to keep their children out of harm's way.

On the other hand, many parents are at least adequate protectors of their children — including, presumably, the 30 percent of mothers who *would* do it over again. But even kind and decent parents or guardians who suspect that their children may have been sexually abused are often reluctant to call the police. The subject at hand may embarrass them, or maybe they're afraid of being wrong or fear retaliation from the suspected abuser. Perhaps they're unwilling to acknowledge, to themselves as well as to others, that they have failed to protect their child as well as they might have. When, like Tiffany's grandmother, they overcome their doubts and summon their courage, they often have difficulty finding anyone who will take their suspicions seriously.

"One day Tiffany was bleeding from her rectum," the grandmother recalled, "so I called her mother and I told her. She said, 'Well, it could be from the detergent, or maybe she's constipated.' But it wasn't just the bleeding. Ralphie is her mother's boyfriend, and Tiffany had started talking about her and Ralphie playing mommy and daddy. She said, 'It feels good. I love him.' I didn't know what she was talking about. Then she came down with a sore mouth. She said her tongue hurt her. So I told this to her mother one Sunday afternoon. She said, 'Well, she should have a sore tongue, because she tells a lot of lies.' "

To the child's grandmother, it seemed as though Tiffany's personality had undergone a change. "She was always so outgoing," the woman said. "But she got real withdrawn, and she looked tired. She started wetting the bed. She said, 'I can't talk to you,' and when she did talk she had a horrible vocabulary. Then she'd say, 'Where's your camera? What did you do with your camera?' She'd start posing, like when we took pictures she'd pose with her legs up. One day we were coming home in the car, and she said, 'Grandma, take off all your clothes. I'm going to take your picture.' This went on for a while before I started putting two and two together — the soreness between her legs, the sore tongue, all these things she was saying. I started thinking this must be a fact, Ralphie really is doing these things to her.

"I took her to the pediatrician, a lady doctor. The doctor said, 'Well, everything seems to be all right.' I didn't tell her what Tiffany was saying, because I wasn't sure and I didn't want to get in any trouble. Because children do fantasize, or so I was told. So I asked my own doctor's wife. I said, 'Could this be possible, or is she imagining these things? I want to be sure that these things are actually occurring, because I don't want to go to jail. I'm scared to death to accuse anybody if it's not so.'

"Then I saw it advertised on TV about the hotline, who to tell if you suspect anything. I called the hotline, to see if we could prove that this was true or what. They gave me three different numbers to call, clinics where they do child therapy. I called one of the clinics, but this woman was so busy that she never called me back. I kept calling her every day. She finally said her boss was out sick. She said, 'Well, you'll have to wait until he comes back. He had an accident.' So I waited another whole week. Then they called and gave us an appointment. Two days later the police came and took a report. They sent a caseworker with the anatomical dolls, and he said, 'Definitely, this child has been molested.' He said, 'You keep a record of whatever she tells you.' So I started writing it all down.

"They gave me temporary custody of Tiffany, and they started an investigation. But when we got to the police station that day, Tiffany's mother was there, and she called Tiffany into a room. I thought the caseworker was in there with them, but it turned out they were alone. When Tiffany came out she said, 'Mommy said she'd beat me if I talk about Ralphie. Ralphie is a good boy, Grandma, and I can't talk about him.' I talked to her mother later, and I said, 'What did you tell that child?' She said, 'You went and reported Ralph, and he's innocent. Ralph did not do this, and you're in trouble.' She threatened me several times. She said, 'I'm going to get even with you if it's the last thing I do.'

"There was no state's attorney to question this child. We waited and waited. Finally they told me the courts won't do anything about a three-year-old, because she's too young to get on the stand. They told me, 'No judge is going to stand for that.' They told me there was no physical evidence, because the hymen grows back on small children. But they let me keep custody of her, and I'm trying to get permanent custody. She doesn't want to go back to live with her mother, and she doesn't want anything to do with Ralph. Her mother has only asked for two visitations in seven and a half months, but she's trying to get her daughter back. All the cases are continued five times. They're so overloaded. The caseworker told me they're refusing people, there's so much sexual abuse among children."

THIRTEEN

Society

THE WINGSPREAD conference was organized by the National Committee for the Prevention of Child Abuse, which for the past several years has conducted an extensive public service campaign aimed at adults who beat and batter children. "Take time out," the committee's slogan goes, "don't take it out on your kids." No one who has heard the announcements can help wondering whether such appeals really make a difference, but apparently they do. A decade ago, researchers at the Universities of Rhode Island and New Hampshire conducted a nationwide survey in which hundreds of parents were asked whether they had displayed any form of violence toward their children during the previous year. The categories ranged from pushing, grabbing, and spanking, to punching, biting, kicking, and beating, to using or threatening the use of a gun or a knife. When the same survey was repeated a decade later, the researchers found that while the overall level of violence by parents against children had remained about the same, the use of the severest punishments had diminished by 47 percent.

In attempting to explain the decrease, the study pointed to some social trends that might have made a difference. One was that many couples were marrying later than before, and more mature parents are statistically less likely to inflict serious violence on their children. Another was that many families were having fewer children, which meant there were fewer unwanted children, and unwanted children are more likely to become the victims of physical abuse. The researchers also considered the possibility that those parents who claimed not to have brutalized their children were lying. But they pointed out that whether or not the real incidence of serious physical violence against children had decreased, many parents were at least more reluctant to acknowledge beating their children. "Even if the change is only one of attitudes," they wrote, "we believe this is significant for a ten-year period, a change that may well lead to an actual change in behavior. If all we have accomplished in the last ten years is to raise parents' consciousness about the inappropriateness of violence, then we have begun the process of reducing violence towards children."[1]

There are any number of public service campaigns aimed at Americans who abuse drugs and alcohol, but so far none has been directed at those who have sex with children. Was it possible, the Wingspread group wondered, that the public service approach might persuade those who sexually abused children to stop or even turn themselves in? One of the conference participants, the University of Chicago's Jon Conte, showed the group a videotape of a public service announcement he had written. Narrated by Mike Farrell, the actor who played B. J. Hunnicutt on the television series "M*A*S*H," it was short and to the point: "If you are a man and you are sexually involved with children, you may be saying to yourself, 'She likes it,' or 'He asked for it,' or 'I'm teaching her about sex.' You're lying to yourself. Real men are not involved sexually with children. If there's any part of you that really cares about that child, stop it. Get help now."

The possibility that such an appeal might have some effect is supported by a Seattle study of 175 child sexual abusers, all of them men, who were asked whether hearing or seeing a public service message would have kept them from abusing their victims. Nearly three-quarters of the men said it would have stopped them cold; only one in ten said it would have had no impact at all.[2] The ideal message, the abusers said, should stress the options that were available — that it was possible, for example, to avoid jail through a pretrial diversion program — compared to the consequences if the abuse were reported by the victim. "I never really knew there was help for this," one of the men said. "I thought it was just that you went to jail, period."

Rather than use a celebrity to present the message, the abusers thought it would be more effective to use a real abuser, or for that matter a real victim. One of the men even composed his own sample message: "I am a sex offender," he wrote. "I was discovered two years ago. My entire family has been hurt. I have been to jail and had to pay numerous fines and court costs. I am presently in treatment. That is not cheap either. I hope to be cured and to learn to control my problem. It hasn't been easy. I wish I never would have started. I knew what I was doing was wrong at the time, and I should have stopped. Please don't go through what I've gone through. Seek help and stop. Believe me, it's just not worth it!"

Those child abusers who actually turn themselves in to the police, and they add up to a tiny number, usually do so only when it begins to look as though their victims are about to blow the whistle. If public service messages are ever broadcast, they will probably have the greatest impact on men who have only recently begun to abuse. A third of the men in the Seattle study said they would have been most vulnerable to such an announcement just after they began molesting children. Asking a neophyte abuser to stop and seek help may be asking him to give up something he doesn't really want in the first place, but if such an approach works, it is most likely to work with middle-class child molesters, those with good jobs, homes, families, and reputations who have the most to lose. It is also worth remembering that abusers who say they would have been deterred by the public service approach have already been caught and convicted.

It is the dedicated pedophile who is least likely to be moved by any public appeal, and David Finkelhor, another of the Wingspread participants, suggested that most of those who abuse children do so in part because they are convinced that they will never be found out. A public service campaign, Finkelhor thought, might at least increase the abuser's awareness of his chances of getting caught, but it is difficult to persuade the narcissistic abuser that he's as vulnerable to the law as ordinary mortals. Police records are filled with examples of men who have taken extraordinary chances in order to have sex with children, such as the Wisconsin child molester charged with sexually assaulting a five-year-old girl in the visitors' center at the prison where he was incarcerated.

A public service campaign of some sort is probably worth the effort, if only to see what results. But the Wingspread group also thought much more could be done by state and local governments to keep child molesters away from children, particularly in regulated institutions like schools, foster homes, and day-care centers. It has always been the case that some children who are too young to attend school have been cared for outside their homes, but the enormous increase in demand for day care over the last decade has made it a new American institution. Many of the day-care centers that have sprung up in suburbs and city centers hold state and local licenses, but such licenses are no guarantee of anything beyond the fact that minimal health and safety standards are being met — and in most cases they really are minimal. When the federal government drew up a set of minimum standards for day-care centers, a Yale University study found that they were higher than the standards set by forty-seven states.

Only ten states require the head of a licensed day-care center to have any training in child development, and only eight require day-care workers to have any experience at all in caring for children. California day-care teachers need six semester units in early childhood education, but in New York City anyone who is eighteen and can read and write at an eighth-grade level can become a teacher's aide. Thirteen states have no educational or professional requirements for child care workers, and the National Association of Social Workers says that only a quarter of those who earn their living caring for children have any professional training at all. Many day-care centers are owned by nationwide chains that pay their employees the minimum wage. Others pay more, but the national average is still around four dollars an hour. Even those workers who are most committed to children say they do not find the work, which often amounts to a combination of diaper changing and crowd control, very rewarding. Because it is hard to keep qualified and dedicated people in such low-paying, dead-end jobs, day-care centers are targets of opportunity for pedophiles.

Even among licensed day-care facilities, there are wide variations in the quality of care. The best centers may allocate one staff member for every half-dozen children, but in others the ratio is one worker to fifteen or twenty. The greater the ratio, of course, the greater the possibility that a day-care worker can molest children undetected. In hopes of improving the quality of care, several state legislatures are considering imposing more stringent requirements on day-care centers, in terms of both the workers they employ and the number of workers per child. But hiring more, and more qualified, caretakers will also increase the cost of day care. Many day-care programs already charge parents between eighty and a hundred dollars a week, which means that some working mothers with preschool-age children must pay up to a third of the average take-home salary for nonprofessional women. An inevitable result of raising child-care standards is to raise the cost of day care past the point that most single mothers, and even many married couples, can afford, which will drive some day-care centers out of business and others underground.

Improving licensing requirements is a partial solution at best, since the greatest danger to children comes from day-care facilities that are not licensed at all. About two million children are cared for in regulated facilities, but an estimated four million others are looked after in unlicensed ones, many of them private homes that either are too small to need a license or are owned by people who have simply failed to apply for one. Because there is no official record of their existence, such places are never visited by day-care inspectors, which means that there is nothing to prevent a convicted child molester from caring for children in his or her home. A California man convicted of abusing three children in an unlicensed day-care home run by his wife had previously been arrested by police with dozens of photographs of nude children in his possession.

Though they are beyond the government's reach, such unlicensed facilities are not necessarily illegal. In many states, those who care for fewer than a half-dozen children are not required to apply for a license. Licensed centers, however, are not beyond reach, and in an effort to keep known pedophiles away from children, some states have passed laws requiring that new day-care workers be fingerprinted and their records checked against state and federal criminal data bases. But many states do not have such requirements, and some of those that do say they cannot afford to pay the twenty dollars that each record check costs. The lack of funding is unfortunate, because background investigations appear to have some value. When New York City began fingerprinting new child care workers in the wake of the Bronx day-care scandals, 240 of the first six thousand applicants turned out to have criminal records. "It's hard to believe," says a lawyer for the California Department of Social Services, "but we do get people applying for day-care licenses that have sexual molesting convictions. You would think they would realize that when they turn in their fingerprints, we're going to find out."

Fingerprint checks are not infallible, because many child abusers manage to plea-bargain their convictions down to a charge of assault or neglect that does not identify them as a child molester. Even the most thorough background investigation can turn up only those child abusers who have already been caught, and records of convicted child abusers are often incomplete. According to the *Miami Herald*, the Florida Child Abuse Registry was so poorly organized that twelve thousand reports identifying known abusers were thrown out because there was no place to store them. For nearly four decades, California law has required convicted sex offenders to register with the authorities, but according to the *Los Angeles Times*, the law is neither widely obeyed nor effectively enforced. Some offenders never register at all, others fail to tell police when they change their addresses, and many of those who do register give addresses that are false. Only a few other states even require the registration of convicted sex offenders.

Screening those who hold jobs that give them access to children is only a first line of defense. The second defense is to monitor day-care centers and other places where children are at risk of being abused. But not only are day-care licensing standards in most states lax, they are loosely enforced at best. The number of Texas day-care centers has more than doubled in recent years, but a shrinking state budget has cut the number of inspectors in half. Instead of four visits a year, most Texas centers now receive two or even one, but that is still better than the national average. Illinois manages a single visit every year, but California day-care centers are inspected only once every three years. Michigan uses a "self-certification" system, which means that once a day-care home has been licensed, it is never inspected unless someone makes a complaint.

When day-care inspections do occur, they are likely to include merely the most rudimentary checks for such things as the number of teachers and bathrooms per child, which is why most of the child abuse that occurs in day-care centers is only discovered by the parents of its victims. Some inspectors are negligent, but most are simply overworked. In order to get a sense that something is amiss, it is necessary to spend time with the children, and most day-care inspectors do not have the time. Each of the twenty-six inspectors in the San Francisco area is responsible for monitoring nearly 250 facilities, and caseloads in other cities are not much smaller.

One possible solution to the day-care problem might be hiring more inspectors. But hiring more inspectors means spending more public funds, and money for social services has been the first budget item to fall in the face of taxpayer revolts and declining state revenues. Another potential solution is the one hit upon by a handful of enlightened corporations that are trying to hold on to valued employees by moving day-care into the workplace. When a child is being cared for in a corner of the factory or the office building where her mother works, and when the mother is free to visit the child during coffee breaks and lunch, the chances of abuse are greatly diminished. But day care in the workplace is an idea whose time has not yet come. Of the six million employers in this country, only about six hundred, most of them hospitals, offer their employees in-house day care.

The reality, child protection officials say, is that the current level of day-care regulation is about as much as can realistically be hoped for. The primary responsibility for children's safety, they say, must lie with parents. "If the parents aren't alert and the parents don't take care, all the legislation in the world will not make that big a difference," says Ted Dewolf, who oversees Michigan's twenty-five hundred licensed day-care centers. "You've got to get the parents educated so they know what to look for, how to select day care. When they buy a car, they spend an enormous amount of time. They spend very little time in selecting day care for their children."

Day-care centers are not the only places where pedophiles have managed to slip through the large cracks in the child protection system. In April 1985, a nine-year-old girl in Waukegan, Illinois, complained that she was being molested by her elementary school teacher. When police searched the teacher's suburban home, they found more than ten thousand photographs of naked children, among them fourteen former students, which had been taken through a two-way mirror in his bathroom door. The man was convicted of abusing that girl and six of his other students. Only after his arrest did the authorities discover that he had been convicted nearly twenty years before of "taking indecent liberties" with a student. Somehow the man had continued teaching until three other children accused him of abuse. Convicted again, he nevertheless managed to obtain a substitute-teaching certificate and the job that led to his most recent conviction. Any of the schools that had hired the teacher during the two decades he was molesting children could have asked police to check his record. But because they were not required to do so by law, none of them ever did.

School officials in some states claim that they are prohibited by Supreme Court decisions in the realm of privacy from even inquiring whether a prospective teacher has an arrest record. Though such interpretations of the Court's rulings are open to argument, the principal opposition to requiring background checks for teachers comes from the teachers themselves, whose unions have flatly opposed any official attempts at scrutinizing the qualifications of their members. When five Chicago teachers were charged with child abuse during a single two-week period, the city's school board announced that it would begin fingerprinting all prospective teachers. Even though the policy was intended to apply only to the newly hired, the Chicago Teachers Union opposed the plan as "an indictment of all teachers," and union officials pointed out that none of the five teachers arrested had had criminal records.

Another venue regulated by the state that has proved a magnet for child molesters is that of institutional care. Public and private institutions for abused or neglected children have been a fixture in America since the early part of this century, when churches and private charities first recognized that such children should be kept away from adult criminals. Every state now operates at least one children's institution, and most have several, but few are models of safety and care. The foster placement of sexually abused children can involve a number of emotional and physical dangers, but the greatest is that the child will be abused again by those who are responsible for his protection.

The great majority of children who find themselves in juvenile institutions, perhaps as many as 90 percent, have not committed any serious crime. Most are status offenders, which means that their offence, such as running away from home or truancy, would not be against the law if they were not underage. Many have committed no crime at all. Some are physically or emotionally disabled, some have been declared "unmanageable" by their parents, and others are there because they have been physically or sexually abused at home. Like institutions for adults, most of this country's training schools, children's shelters, and guidance centers are overcrowded, understaffed, and in serious need of funds. Because it is difficult to find trained guidance counselors willing to work for low wages in such Dickensian settings, many children's institutions attract sexually abusive men and women.

Three years ago, the state of Oklahoma was rocked by newspaper reports of thousands of cases of physical and sexual abuse of girls and boys by employees of that state's juvenile institutions. Some of the children had been forced to engage in prostitution by those assigned to protect and counsel them, including a senior Oklahoma official who turned out to have a prior record of arrests for sexual abuse. Though the Oklahoma scandal stands as something of a landmark in the annals of child abuse, such horrors are not limited to backward states or small towns. In 1985, after hearing reports that a child prostitution ring was operating out of Los Angeles County's emergency children's shelter, a grand jury uncovered fifty cases of child abuse by staff members during the first six months of that year, most of which had never been reported to police. A three-year federal study of child care institutions in New York found that child guardians had failed to report more than 80 percent of the abuses, including sexual assaults, that occurred under their supervision.

Even when official guardians do not commit such abuses themselves, the supervision they provide can be so lax that their charges risk being preyed on by outsiders. In Chicago, two men and a woman were convicted of having used drugs and threats to recruit a number of young girls for their juvenile prostitution ring from among the residents of the Mary Bartelme Homes, a state-funded institution for neglected children. Several of the girls, some of whom were from middle-class suburban families, had been placed in the facility to get them away from sexually abusive parents.

Because state-run facilities are chronically overcrowded, the warehousing of neglected or unwanted children has become a growth industry in America. There are thousands of private children's homes around the country that provide — for sizable fees — room, board, and schooling for children whose parents no longer want them at home. Lately, a number of states whose children's institutions are filled to overflowing have begun contracting private homes, many of which are operated as a fund-raising device by fundamentalist religious organizations, to take in children who have been abused and neglected by their parents. Because most of those who staff such homes are even less qualified and less closely supervised than warders in public institutions, the potential in such settings for abuse is even greater.

Private foster homes have a better record for protecting children than public institutions, but those who apply to become foster parents are not screened nearly as thoroughly as they might be, nor are they closely supervised. Many of the men and women who care for the two hundred thousand American children living under private foster care are well-meaning couples who are concerned for the welfare of children. Though the stipends paid by state welfare agencies have not increased nearly as fast as inflation, for some, being a foster parent is little more than a source of extra income. Others become foster parents as a means of gaining access to children.

When Liza was nine, her father went to prison for abusing her and her thirteen-year-old sister. Left with no way to make ends meet, Liza's mother moved the family to a shabby hotel in downtown Los Angeles and put the girls to work on the street. "My mom would talk to the men, and then they would come and talk to me," Liza recalls. "They weren't all that smart, but they had a lot of money. We'd tell them what to do, and they'd do anything we'd tell them. It was fun. It was like a game." When the state of California found Liza, it put her in a foster home, a nice two-story house with a swimming pool and a Jacuzzi where a prosperous businessman lived with his family. But Liza's foster father turned out to be like the men her mother had brought to the hotel room. "He used to come in at night and feel me and stuff," she says. "It happened every day, it seemed like. I remember him chasing me and me screaming. I was scared of him, but I didn't know what to do." The man's wife proved unsympathetic. "She told me if I said anything, she was going to tell my social worker that I was messing up in school," Liza says. "Even after I told her that, she still left me in the house with him alone."

The Illinois Department of Child and Family Services says it knows of forty-nine children under its supervision who were sexually abused by their foster parents in 1986, and there are no doubt others who have not come to its attention. Most states perform fingerprint checks on prospective foster parents, but the checks have all the same loopholes as those for day-care workers and teachers, and they can only turn up child abusers who have been convicted. When the New Jersey foster parents program tried to screen out people who had been accused of child abuse as well as those who had been convicted, the American Civil Liberties Union objected to the "abuse of due process" involved, and the plan was scrapped.

Foster homes and day-care centers are at least subject to some governmental regulation. The many private youth organizations in this country are not, and for them keeping child molesters away from children is even more difficult than it is for regulated institutions. The Big Brothers and Big Sisters Association of America has placed what one official calls "a terribly high priority" on screening its eighty thousand volunteers, and the organization has lobbied in several states for legislation that would allow it to check the names of applicants against arrest and conviction records. It has also adopted an extensive vetting process that includes thorough background checks and a series of personal interviews. Other private youth organizations, no less concerned, are prevented by state privacy laws from going any further.

The YMCA's national headquarters has drawn up a set of recommended guidelines to help in selecting those who run its many programs. But each local YMCA is an independent corporation, and beyond urging caution in hiring, there is little the national organization can do to help. The Boy Scouts of America maintains a nationwide list of convicted child abusers that it checks against the names of those who apply to become adult leaders. But the ultimate responsibility for selecting leaders rests with the churches, schools, and other organizations that sponsor individual troops. "The only thing we can do is get the organization to be sure they know the individual," a Boy Scouts executive admits.

In the effort to combat most social problems, the greatest public attention seems to be paid to those areas where it is easiest to accomplish something visibly and quickly, and the sexual abuse of children is no exception. The aspect of child sexual abuse that has been most vigorously attacked by American society in recent years is child pornography, and on the surface the antipornography effort has met with considerable success.

Before 1978, when Congress passed the first federal law prohibiting the production and sale of child pornography, it was possible in this country to purchase more than 250 different magazines filled with pornographic pictures of young children, most of them imported from abroad. The 1978 law did not bar the free exchange or private possession of obscene pictures of young children, but it marked the federal government's first major step toward eradicating a form of commercially available pornography that no one except pedophiles argued was a legitimate expression of free speech. Because of the 1978 law, there is no longer any city in the United States where child pornography is openly sold; virtually all the child pornography produced in this country nowadays is traded and sold among a few thousand practicing pedophiles.[3]

Some commercial child porn is still mailed from abroad, the majority of it from Denmark, Sweden, and the Netherlands, but there appears to be far less than there once was. Denmark legalized all pornography in 1972, but in 1981 it made the production and sale of pornographic pictures of children under fifteen illegal. Pornography has been technically illegal in the Netherlands since the turn of the century, but only during the past two or three years have the antipornography statutes actually been enforced. In view of their recent efforts, Scandinavian officials take offense, and with some justification, at suggestions that their countries are responsible for polluting the United States with child pornography. The chief of Swedish Customs has claimed, and U.S. Customs officers agree, that many of the photos published in Scandinavian magazines are actually made in the United States and Canada by amateur pedophile-photographers and then sent abroad for distribution.

U.S. officials also assert that some Scandinavian distributors are fronts for American producers, and there is some basis for such complaints. A few years ago, investigators tracking an "international child pornography ring" with post office boxes in Sweden and Denmark traced it to a California woman who was netting five hundred thousand dollars a year from her mail-order pornography business. The woman, Catherine Wilson, lived in the affluent

Hancock Park neighborhood of Los Angeles with her five children, a Mercedes-Benz, and a Rolls Royce. The thirty thousand customers on what Wilson called her "golden list," among them an Episcopal priest from Baltimore, sent their orders to one of the Scandinavian addresses. The orders were forwarded to Los Angeles after the money was deposited in a Swiss account. Wilson, driving one of her expensive automobiles, filled the orders by mailing packets of pictures from post offices across the Southwest.

Seizures of illegal pornographic materials from abroad nearly doubled after it became a federal felony to order child pornography by mail. In 1984, more than half of the forty-two hundred shipments of pornography impounded by U.S. Customs included pictures of children. Some foreign producers tried different ruses to get their pictures past the customs inspectors, including sending the material in envelopes stolen from hotels popular with foreign tourists in hopes that they would be mistaken for letters from vacationing Americans. But the ruses have not worked very well, and many producers appear to be giving up the American market altogether rather than go through such machinations. When a California police officer posing as a pedophile sent fourteen letters of inquiry to Scandinavian pornographers in late 1975, most wrote back to say they were no longer shipping their products to the United States. The fact that customs seizures of foreign-produced child pornography have lately begun to decline also suggests that not as much is being shipped through the mail as once was.

The battle against the domestic child pornographers is a different story. Prosecutions of domestic producers have increased, from thirty-four in all of 1984 to more than a hundred during the first six months of 1986. But those on the side of law enforcement say that such cases are the hardest to put together, because the pedophiles who sell or trade such material are extraordinarily careful about whom they deal with. An example is Earl William Magoun, the sixty-year-old pornographer to whom Walter Holbrook sold the photographs of the children he sexually abused. Magoun did his mail-order business under the name "Betty Adams," and one policeman says that "until Betty Adams knew who you were and knew that you weren't a cop, he generally didn't put out the child pornography or the animal stuff until you had bought his bondage and torture pictures, or bought the spanking pictures or the nun pictures. These people are not stupid." Another child pornographer who held a full-time job with the New York State Department of Tax and Finance used the department's computer to make sure his prospective customers were who they said they were.

To make such prosecutions even more difficult, in the absence of a live victim it is often impossible to prove the age of the children at the time they were photographed. There is little problem where very young children are concerned, but older children and teenagers are another matter. Prosecutors can call physiologists to testify that the child in question was probably not more than seventeen, but expert opinions are open to interpretation, and such testimony does not always result in a conviction. Another technique used by law enforcement officials has been to put photo processing labs on notice that developing child pornography is a federal crime, and that they are required by law to notify authorities whenever such photos are submitted for developing. The effort has produced some convictions, but these are mostly a matter of luck, since most photographs are now processed with automated equipment and are never seen by anyone. With the advent of inexpensive home video recorders, it is no longer necessary for pornographers to rely on the services of professional developers. Not only do VCRs make the production of child pornography much easier, but it is also possible to duplicate a particular tape any number of times by connecting one machine to another.

Some of the loopholes contained in the 1978 law were tightened in 1984, when Congress prohibited the free exchange of child pornography, a common practice among pedophiles who trade pictures of children like baseball cards. Moreover, the revised statute does away with the requirement that sexually explicit pictures of children must also qualify as lewd or obscene in order to be illegal.[4] Penalties for violating the anti-child-pornography statutes were increased tenfold, to a maximum of two hundred thousand dollars and fifteen years in prison. A few important loopholes, however, remain. The new law, like the old one, covers only "visual depictions" and not written materials, and because the federal laws still apply only to interstate trafficking, the private possession of child pornography is still legal, except in the six states that forbid it. Most constitutional scholars doubt that the Supreme Court, which over the years has drawn firm distinctions between private and public conduct, would ever uphold a federal statute prohibiting the private possession of child pornography.

Some civil libertarians argue that any discussion of what to do about child pornography must go beyond its intrinsic repugnance to the role it plays in actually encouraging the sexual abuse of children. Though it has been debated avidly for years, the question of what effect pornography has on the viewer is still unresolved. Nearly two decades ago, when questions were raised about whether viewing adult pornography encouraged sex crimes by adults against other adults, a commission appointed by President Nixon concluded that pornography had no significant impact on the behavior of the viewer. Though the Nixon commission's conclusions were backed up by scientific research, a new commission appointed by President Reagan concluded last year that viewing some forms of violent pornography does contribute to violent sexual behavior.

Unlike its predecessor panel, the Reagan commission did no quantitative research of its own, choosing instead to hear dozens of hours of testimony from experts who were mostly connected in some way with law enforcement. When a few social scientists testified that viewing pornography had no perceptible effect on sexual behavior, the commission chose largely to ignore their testimony. Judith Becker of the New York State Psychiatric Institute, the only real scientist on the panel, was dismayed. "I've been working with sex offenders for eleven years," Becker said, "and I would think that if there were a link between pornography and sexual behavior, we would have found it before now."

The Reagan commission did not specifically consider the question of whether child pornography contributes to the sexual abuse of children. But it is worth nothing that, while graphic pornography featuring children first became commercially available less than twenty years ago, there appears to be nothing new about sex crimes against children. Nor does there seem to be a connection in other cultures where such pornography has been even more widely available. A recent Swedish survey of a thousand citizens between the ages of eight and seventy found that only 9 percent of the women and 3 percent of the men admitted having been abused as children. James Fallows, a former speechwriter for Jimmy Carter who recently moved his family to Japan, has reflected on the fact that Japan is awash in cheap pornography that focuses on young girls "being accosted, surprised, tied up, beaten, knifed, tortured, and in general given a hard time." Fallows concluded that "in the United States more and more people are claiming that pornography contributes to sex crimes. If you look at Japan — with its high level of violent stimulation but reportedly low incidence of rape and assault — you have your doubts."[5]

Such evidence as exists, in fact, tends to deny the possibility of a connection between child pornography and abusive behavior. Nearly three-quarters of 531 child abusers studied by Judith Becker and Gene Able at the New York State Psychiatric Institute told researchers that while they might have viewed child pornography at some point during their lives, it could not be held responsible for their abusive behavior. Mainly because of such studies, most researchers now believe that an interest in child pornography follows, rather than precedes, a sexual interest in children. One is Rob Freeman-Longo, a researcher at Oregon State Hospital, who has studied the question extensively and who flatly maintains that "pornography does not create sex offenses. It doesn't make men go out and commit sex crimes.

"Some of these fixated pedophiles," Freeman-Longo says, "the better part of their waking hours are spent fantasizing about children. What pornography does do for the man who has those kinds of fantasies is that it reinforces that. A man doesn't need pornography to go out and molest a child. The absence of pornography has never stopped a child molester from molesting a kid." Freeman-Longo also points out that pornography is in the eye of the beholder. "A pedophile can look at the children's underwear section of a Sears catalogue and become aroused," he says. "He can read *Boy's Life* magazine and watch films on the Scouting Jamboree and get a throbbing erection, and those are totally nonpornographic materials."

The difficulty of eradicating underground child pornography, the constitutional protections for private behavior, and the doubts about whether child pornography actively contributes to child abuse have led some to question whether more and stricter antipornography laws are worth the effort required to pass them. In raising such questions, however, it is critical to draw a distinction between the production of child pornography and its reproduction, distribution, and possession. No one is suggesting that the effort to stamp out the actual production of child pornography be abandoned or even scaled down, since in order to produce such pornography it is necessary to sexually abuse a child. But the possibility must be considered that a more intensive effort to wipe out the clandestine exchange of existing child pornography amounts to treating the symptom and not the disease.

The argument that the resources necessary to broaden the battle against child porn might be better spent in arresting the child molesters themselves was offered by a staff lawyer for the American Civil Liberties Union who testified before the Reagan pornography commission. "There have been other attempts to get at the problems in a society by regulating speech," the ACLU attorney said, "and those attempts have not worked. Attempts to regulate child pornography are a perfect example. Regulating speech does not stop the crime, so I suggest to you to reject the attempt to link pornography with rape, sexual assault, and organized crime. Go after the rapist, go after organized crime, go after those who sexually abuse children."

The fact that child pornography has been removed from public view makes an important statement about society's view of child sexual abuse. But it is equally important that the same society stop sending a double message about its view of children as sexual objects. While the prohibition against sex with children is declared in a loud voice, the unspoken idea that sex with children might be acceptable after all is communicated in a number of more subtle ways, particularly the sexualization of children in the mass media and in advertising. Among the questions overlooked in the pornography debate is the issue of when artistic or humorous portrayals of children in an erotic vein cease to be art or humor and become something else.

Roman Polanski, the Polish film director, is remembered for fleeing the country after pleading guilty to having had intercourse with a thirteen-year-old Los Angeles girl. What is less often remembered is that Polanski abused the girl only after photographing her nude for the same popular French fashion magazine that had previously published seven pages of David Hamilton's photographs.[6] Though pictures of children undressed are not illegal in themselves unless they are deemed to be "sexually explicit," such photographs have been relatively rare in legitimate American publications. A few have appeared in the trendier fashion magazines, and *Playboy* has published nude photographs of Brooke Shields taken when she was ten. (Prints of those pictures now sell for five hundred dollars apiece. The Manhattan photographer who took them with the approval of Shields's mother calls Shields "the first prepubescent sex symbol in the world.")

The portrayal of young girls in a sexual light for commercial purposes seems to have reached its apogee in the many television and print advertisements by the makers of expensive blue jeans. The first examples of the genre, created for Calvin Klein, featured a sultry Brooke Shields confiding that nothing came between her and her "Calvins." A television campaign by rival jeansmaker Jordache that showed even younger models dancing suggestively was taken off the air after the company and the networks received a torrent of viewer complaints. Guess Industries, which manufactures its own brand of blue jeans, has produced a still more controversial magazine spot in which two young girls of indeterminate age, one wearing a torn dress and the other a slip, embrace in a woodsy dell. Such images are not child pornography. Rather, the concern is with the subliminal message they send. Most pedophiles know that sex with children is taboo, but when they see advertisements that use suggestive pictures of adolescent and even preadolescent girls to sell clothing, perfume, and shampoo, they might be forgiven for concluding that the same society that condemns them so loudly in public is speaking with more than one voice.

The message about double messages hasn't yet gotten through to the United States Congress, as became clear when several members expressed their outrage over a U.S. Justice Department study of the sexual portrayal of children in *Playboy*, *Penthouse*, and *Hustler*, the three leading "men's magazines," which together are read each month by one American in ten. One of those who objected was Pennsylvania senator Arlen Spector, whose own subcommittee three months earlier had heard Joseph Henry testify about his experiences as a pedophile. Spector, quick to attack the study as a $750,000 example of idiocy by the Reagan Administration, said he had "never seen pictures of crimes against children appear in those magazines."

Perhaps not, but it is difficult to see how anyone could overlook *Hustler's* regular full-page cartoon featuring the continuing efforts of "Chester the Molester" to ensnare small girls. In one cartoon, Chester lurks behind a fence while a very young girl approaches a bag of candy he has placed as a lure on the sidewalk. In another, he hides in some bushes as an equally young girl walks by, his penis protruding from the leaves beneath a sign that reads "Free Hot Dog!" Larry Flynt, the publisher of *Hustler*, calls child abusers "disgusting perverts," and takes credit for having "spoken out against this problem long before it became the hot topic it is today." Like *Hustler*, *Penthouse* is on record as opposing the sexual abuse of children. But while columnist Emily Prager fulminates about sexual abuse in day-care centers and "kiddie porn," *Penthouse* publishes nude photographs of a thirty-five-year-old mother and her (barely) eighteen-year-old daughter touching one another more than a little suggestively.

Hugh Hefner, the publisher of *Playboy*, has also taken a strong public stand against child sexual abuse. Hefner has even turned over his sybaritic Los Angeles mansion for a party that raised several thousand dollars to help build a Hollywood shelter for child prostitutes. A report on the party appeared in the same issue of *Playboy* as a cartoon showing a factory where assembly-line workers are adjusting the voice boxes of talking dolls. All of the dolls in the cartoon say "Momma" except for the one being adjusted by a leering technician who resembles Chester the Molester, which says, "Wanna have a party, big boy?" Such cartoons do not approach the legal definition of child pornography. But there is a danger that cartoons poking fun at child molesters will leave some readers, including the molesters themselves, with the impression that society really does not take such offenses very seriously.

A good measure of social change in any society, in fact, is the texture of its humor. A decade ago, a frequently repeated joke concerned two child molesters who were discussing their latest conquests. "Lemme tell ya about the eight-year-old kid I met last night," the first molester says. When the second molester hears the child's age, he makes a face. "I know, I know," his friend quickly adds, "but she had the body of a four-year-old." Except in places like *Hustler* and *Playboy*, child-molester jokes aren't seen or heard very often anymore, and there can be little question that social attitudes about the sexual abuse of children are beginning to change. But changing the public perception of a problem is not the same as resolving the problem itself.

In November 1985, more than two years after Jim Rud was arrested in Jordan, more than a year after the first indictments had been handed down in the McMartin case, three thousand child therapists, clinical researchers, prosecutors, physicians, teachers, police officers, and social workers, including all the members of the original Wingspread group, assembled in Chicago for the Seventh National Conference on Child Abuse and Neglect. It was the largest gathering of its kind in history, and those in attendance knew more than anybody about the dangers and dimensions of sexual abuse in America. They had also done more than anybody to raise the public perception of the problem, but now they found themselves divided over whether some solution to it would ever be found.

Jim Gabarino, a former professor at Pennsylvania State University who now heads the Erikson Institute for Advanced Study in Child Development, was among the most optimistic. Gabarino asked the congregants to think for a moment about all of the other ills and evils that had been abolished in the last hundred years — slavery, cholera, smallpox, maternal death in childbirth — through the force of advocacy, research, social engineering, and sheer good will. It is far easier to be a child these days, Gabarino said, than it was a hundred years ago. Society no longer puts children to work at an early age, no longer indentures them or marries them off at twelve. Instead, we have compulsory education, state and federal child protection agencies, and child abuse reporting laws. What was once considered strict discipline is now called physical assault against children. With enough ingenuity and gumption, Gabarino seemed to be saying, we will find a solution in time.

But Fernando Guerra, a professor of pediatric medicine from the University of Texas, didn't agree. "As I spend more time in the practice of pediatrics," he told the conference, "I am convinced that we can no longer stop the tremendously overpowering problem of child abuse and neglect. There are people in each of our communities who are totally overwhelmed by stressful events, who face one crisis after another, and the groups that remain at greatest risk continue to fall outside the system of resources that has been developed to do something about this." Michael Wald, a law professor from Stanford, concurred. "Unless we fundamentally change the type of society that we are," he said, "there really is no hope for child protection."

If such fundamental change seems beyond reach, it may be because some of the same trends that appear to correlate with child abuse — the disintegration of the nuclear family, an increase in the numbers of working couples and single and divorced mothers, more second and third marriages, the emergence of a permanent underclass, and an apparent increase in the number of sexually abused children — show no sign of reversing themselves. Even if they did, it seems unlikely that child sexual abuse can ever be eradicated, or even significantly diminished, by a society that has been unable to do the same for alcohol and drug abuse or the physical mistreatment of children. Perhaps the sexual attraction to children is so fundamental and so powerful that it can never be erased. But in spite of the obstacles and frustrations involved, not to redouble the attempt would be to relinquish any claim to civilization and humanity. Dr. Jaap Doek, president of the International Society for the Prevention of Child Abuse, put it best when he declared that "the effort to bring about the abolition of child abuse must be made. It may be doomed to failure, but to make no effort at all is far worse than failure. It is demeaning to the human spirit."

While child abuse researchers continue to seek the elusive remedy, some child molesters offer a solution of their own. Sex with children is wrong, they say, only because society says it's wrong; the way to resolve the problem is simply to stop calling it a problem. It may be true, as the pedophiles contend, that some children — it must be a small number — not only survive a sexual relationship with an adult but benefit from it in some way. It is probably also true that there are some pedophiles who would never conceive of forcing a child to engage in sex against his or her will, and whose narcissistic interest is in what they see as the fair exchange of pleasure for pleasure.

But everything that is known about how children grow up suggests that it is ultimately destructive for the huge majority of them to be plunged into an emotional and physical relationship with an adult. The trouble with such a relationship is that it places a child of any age at a developmental level it has not yet achieved on its own. Any sexual relationship involves much more than just sex, and when adults have sex with children, there is a clear danger of emotional exploitation by the more powerful member of what Freud termed "the incongruous pair." Henry Giaretto puts it most succinctly when he says, "It's like matching a high school boxer with Muhammad Ali."

To say that society will sanction sex between adults and those few children who might not be harmed by the experience is absurd. No one can make a determination about the potential for harm — neither society nor the pedophile, and least of all the child. What society does instead is the only thing it can do: it issues a flat prohibition against having sex with children. Claude Levi-Strauss observed that people do not choose their cultures, they are "delivered into" them. Because they are, the pedophile's logic is in some sense ultimately correct. Sex with children *is* wrong because society says it's wrong. No better reason is required.

NOTES

Preface

1. Hawkins was defeated for reelection in November 1986.

1. Questions

1. Douglas J. Besharov, " 'Doing Something' about Child Abuse," *Harvard Journal of Law and Public Policy* 8 (1985): 539–589.
2. New York: Lyle Stuart, 1986.
3. Hanke Gratteau and R. Bruce Dold, *Chicago Tribune*, Oct. 6, 1986, p. 1.

2. Numbers

1. A. C. Kinsey, W. B. Pomeroy, C. E. Martin, and P. H. Gebhard, *Sexual Behavior in the Human Female* (Philadelphia: W. B. Saunders Co., 1948).
2. In what is considered the classic essay on the *Kinsey Report*, Lionel Trilling notes that "the way for the Report was prepared by Freud, but Freud, in all the years of his activity, never had the currency or authority with the public that the Report has achieved in a matter of weeks."
3. S. K. Weinberg, *Incest Behavior* (Secaucus: Citadel Press, 1955).
4. David Finkelhor, *Sexually Victimized Children* (New York: The Free Press, 1979).
5. Diana E. H. Russell, "The Incidence and Prevalence of Intrafamilial and Extrafamilial Sexual Abuse of Female Children," *International Journal of Child Abuse and Neglect* 7 (1983): 133–139. Reprinted in *Sexual Exploitation* (Beverly Hills: Sage Publications, 1984).
6. Child sexual abuse is generally defined as what happens to victims under eighteen, since in most states that is the age of consent. The distinction is really artificial. A recent study by the Association of American Colleges found that "gang rapes" of college coeds had taken place on more than fifty campuses over a two-year period, 90 percent of them at fraternity parties. "On some campuses, we heard reports of gang rapes happening every week at parties," said Julie Ehrhart, the report's author.
7. In two-thirds of the cases, the abuse only happened once. But in 20 percent it had gone on for up to a year, and in 15 percent for up to ten years. Lewis's findings are summarized in the *Los Angeles Times* in two articles published on August 25 and 26, 1985, both on page 1.
8. Because of the large sample size, Lewis's margin of error was quite small — less than 2 percent, compared with around 2.5 percent for a standard Gallup or Harris survey. This meant that the percentages in the *Times* survey might differ from reality by two percentage points in either direction, but no more.

9. Gail E. Wyatt, "The Sexual Abuse of Afro-American and White-American Women in Childhood," *International Journal of Child Abuse and Neglect* 9 (1985), 507–519.

10. Diana E. H. Russell, "The Prevalence and Seriousness of Incestuous Abuse: Stepfathers vs. Biological Fathers," *International Journal of Child Abuse and Neglect* 8 (1984): 15–22.

11. *Sexual Offences Against Children: Report of the Committee on Sexual Offences Against Children and Youths* (Ottawa: Canadian Government Publishing Centre, 1984).

12. Anthony W. Baker and Sylvia P. Duncan, "Child Sexual Abuse: A Study of Prevalence in Great Britain," *International Journal of Child Abuse and Neglect* 9 (1985): 457–467.

13. G. Gorer, *Himalayan Village* (London: Michael Joseph, 1938).

14. C. S. Ford and Frank A. Beach, *Patterns of Sexual Behavior* (New York: Harper & Row, 1951).

15. For a discussion of the outbreeding propensities of chimpanzees and elephants, see W. Arens, *The Original Sin: Incest and Its Meaning* (Oxford: Oxford University Press, 1986).

16. Guido Ruggerio, *The Boundaries of Eros: Sex Crime and Sexuality in Renaissance Venice* (Oxford: Oxford University Press, 1984).

17. *Centuries of Childhood* (New York: Alfred A. Knopf, 1962), 33. Aries also sees the conception of children as little adults reflected in the styles of their clothing. Until the seventeenth century, he writes, "as soon as the child abandoned his swaddling-band — the band of cloth that was wound tightly round his body in babyhood — he was dressed just like the other men and women of his class."

18. Jeffrey M. Masson, *The Assault on Truth: Freud's Suppression of the Seduction Theory* (New York: Farrar, Straus & Giroux, 1984), 25.

19. Letter from Freud to Fliess dated September 21, 1897, quoted in Masson, 108–110.

20. In recent years, there has been speculation about the possibility that Freud was himself a childhood victim of incest. In the letter to Fliess, Freud notes that one of the factors leading to his decision was his recognition that, if the seduction theory were allowed to stand, "in all cases the father, not excluding my own, had to be accused of being perverse. . . ." What Freud meant by this remains unclear, and has become the subject of much conjecture. According to one interpretation, he might have been suggesting that to consider his own father capable of such perversity proved the implausibility of the seduction theory. Others have read the phrase as a veiled hint that Freud or his siblings might have been sexually abused as children. In *Freud and His Father* (New York: W. W. Norton & Co., 1986), Marianne Krull raises the possibility that Freud abandoned the seduction theory in part because to continue with it would have required him to acknowledge that he "had come up against the most crucial event in his self-analysis: he had reached the point where he had to hold his father responsible for his own neurotic symptoms," and would have been forced to accuse his own father of being a seducer of children. There is no evidence that Jacob Freud ever sexually abused his own children. But Krull also writes of the close relationship between the young Sigmund Freud and his nursemaid, and she speculates

on the possibility of a sexual relationship between Freud's mother and one of his much older half-brothers. Freud's affair much later in life with Minna Bernays, his wife's sister, has also been speculated upon by Peter Swales and others.

21. Freud suggested that an integral part of this equation was a son's unconscious wish to murder his father, in order to get him out of the way. Matricide is a rare event, but it is a matter of record that many more sons kill their mothers than their fathers, which points up an element of oedipal theory that is often overlooked — the son's unconscious hatred of his mother because of his perception that, in preferring the father, she has rejected him as a love object.

22. Despite the numerous attempts by historians of psychoanalysis to explain what Freud meant, the man himself often remains the best expositor of his theories. Nowhere is there a better description of repression than the one he offered in a 1909 lecture at Clark University in Worcester, Massachusetts:

> Let us suppose that in this lecture room and among this audience, whose exemplary quiet and attentiveness I cannot sufficiently commend, there is nevertheless someone who is causing a disturbance and whose ill-mannered laughter, chattering, and shuffling with his feet are distracting my attention from my task. I have to announce that I cannot proceed with my lecture; and thereupon three or four of you who are strong men stand up and, after a short struggle, put the interrupter outside the door. So now he is "repressed," and I can continue my lecture. But in order that the interruption shall not be repeated, in case the individual who has been expelled should try to enter the room once more, the gentlemen who have put my will into effect place their chairs up against the door and thus establish a "resistance" after the repression has been accomplished. If you will now translate the two localities concerned into psychical terms as the "conscious" and the "unconscious," you will have before you a fairly good picture of the process of repression . . . [but if] you come to think of it, the removal of the interrupter and the posting of the guardians at the door may not mean the end of the story. It may very well be that the individual who has been expelled, and who has now become embittered and reckless, will cause us further trouble. It is true that he is no longer among us; we are free from his presence, from his insulting laughter and his sotto voce comments. But in some respects, nevertheless, the repression has been unsuccessful; for now he is making an intolerable exhibition of himself outside the room, and his shouting and banging on the door with his fists interfere with my lecture even more than his bad behavior did before. In these circumstances we could not fail to be delighted if your respected president, Dr. Stanley Hall, should be willing to assume the role of mediator and peacemaker. He would have a talk with the unruly person outside and would then come to us with a request that he should be readmitted after all: he himself would guarantee that the man would now behave better. On Dr. Hall's authority we decide to lift the repression, and peace and quiet are restored. This presents what is really no bad picture of the physician's task in the psycho-analytic treatment of the neuroses.

The entire lecture is reprinted in *Five Lectures on Psycho-Analysis*, translated and edited by James Strachey (New York: W. W. Norton & Company, 1977).

23. In *The Psychoanalytic Theory of Neurosis* (New York: W. W. Norton, 1945), Otto Fenichel admits that "It is not easy to answer the question about castration anxiety in women. First, it can be asserted that the Oedipus complex in women actually is not combated to the same degree and with the same decisiveness as it is in men. There are many more women who all their life long remain bound to their father or to father figures, or in some way betray the relationship of their love object to their father, than there are men who have not overcome their mother fixation."

24. From then on, it was the oedipal experience Freudian psychoanalysis would focus on, by breaking through the repressive barrier and integrating the childish fears and longings into the whole of the adult personality. As Otto Fenichel explained it half a century later, "after the infantile defenses have been canceled, the isolation is undone and the warded-off strivings are connected again with the total personality. They now participate in the maturity of the personality; infantile drives turn into adult ones, which can be discharged. Thereafter, remainders can be handled by sublimation or by other more effective types of suppression."

25. Masson, 147.

26. Masson, 148.

27. Letter from Anna Freud to J. M. Masson, dated September 10, 1981, quoted by Masson.

4. Abusers

1. Able has since joined the faculty of Emory University in Atlanta.

2. Heinz Kohut, *The Analysis of the Self* (New York: International Universities Press, 1971).

3. Christopher Lasch, *The Culture of Narcissism* (New York: W. W. Norton & Co., 1979).

4. Though he does not specifically speak about incestuous parents, in *The Restoration of the Self* (New York: International Universities Press, 1977) Kohut writes that "the seductive parent is not primarily harmful to the child because of his seductiveness; it is his disturbed empathic capacity (of which the grossly sexual behavior is only a symptom) that, by depriving the child of maturation-promoting responses, sets up the chain of events leading to psychological illness." And: "The child's deprivation from the side of the parental self-object is not as easily discerned — indeed, evaluated in terms of behavior, these parents give an appearance of overcloseness to their children. But the appearance is deceptive, for these parents are unable to respond to their children's changing narcissistic requirements, are unable to obtain narcissistic fulfillment by participating in their children's growth, because they are using their children for their own narcissistic needs."

5. Lasch writes that "the fusion of pregenital and Oedipal impulses in the service of aggression encourages polymorphous perversity." Kohut suggests that the sexuality of the acute narcissist tends toward the perverse both because he can "trust no source of satisfaction" and as a means of relieving the "painful narcissistic tension" created by the conflict between self-love and self-hate.

6. In mid-1987 Michael Reagan, the President's adopted son, disclosed that he had been sexually abused for a solid year at the age of seven by a day-camp counselor who had taken the place of his distant movie-star father in the boy's affections. It was because of that experience, Reagan said, that he had feared for many years that he might really be a homosexual.

5. Families

1. The Appalachian stereotype was reinforced in late 1986, when police in the tiny mountain community of Salyersville, Kentucky, charged seventeen members of seven related families with the sexual abuse of two dozen of their children, ranging in age from nine months to eleven years. "From all appearances, we're talking cousins, uncles, aunts, sisters, brothers, fathers, mothers, and grandmothers," one state trooper said.

2. In *The Psychoanalytic Theory of Neurosis* (New York: W. W. Norton & Co., 1945), Otto Fenichel writes that "in any sort of permanent community there are always adults who serve as substitutes for the parents, but the fact that they were not the real parents will reflect itself in the special form of the Oedipus complex . . . [i]t would be wrong to imagine that in childhood there are no other love objects than the parent of the opposite sex. Also siblings, uncles, aunts, grandparents, friends, and acquaintances of the parent may be of decisive influence."

3. *The New York Review of Books*, December 4, 1986, p. 39.

4. U.S. Children's Bureau, *National Study of Social Services to Children and Their Families* (Washington: U.S. Department of Health, Education and Welfare, 1979), 120.

6. Pedophiles

1. Although Sonenschein was convicted for the dissemination of child pornography, his conviction was later reversed by a Texas appeals court, which maintained that prosecutors had not presented enough evidence to corroborate the testimony of their star witness — the man to whom Sonenschein had allegedly given the photograph. The state is appealing the reversal.

2. Testimony of Joseph Henry. U.S. Congress. Senate. Committee on Governmental Affairs. *Child Pornography and Pedophilia.* 2 vols. 99th Cong., 1st sess., 1985.

3. Testimony of Bruce Selcraig. U.S. Congress. Senate. Committee on Governmental Affairs. *Child Pornography and Pedophilia.* 2 vols. 99th Cong., 1st sess., 1985.

4. To support this position, pedophiles often cite a study by a Dutch psychologist, Dr. Frits Bernard, who claims to have discovered a number of adults who had sex as children and were unharmed by the experience. A few researchers in this country have also reported encountering such adults. A study of sixteen New York City–area adolescents who had had sex with their parents and other adults was published some years ago by Lauretta Bender and Abram Blau in the *American Journal of Orthopsychiatry* 7 (1937). The researchers noted that "[t]he most remarkable feature presented by these children . . . was that they showed less evidence of fear, anxiety, guilt, or psychic trauma than might be expected. On the contrary, they more frequently exhibited either a frank, objective attitude or they were bold, flaunting, and even brazen about the situation . . . [t]he emotional reaction of these children was in marked contrast to that [of] their adult guardians, which was one of horrified anxiety and apprehensiveness regarding the future of the child . . . [a]nother striking characteristic shown by these children was that they had unusually attractive and charming personalities. They made personal contacts very easily."

5. The pedophiles are particularly fond of quoting Alfred Kinsey's assertion, in *Sexual Behavior in the Human Female*, that "it is difficult to understand why a

child, except for its cultural conditioning, should be disturbed at having its genitalia touched, or disturbed at seeing the genitalia of other persons, or disturbed at even more specific sexual contacts."

6. Unpublished data compiled by Rob Freeman-Longo, director, Sex Offender Unit, Oregon State Hospital, Salem, Oregon.

7. Lewis Carroll was the pen name of nineteenth-century Oxford mathematician Charles Dodgson, the author of the classic children's stories *Alice's Adventures in Wonderland* and *Through the Looking-Glass*. Dodgson's penchant for photographing young girls in various stages of undress is less well known.

8. J. A. Inciardi, Division of Criminal Justice, University of Delaware. U.S. Congress. Senate. Committee on Governmental Affairs. *Child Pornography and Pedophilia*. 2 vols. 99th Cong., 1st sess., 1985.

9. Testimony of Joseph Henry. U.S. Congress. Senate. Committee on Governmental Affairs. *Child Pornography and Pedophilia*. 2 vols. 99th Cong., 1st sess., 1985.

10. Costello, John, *Virtue under Fire* (Boston: Little, Brown and Company, 1986).

11. Kenneth V. Lanning and Ann W. Burgess, "Child Pornography and Sex Rings," *FBI Law Enforcement Bulletin*, January 1984, p. 10.

12. Testimony of Joseph Henry. U.S. Congress. Senate. Committee on Governmental Affairs. *Child Pornography and Pedophilia*. 2 vols. 99th Cong., 1st sess., 1985.

13. Luis Johnson, sentenced to 527 years—a California record—is being held on death row at San Quentin, the only place where prison authorities say they can protect him from the other inmates. Whether or not they succeed, Johnson will die in prison. Not so, perhaps, Alex Cabarga, whose 208-year sentence was struck down last year as "unconstitutionally excessive" by a three-judge California appeals court. Calling Cabarga Johnson's "third victim," the court sent the case back for resentencing.

9. Lawyers

1. Findings based on the examination of 247 Denver, Colorado, girls under age thirteen, reported by Hendrika B. Cantwell in the *International Journal of Child Abuse and Neglect* 6 (1983):75. "Enlarged" was defined as a vaginal opening dilated to more than four centimeters in diameter.

2. At the moment, medical technology permits prosecutors to argue only that a defendant *might have* committed a particular crime, since samples of blood, semen, hair, or skin cells taken from the victim of an assault can be assigned to one of several broad genetic categories. Because such evidence can also be used to show that a defendant who does not fall into the given category could not have committed the crime in question, it often proves to be exculpatory. But a very new technique being developed in England, which involves the analysis of the nuclear DNA contained in skin cells and bodily fluids, may make it possible to link a semen sample or a pubic hair with a particular individual.

3. Jan Hollingsworth, *Unspeakable Acts* (New York: Congdon & Weed, 1986).

4. A study by Jon R. Conte and Lucy Berliner of eighty-four Seattle men charged with child sexual abuse found that sixty-two pleaded guilty before trial. See "Prosecution of the Offender in Cases of Sexual Assault against Children," *Victimology* 6 (1981):102–109.

10. Justice

1. As with other fundamental constitutional questions, the answer will probably not come all at once. Rather, it is likely to emerge over several years, in the form of decisions in a series of related cases. In one such case, decided in February 1987, the Supreme Court said that a father accused of sexually abusing his daughters did not have the right to examine confidential state records for clues to who had accused him. A potentially more significant opinion was handed down in June of the same year, when the Court suggested — really for the first time — that it might be willing to provide substantial special protections for the victims of child abuse, and at the expense of those accused of having abused them. By a vote of six to three, the justices ruled that a defendant in a Kentucky child abuse case did not have a constitutional right to attend a pretrial competency hearing for his victims. The ruling reinstated the conviction of a man who had been found guilty of sodomizing three young children but whose sentence had been overturned by the Kentucky supreme court on the ground that the trial judge's decision to exclude the man from the victims' competency hearing had violated his Sixth Amendment rights. Writing for the majority, Associate Justice Harry A. Blackmun noted that the Sixth Amendment guaranteed a defendant the right to be present at any stage of the criminal proceeding that is critical to the outcome of the proceeding, "if his presence would contribute to the fairness of the procedure." But the defendant's presence at a competency hearing was deemed not to be critical, since it had not involved the discussion of substantiative testimony by any of the victims. In its decision, the Court did not address any of the really big questions raised by child abuse cases, such as whether such a defendant has a right to confront his or her accuser at the trial itself.
2. *Los Angeles Times*, February 11, 1985, p. 14.

11. Therapy

1. Peggy Smith, Marvin Bohnstedt, Elizabeth Lennon, and Kathleen Grove, "Long-Term Correlates of Child Victimization: Consequences of Intervention and Non-Intervention," National Center on Child Abuse and Neglect, 1985.
2. Judith V. Becker, Jerry Cunningham-Rathner, Meg S. Kaplan, "The Adolescent Sexual Perpetrator" (in press).

12. Prevention

1. New York: Tom Doherty Associates, 1985.
2. Jon R. Conte, Carole Rosen, and Leslee Saperstein, "An Analysis of Programs to Prevent the Sexual Victimization of Children," presented to the Fifth International Congress on Child Abuse and Neglect, September 16–19, 1984. Montreal, Canada.
3. Douglas J. Besharov, " 'Doing Something' about Child Abuse," *Harvard Journal of Law and Public Policy* 8 (1985): 539–589.
4. October 10, 1984, Part II, p. 1.
5. C. Henry Kempe, "The Pediatrician's Role in Child Advocacy and Preventive Pediatrics," *American Journal of Diseases of Children* 132 (1978): 255–260.

6. For a full account of the Bartholome case, see the *Los Angeles Times* for Sunday, October 19, 1986, Part II, p. 1.

13. Society

1. Richard J. Gelles, College of Arts and Sciences, University of Rhode Island, and Murray A. Straus, Department of Sociology, University of New Hampshire. Paper presented at the Seventh National Conference on Child Abuse and Neglect, Chicago, November 11, 1985.
2. Timothy A. Smith and Jon R. Conte, unpublished data taken from a survey of offenders at Northwest Treatment Associates, Seattle, Washington, 1984.
3. Following a year-long investigation, the Senate Permanent Subcommittee on Investigations concluded that there were, at most, about two thousand pedophile-pornographers at work in this country, that organized crime played no part in the trade, and that "what commercial child pornography does exist in the United States constitutes a small portion of the overall pornography market and is deeply underground."
4. Pornography featuring adults must still meet the obscenity test, as embodied in the Supreme Court's 1973 decision in *Miller v. California*, before it can be judged illegal. Such a test, the Court wrote, should determine whether an "average person," applying contemporary community standards, would find that the work in question, taken as a whole, appeals to the "prurient interest," whether it depicts sexual conduct "in a patently offensive way," and whether the work, taken as a whole, "lacks serious literary, artistic, political, or scientific value."
5. *Atlantic Monthly*, September 1986, p. 37.
6. Roman Polanski, *Roman* (New York: Ballantine Books, 1985), 358.

INDEX